B&T 23.50

LITERATURE IN PROTESTANT ENGLAND, 1560-1660

Literature in Protestant England 1560-1660

Alan Sinfield

CROOM HELM
London & Canberra

BARNES & NOBLE BOOKS
Totowa, New Jersey

© 1983 Alan Sinfield
Croom Helm Ltd, Provident House, Burrell Row,
Beckenham, Kent BR3 1AT

British Library Cataloguing in Publication Data

Sinfield, Alan
 Literature in Protestant England 1560-1660.
 1. English literature – Early modern, 1500-1700 –
 History and criticism
 I. Title
 820.9'003   PR421

ISBN 0-7099-2367-8

First published in the USA 1983 by
BARNES & NOBLE BOOKS,
81 ADAMS DRIVE,
TOTOWA, New Jersey, 07512

Library of Congress Cataloging in Publication Data

Sinfield, Alan.
 Literature in Protestant England, 1560-1660.
 Bibliography: p.
 Includes index.
 1. English literature – Early modern, 1500-1700 –
History and criticism. 2. Christianity and literature.
3. Protestantism and literature. 4. Reformation –
England. 5. Great Britain – Intellectual life – 16th
century. I. Title.
PR419.R4S58   1983   820'.9'382   82-18408
ISBN 0-389-20341-6

Printed and bound in Great Britain
by Billing & Sons, Worcester

Contents

To My Mother

Foreword

This book grew out of an interest in Philip Sidney, which threw up the question of the relationship between his imaginative writing and his involvement, politically, with Elizabethan puritanism. As I explored the historical context, it became apparent that literary "history" was working from constructions of the nature of puritanism and of orthodoxy, and of their relationships with literature, which were at odds with those used by historians. The Elizabethan Church, doctrinally, was broadly Calvinist: the "via media" (to which puritans objected) mainly concerned liturgy and organization.   A.G. Dickens remarks in *The English Reformation*: "Even Archbishop Whitgift [1583-1604], who so fiercely disciplined Puritan mislikers of the surplice, did not differ from them upon the essential points of theology.   He was a strict Calvinist . . ." (Batsford, 1964, p. 313).   To Michael Walzer, Sidney and his associates represented an "ideal alternative to the courtier: animated by a fine sense of personal virtue, they were conditioned at the same time by a new Calvinist zeal" (*The Revolution of the Saints* [Harvard University Press, 1965], p. 241).

So it was necessary to take Calvinism seriously, as the Elizabethans had done.   Study of their theological and devotional writing revealed a confident and elaborate attempt to render coherent, persuasive and effective a doctrine which is (for the most part) alien to us—I have drawn upon these primary sources in this book where appropriate, hoping to convey something of the manner in which Elizabethans and Jacobeans handled the issues (the editions from which I have cited are listed on pp. 153-56).   The problems and contradictions also came into focus. When literature of the period is set into this context, its relationships with official religious doctrine emerge as diverse, provocative and significant.   This book is organized around aspects of those relationships.

As the work proceeded it became apparent that its contextualising of literature is more radical than is customary; that the historical setting does not mainly point up the centrality of the literature.   The book is almost entirely about literary

texts, but whilst they are not treated as passively reflecting
their context, neither are they perceived as transcending it.
Nor is Christianity accorded the vague deference—as an adjacent
and incorporable scheme of transcendence—which is common
in literary studies of the period.   Arguably, the thoroughgoing
contextualising of literature here attempted makes literature
not less but more important, but it runs counter to prevailing
assumptions.   The questioning of these assumptions in structuralist
and Marxist work and (most relevantly) in cultural studies made
it possible to theorize the stance of this book, and chapter I
attempts to explain the approach taken and to locate it within
current thought.

It is a pleasure to record the support of many friends.
Members of the University of Sussex have contributed to discuss-
ions of parts of the book which were delivered as papers.   Those
who have read all or some of the typescript and offered valuable
advice include Martin Monks, Maurice Evans, Laurence Lerner,
A.D. Nuttall, Stephen Medcalf, John Russell Brown, Peter
Stallybrass, Adrian Pinnington, Jen Green and Jonathan Dollimore
(who also helped with the proofs).   Urgent conversations with
many friends have assisted the formation of the general approach
I have taken, including Martin Monks, David Morse, Mark Sinfield,
Graham Usher, Cedric Watts and David Williams; members of
the Sussex University Literature Teaching Politics group: David
Forgacs, Frank Gloversmith, Ann Jones, Cora Kaplan, Ulrike
Meinhof, Peter Stallybrass, Allon White; and especially Jonathan
Dollimore, whose concurrent work in related areas has proved
stimulating in the completion of the book (see his *Radical Tragedy*
[Harvester, 1983]).

These acknowledgments do not distinguish generous enthusiasts
from challenging sceptics; nor do they distinguish certain special
personal supports.   The latter could not be adequately specified
here, or, I think, anywhere.   The book can be dedicated only
to my mother, from whom I must have acquired persistence.

Alan Sinfield

Brighton and Rhydycroesau

1 Theoretical perspectives

This book is a study of Renaissance literature in relation to a major part of its historical context. It is not about *all* the context; it does not pretend to full and rounded coverage. It focusses with special intensity one aspect—protestant Christianity. The advantages of highlighting this aspect are several: it is significant for a range of important writing in the period; it is widely misunderstood; and it brings into question traditional attitudes to literature.

The major historical studies of the Reformation show that the English Church preached a provocative, hard-line theology which has little in common with modern Anglicanism; see Charles and Katherine George, *The Protestant Mind of the English Reformation* (Princeton, 1961); Christopher Hill, *Society and Puritanism in Pre-Revolutionary England* (Secker and Warburg, 1964; Panther, 1969); A. G. Dickens, *The English Reformation* (Batsford, 1964); Keith Thomas, *Religion and the Decline of Magic* (Weidenfeld and Nicolson, 1971; Peregrine, 1978); Nicholas Tyacke, "Puritanism, Arminianism, and Counter-Revolution," in *The Origins of the English Civil War*, ed. Conrad Russell (Mamillan, 1973). My second chapter expounds this doctrine, which seems to us so stern, unfamiliar, unsympathetic and problematic; shows the extent of its influence; elaborates its implications; and tries to explain why it made sense at the time.

Three fundamental questions about literary studies and the literature written in the wake of the Reformation pose themselves. One is why the religious orthodoxy of the period is so little regarded in literary studies. (1) A second is what the status and functions of orthodoxy might be in society, particularly in relation to the literary work. A third is how it can be (as I believe) that attending to the strangeness and inadequacy of Reformation Christianity can enhance our appreciation of the literature. (These questions are opened up in my article, "Against Appropriation," *Essays in Criticism*, XXXI [1981], 181-95.)

The rigours and contradictions of Reformation doctrine are often obscured in critical studies written within the dominant cultural tradition because that tradition holds that literature expresses enduring human values; moreover, that such is its rationale and the criterion by which we should evaluate it.

Hence the tendency to centralize a more benign "Christian Humanism"—a rational, moderate faith like that of Erasmus, characterized by a calm spirituality, a commitment to the ethical principles of Jesus' "Sermon on the Mount," a conviction that "redemption" is available to all persons of good will, and a belief in the power of people (including pagans) to intuit God's purpose for the world and to express it in literature. This outlook is not foreign to the period, but most of the important writers manifest a far more complex and anxious attitude, strongly aware of its latent contradictions as they were foregrounded by orthodox protestantism. The appeal of "Christian Humanism" to many modern interpreters is that it is either close to their own outlook or can without too much strain be reconciled with it. Thus they appear to confirm their ideology from celebrated literature, and to ratify their idealist assumptions.

In this critical tradition, even the historical scholar will feel that he or she should slant interpretation towards what is acceptable to the modern reader (i.e. the "universal" dimension of the text!). Theodore Spencer's *Shakespeare and the Nature of Man* (2nd edn, 1966) is full of valuable contextual material, but Spencer holds that Shakespeare's tragedies "take on a symbolic and universal meaning" (p. 94). This leads Spencer, at points, subtly to adapt his historical material. Take the Witches in *Macbeth* . We don't now believe in witchcraft or, possibly, in any form of supernatural intervention; further, the concept is repellent, for it was used to justify the persecution, torture and killing of numbers of women. Spencer refers to the Witches as one of "the abstractions that are developed from the human mind" and as "a final dramatic realization of the Elizabethan dramatic convention which invariably tended to see individual human experience in relation to some power—God, the stars, or Fortune— larger than itself" (p. 157). But in a society where witchcraft is generally credited, the appearance in a play of personages who say and do witchlike things must, in the absence of some counter-indication, be taken as meaning, not "abstractions," but *witches*. And the Elizabethan tendency to see human experience in relation to a power larger than itself was not a "dramatic convention" but a fundamental item of belief. Spencer places a genial humanistic gloss upon such superstitions rather than admit that *Macbeth*, in certain major aspects, has a less than "universal meaning."

The second question posed by my approach concerns the status and functions of an orthodoxy and its relations with the literary work. My claim that the "Christian Humanism" often identified in the period must be reconsidered in the light of historians' accounts of contemporary doctrine does *not* mean that everyone is supposed to have held Calvinist beliefs. We do not have much idea in principle of what it means "to hold a belief," and we know that thought and behaviour are in practice criss-crossed by assumptions of which we are only half aware and which, if pressed, would prove radically divergent. Moreover, people do not always believe what they are told to believe; the reiteration of a doctrine by authority may indicate not that it was generally accepted, but that it was widely mistrusted.

On the one hand, protestantism was the most fully articulated system of belief and it had the authority of state, church and educational system. Such an orthodoxy cannot for an indefinite period be at odds with generally held attitudes, at least among influential groups. We may regard protestant Christianity as the explicit and systematic formulation of a hierarchical, indeed tyrannical, attitude to human affairs, which was manifest in state and local courts, in schools and in the family. The "loving care" attributed to the protestant God seems very like that which people experienced in human power relations. On the other hand, other structures of ideas were available to Elizabethans and Jacobeans. Pagan literature was immensely potent and endorsed by sixteenth-century humanists, but at odds with protestantism (as we shall see) in respect of human potential, ethics, literature, religion, sexuality and politics. The nascent empiricism associated with Machiavelli and Bacon also promoted a rival view of the world. This protestantism did not endure, so its dominance was evidently not total. We need a theory which will speak to the authoritative role of official doctrine and to the opportunities for dissidence and change, and to the relationships between them.

> The dominant culture of a complex society is never a homogenous structure. It is layered, reflecting different interests within the dominant class (e.g. an aristocratic versus a bourgeois outlook), containing different traces from the past (e.g. religious ideas within a largely secular culture), as well as emergent elements in the present. Subordinate cultures will not always be in open conflict with it. They may, for long periods, coexist with it, negotiate the spaces and gaps in it, make inroads into it, "warrenning it from within." (2)

Sixteenth and seventeenth-century culture manifests just such a complex and mobile structure. Official insistence upon an orthodoxy in religious and social doctrine—and we are talking here about a one-party state—is an attempt to determine the hierarchy of relationships within culture and to regulate change. Within certain limits, it may not matter what the orthodoxy is: the claim of total authority through the suppression of alternatives (which are identified as the enemy, as "AntiChrist") effects the main function of legitimating social control.

3

The outcome will depend upon the appropriateness of officially approved belief to actual developing conditions. In any conceivable society, the analyst will be able to perceive strains and stresses which can be contained only by a generous rate of adaptation or by extremes of physical force. Sixteenth and seventeenth-century society experienced diverse, difficult and rapid changes in most aspects of life, and the social and religious orthodoxy was not adequate to them.

> All these changes, religious and economic, were hard to absorb within a social theory which was based on the notion of a stable social order and unanimity in religious and political purposes. The notion of every man in his place was hard to combine with the effect of inflation on the social structure, and the notion that it was a meaningful limitation on the king's power to say that "the king's perogative stretcheth not to the doing of any wrong" was hard to preserve when almost every action of the king's was thought wrong by some group of his subjects. Many of the tensions of this period resulted from the incompatibility between social facts and social ideas. (Conrad Russell, *The Crisis of Parliaments* [Oxford University Press, 1971], pp. 195-6)

We will observe the internal contradictions of protestant religious orthodoxy, as its proponents struggled to incorporate diverse objectives within a single structure, and the relationships—of disjunction, negotiation, subversion and opposition—between protestantism and other ideological formations. Hence my subtitle, "a study in cultural dislocation."

"Culture" may be defined as "that level at which social groups develop distinct patterns of life, and give *expressive form* to their social and material life-experience" (Hall &c., *Resistance Through Rituals*, p. 10). In societies which have print and urbanization but not electronic media, literature and theatre will probably be principal vehicles of culture. Through them, with the diverse objectives I have described, culture will be developed. And in the sixteenth and seventeenth centuries protestantism must have constituted a crucial frame of reference. Those who tried to adapt or by-pass it must have felt it as a presence to be negotiated; even those who sought to repudiate it had to acknowledge it.

We may think of the literary text as a particularising pattern laid across the (changing) grid of social possibilities. It heightens and affirms some customary structures, disconfirms others, and perhaps discovers new lines of force. It contributes to culture through its tendency to strengthen certain kinds of perception and to discourage others. Of course, it has its own practices—institutions and conventions. Plays (for instance) were subjected to different governmental pressures from those which bore upon sermons; they inherited and were able to develop a different language (of speech, gesture and spectacle). Nevertheless, the fictive constructions of literature cannot be separated from their role in the production of culture; to suppose otherwise would be to deprive them of most of their potential significance. We must learn to *read*, very carefully, the mediating practices through which meaning is constructed in a particular literary form. Then we may perceive, as Raymond Williams puts it, how "the 'persons' are 'created' to show that people are 'like this' and their relations 'like this'" (*Marxism and Literature*, Oxford University Press, 1977; p. 209). The literary text, as we involve ourselves in it, constitutes an invitation to agree that the world is, importantly, thus. So it effects a commentary upon, and hence an intervention in, contemporary attitudes.

This book traces the interactions of literature with protestant orthodoxy in a dislocated culture. Chapter III is about the divergence of protestant and humanist ideas of human potential and the role of literature; chapter IV is about contradictions in the doctrine of love and marriage. Spenser, Sidney, Shakespeare, Donne and Milton are important in these chapters, and they attempt, in very different ways, an accommodation within the divergent pressures of protestantism and between protestantism and other modes of thought. Chapters V and VI analyse how some tragedians engaged in a subversion or repudiation of protestantism. Tragedy, after all, lays claim to the same area of significance as religion, and many of its inherited forms were pagan. Occasionally, I think, the challenge to religion was purposeful, but quite often it was only half conscious, an anxious and confused reaction to a provocative theology. The final chapter is about how this protestantism disintegrated under the strain of internal and external contradictions, and in the process helped to stimulate secularism.

We must ask, finally, about the relevance of all this in the modern world. The common assumption is that permanent "human values" guarantee the continuing significance of "great literature." But this position is becoming less effective in Renaissance studies, as concern about the patriarchal basis of very many texts is added to scepticism and ignorance about religion and disquiet about hierarchical assumptions in politics. It is increasingly difficult to involve the non-professional reader in Renaissance studies on the basis of harmony of values.

The approach taken in this book reverses the principle of relevance. Earlier writing illuminates our society not because it appeals to enduring human needs, but because it offers an alternative perspective. We gain a vantage-point upon our own attitudes, and specially those which operate commonly as unexamined assumptions, by involving ourselves in an alien world-view. Brecht complained: "When our theatres perform plays of other periods they like to annihilate distance, fill in the gap, gloss over the differences. But what comes then of our delight in comparisons, in distance, in dissimilarity—which is at the same time a delight in what is close and proper to ourselves?" (*Brecht on Theatre*, trans. John Willett [Methuen, 1978], p. 276). Study of another culture is like returning from a stay in another country: we become conscious of habitual features, more able to assess the constraints of our own ideology. Confirmation of ourselves breeds complacency, difference stimulates.

Notes

1.   But see William R. Elton, *"King Lear" and the Gods* (Huntington Library, 1968); Roland Mushat Frye, *Shakespeare and Christian Doctrine* (Princeton, 1963); William G. Halewood, *The Poetry of Grace* (Yale, 1970); Robert G. Hunter, *Shakespeare and the Mystery of the Gods* (University of Georgia, 1976); Stanley Eugene Fish, *Surprised By Sin* (Macmillan, 1967); Margot Heinemann, *Puritanism and Theatre* (Cambridge, 1980); Barbara Lewalski, *Milton's Brief Epic* (Brown University and Methuen, 1966), and *Protestant Poetics and the Seventeenth-Century Religious Lyric* (Princeton, 1979); Dominic Baker-Smith, "Religion and John Webster" in *John Webster*, ed. Brian Morris (Benn, 1970); Paul R. Sellin, "The Hidden God" in *The Darker Vision of the Renaissance*, ed. R.S. Kinsman (University of California, 1974); Stevie Davies, *Renaissance Views of Man* (Manchester University Press, 1978); and, by the present author: "Sidney and Du Bartas," *Comparative Literature*, XXVII (1975), 8-20; "Astrophil's Self-Deception," *Essays in Criticism*, XXVIII (1978), 1-18; "Sidney, Du Plessis-Mornay and the Pagans," *Philological Quarterly*, LVIII (1979), 26-39; "Sidney and Astrophil," *Studies in English Literature 1500-1900*, XX (1980), 25-41; "Hamlet's Special Providence," *Shakespeare Survey*, XXXIII (1980), 89-98.

2.   John Clarke, Stuart Hall, Tony Jefferson and Brian Roberts, "Subcultures, Cultures and Class," in *Resistance Through Rituals*, ed. Stuart Hall and Tony Jefferson (Hutchinson and the Centre for Contemporary Cultural Studies, 1976), p.12; the final phrase is quoted from E.P. Thompson, "The Peculiarities of the English."

2 Protestantism: a belief of contradictories

> That which taketh away the reputation of wisdom
> in him that formeth a religion . . . is the
> enjoining of a belief of contradictories.
> (Hobbes, *Leviathan*, p. 179)

Hobbes asserts that a contradictory theology eventually undermines itself: people stop believing it. This book is about the interaction between literature and Reformation Christianity—a system of belief which evidently convinced many, but which confronted in a particularly strong form the characteristic problems of monotheism. Protestants attempted a bold and provocative resolution, but eventually it collapsed under the weight of its own contradictions. As writers struggled to make sense of their world they acknowledged, inevitably, the demands and tensions of contemporary religion.

Protestants sought to establish for all the faithful an intense and personal relationship between the individual and God. They were not content that religion should consist of casual or external observance. Hence the attack on the mediatory functions by which the Church had traditionally interposed itself—saints, the Latin Bible and ritual, the priest, indulgences. In the Homily "Of Good Works" Elizabethans were given a list

> of papistical superstitions and abuses, as of Beads, of
> Lady Psalters and Rosaries, of Fifteen Os, of St Bernard's
> Verses, of St Agatha's Letters, of Purgatory, of Masses
> Satisfactory, of Stations and Jubilees, of feigned Reliques,
> of Hallowed Beads, Bells, Bread, Water, Palms, Candles,
> Fire, and such other, of superstitious Fastings, of
> Fraternities (or Brotherhoods), of Pardons, with such like
> merchandise. (*Homilies*, p. 60)

Reformers held that religion had become a matter of superstition and routine performance, too often corrupted by the movement of cash. The Homily commands a more inward ideal of Christian service: "First you must have an assured faith in God, and give yourselves wholly unto him, love him in prosperity and adversity, and dread to offend him evermore. Then, for his sake, love all men, friends and foes" (p. 61).

This emphasis upon an immediate and personal relationship with God is apparent in the diverse accents of the religious poetry of Donne and Herbert:

> But as I rav'd and grew more fierce and wild
> At every word,
> Me thoughts I heard one calling, *Child:*
> And I reply'd, *My Lord.*
> (Herbert, "The Collar")

But by taking from the Church the responsibility for the quality of the relationship between people and God the Reformation placed a burden upon every believer. How can one gain God's favour?

The only safe answer was that one can't: one can be pleasing to God only through God's extraordinary generosity. Luther declared in *The Bondage of the Will* (1524): "No man can be thoroughly humbled until he knows that his salvation is utterly beyond his own powers, devices, endeavours, will, and works, and depends entirely on the choice, will, and work of another, namely, of God alone" (*Luther and Erasmus*, p. 137). We can do nothing whatsoever to merit divine grace, we can only be given it. In ourselves we are worthless; we cannot ascend, only be lifted up. Hence the abrupt ending of "The Collar." Despite the undercurrent of religious imagery (a thorn, blood-letting, the wine and corn of the communion service), which reminds the reader of Christ's sacrifice, Herbert gets further and further from God—"more fierce and wild." The reversal is caused sheerly by divine intervention: "I heard one calling, *Child."* The poet's response is unexplored, even automatic. He has no real choice, it is not his achievement but something which God does to him.

The protestant belief that salvation is entirely dependent upon the unmerited gift of divine grace was not new; the reformers drew continually upon the church fathers, especially Augustine. If God is the all-powerful creator, it is difficult to avoid the ultimate conclusion that he has determined everything. Aquinas granted as much (*Summa Theologica*, I, q.23, a.1); Milton struggled awkwardly with the problem in *Paradise Lost*, book III. But the political and social conditions of the sixteenth century facilitated an institutional split in Christendom, and the consequence was a polarisation and hardening of doctrine. Issues which in other times were accommodated by logical evasions and evocative phraseology were teased out and stated in uncompromising terms, and the problems which ultimately confront all traditional Christianity come sharply into focus.

Protestant thought, by its insistence on divine power and human wretchedness, imposed upon its adherents fundamental

psychological and ethical difficulties.   Medieval Catholics had
proposed a harmonious co-operation between God and humanity.
They too held that there can be no merit without grace, but
they also declared that there can be no blessedness without merit.
Thus God descends to mankind offering salvation, and mankind
in response ascends to God.   The reformers rejected this compromise, and with it the sense of continuity and shared purpose
between human and divine.   They established instead a universe
divided in deep and perpetual strife—between God's wisdom and
our benighted recalcitrance, our ultimate goal and our present
uncertainty, the elect and the reprobate.   We are sunk in sin
unless God reclaims us; then we are immediately among the
saints.   Luther declared:

> there are two kingdoms in the world, which are bitterly
> opposed to each other.   In one of them Satan reigns. . . .
> He holds captive to his will all who are not snatched away
> from him by the Spirit of Christ. . . . In the other kingdom,
> Christ reigns, and his kingdom ceaselessly resists and makes
> war on the kingdom of Satan.   *(Luther and Erasmus,*
> pp. 327-28)

This is the anxious and combative religion of Donne's besieged
citadel:

> I, like an usurped town, to another due,
> Labour to admit you, but oh, to no end,
> .   .   .   .
> Take me to you, imprison me, for I
> Except you enthral me, never shall be free,
> Nor ever chaste, except you ravish me.
> ("Holy Sonnet" 14)

The determination to create a more immediate relationship
between humanity and God, therefore, paradoxically placed a
vast and uncertain gulf between them.   Hugh Latimer explained
in a sermon of 19 December, 1529:

> the more we know our feeble nature, and set less by it,
> the more we shall conceive and know in our hearts what
> God hath done for us; and the more we know what God hath
> done for us, the less we shall set by ourselves, and the more
> we shall love and please God: so that in no condition we
> shall either know ourselves or God, except we do utterly
> confess ourselves to be mere vileness and corruption.
> *(Selected Sermons,* p. 9)

We approach God by learning how distinct, through our wickedness,
we are from him.   The invitation to advance is conditional upon
our acknowledgement that we are unable, of ourselves, to do
so.   William Perkins sets it out in *An Instruction touching Religious*

Worship (1601):

> The principal worship of God hath two parts.   One is to
> yield subjection to him, the other to draw near to him and
> to cleave unto him.   By the first we put a difference between
> ourselves and God, by reason of the greatness of his majesty.
> By the other we make ourselves one with him as with the
> fountain of goodness.   *(Work,* p. 313)

Perkins does not say that we first humble ourselves then become
one with God, as might a medieval mystic.   The two "parts"
are to be simultaneous and continuous, the tension is permanent.
    The ethical problem which is foregrounded in Reformation
Christianity concerns the uncompromising recognition of divine
power.   God's power and goodness are always difficult to reconcile
(if God is omnipotent and good, why does he not make things
better?): protestants chose to emphasize God's control over the
universe at the expense, or so it seems to most people today,
of his goodness.
    The reformers established divine power by insisting that
no one can merit salvation and it is up to God whom he will
elect.   They held that his mercy resides in the fact that he
chooses to rescue any of us.   But this leaves the reprobate no
opportunity to avoid condemnation, and raises a question about
the goodness of a deity who has created many for inevitable
damnation.   It is difficult but crucial for the modern reader
to appreciate that many protestants did not consider this to
be unjust.   In William Lawne's *Abridgement of Calvin's Institutes
of the Christian Religion* (1583) objections are treated in dialogue
form.   God's mercy is asserted, but so is his power to determine
who shall be saved:

> All are guilty: but the mercy of God relieveth and
> succoureth certain.
> *Objection.* Let it succour all.
> *Answer.* It is meet that by punishing he likewise show
> himself to be a just judge.   (p. 224)

This dialogue stands at a watershed in modern ethical development.
Calvin and Lawne recognize the generous possibility in the objection,
but they dismiss it.   For them the need for authority and punishment overrides the claims of equity and generosity.   The objector
quotes St Paul's statement, "God will have all to be saved" (1
Timothy, 2:4); the reply is from Exodus: "I will have mercy on
whom I will have mercy" (33:19; p. 230).   The objector holds,
with some biblical support, that God means to save everyone,
but most protestants could not envisage divine mercy without
divine judgement.   The objector's argument only gradually undermined Calvinist orthodoxy.
    This is the theology Donne adopted with his conversion.
Much of the struggle in the "Holy Sonnets" is with its rigours.

Donne accepts the protestant view of his own unworthiness:
"I have sinned, and sinned, and only he, / Who could do no iniquity,
hath died" (11).   Christ's sacrifice witnesses to divine mercy,
but suppose Donne is not among the few to whom it is extended?—
"Oh I shall soon despair, when I do see / That thou lov'st mankind
well, yet wilt not choose me" (2).   He would repent, but that
too is in God's gift; only he can "give thee that grace to begin"·
(4).   In one sonnet at least Donne allows a trace of resentment:
"And mercy being easy, and glorious / To God, in his stern wrath,
why threatens he?" (9).   Like Lawne's objector, Donne wonders
why God does not "succour all," but the complaint is itself a
gross sin and he at once withdraws, with the Pauline cut-off
which Lawne uses in a similar context: "But who am I, that dare
dispute with thee / Oh God?" (Romans, 9:20; Lawne, p. 220).
      John Carey in his book *John Donne: Life, Mind and Art*
(Faber and Faber, 1981) sees all this as a specially personal alarm
consequent upon Donne's change from Catholicism.   But most
sixteenth-century protestants had been born Catholics, and the
structure of Donne's anxiety—though he was indeed strenuously
aware of this, as of other complexities—was by no means merely
personal.   (In fact, Carey's interesting analysis suffers from
an inadequate theory of the relationship between individual and
social ideology, as we see in a comment like this: "Donne's renunciation of Catholicism left him writhing in the trap which was
always set to catch the Protestant soul"—p. 55.   Carey recognizes
that the problem was common to "the Protestant soul" but at
the same time tries to give priority to "Donne's renunciation."
He does not distinguish the particular personal pressure in Donne's
writing—for instance, the brinkmanship with which he raises
problems which he cannot permit to reach their ultimate expression—
and the characteristic configuration of Reformation thought.
Two unbalanced consequences follow: on the one hand, Donne
is made to suffer all the problems of official doctrine without
any apparent support in social experience; and on the other,
Reformation theology is found to be the villain behind every
personal trait which Carey considers culpable.)
      The Reformation belief of contradictories created a universe
of strife and tension.   It insisted on the need for grace whilst
denying any means to obtain it.   It claimed that God is aware
of every movement of the individual spirit whilst emphasizing
the inevitability of sin.   And it posited a good and just divinity
who damns the larger proportion of his people without their
being able to affect the issue.   Theologians shuffled their texts
and arguments to make it appear gracious and logically consistent;
creative writers wrestled, with more and less conviction, to accommodate it to their intuitions about humanity.   Finally, Hobbes
was right and most people rejected it.

* * * * * *

The notion is still about, though not among historians, that the
Elizabethan religious settlement of 1558 was a compromise,
that the extremities of protestant experience as I have described
them are therefore inapplicable and that the vast majority of
informed English people inhabited a stable and harmonious universe
guaranteed by a manifestly benign deity.   This is not so.
    Of course, we cannot tell what most people actually believed
around the year 1600.   Heavy penalties (including torture and
death) attended the expression of opinions—papist, sectarian
atheistical or pagan—which diverged from official doctrine.   Many
people must have retained a perhaps confused attachment to
Catholic practices.   And there is considerable evidence that
many had little comprehension of Christian thought of any kind.
Church courts were exercised with bizarre cases of ignorance
and irreverence, and protestant activists complained continually
of the lack of preachers to inform the people.   William Perkins
listed some of the current "errors" in a preface to *The
Foundation of Christian Religion* (1590)—"That howsoever a
man live, yet if he call upon God on his deathbed and say, Lord
have mercy upon me, and so go away like a lamb, he is certainly
saved"; "That a man may go to wizards, called wise men, for
counsel, because God hath provided a salve for every sore"
(*Work*, pp. 142, 144).
    The problem of identifying belief is lessened in the present
study by the fact that literature was written by educated men
who understood very well what they were supposed to believe.
They did not necessarily accept it, but they could not avoid taking
account of it.   Many of them were instructed at Oxford or
Cambridge, which were still mainly training centres for the ministry
and where only teachers approved by the church hierarchy were
permitted.
    The official doctrine of the Elizabethan Church was Calvinist,
as Archbishop Grindal insisted in a letter to the Strasburg Calvinist,
Hierom Zanchius (1571/72): "As for *doctrine*, hitherto we retain
it unshaken and unadulterated in our churches. . . . all our controversy has flowed from *discipline*" (Grindal, *Remains*, p. 339).
As Grindal explains, the puritan wing of the Church was worried
not about doctrine but about authority and the wearing of a
cap and surplice which could not be justified from Scripture.
The fact is that the Queen and some of her advisers did not
care much what people believed so long as they kept the peace.
    The doctrine of the English Church was set out in the Thirty-
nine Articles (finalised in 1571 and now published at the end
of the Anglican Prayer Book).   They were ordered to be read
in church several times a year and repeated by the faithful as
a condition of participation at Communion.   Article 10 states
firmly that man "cannot turn and prepare himself, by his own
natural strength and good works, to faith, and calling upon God:
Wherefore we have no power to do good works pleasant and acceptable to God without the grace of God by Christ preventing us"
(i.e. "going before us").   The Homilies were appointed to be

read in churches whenever there was not a sermon. In "The Salvation of Mankind" congregations were told that "justification is the office of God only; and is not a thing which we render unto him, but which we receive of him." The phrase "justification by faith" does not mean

> that this our own act, to believe in Christ, or this our faith in Christ, which is within us, doth justify us and deserve our justification unto us; for that were to count ourselves to be justified by some act or virtue that is within ourselves. . . . We must trust only in God's mercy. (*Homilies*, pp. 26-27)

The Elizabethan Church looked not to Wittenberg, where Luther's successors had moderated his doctrine, but to Geneva. The libraries of theological students at the turn of the century were replete with works by Calvin, Peter Martyr, Beza and Bullinger; the sermons of the Calvinist preacher William Perkins were a chief feature of life at Cambridge between 1592 and 1602; the standard Bible was the Geneva version (1557), with marginal comments to point the right interpretation.

The Elizabethan Church was officially committed also to the corollary of locating the possibility of grace entirely with God: the doctrine of election and reprobation. The seventeenth of the Thirty-nine Articles asserts:

> Predestination to Life is the everlasting purpose of God, whereby (before the foundations of the world were laid) he hath constantly decreed by his counsel secret to us, to deliver from curse and damnation those whom he hath chosen. . . . for curious and carnal persons, lacking the Spirit of Christ, to have continually before their eyes the sentence of God's predestination, is a most dangerous downfall. . . .

This article compromises only in so far as it leaves the loophole (which Milton was to exploit) that the end of some people might be undecided.

This strong version of protestant thought was hardly disputed in the English Church before 1600. In the 1590s William Barrett and Peter Baro questioned predestination at Cambridge; to still the controversy Archbishop Whitgift (no puritan) promulgated the Lambeth Articles (1595), stating unequivocally that "God from eternity predestined certain men to life and condemned others to death." Lancelot Andrewes disagreed and the Queen objected, but Whitgift declared that the articles "must be so taken and used as our private judgements, thinking them to be true and correspondent to the doctrine professed in this church of England, and established by the laws of the land." He told the vice-chancellor at Cambridge "to take care that nothing he publicly taught to the contrary" (Whitgift, *Works*, III, 612). Richard Hooker was commissioned by the bishops to defend episcopacy and in the process argued back towards the papist view of human capacity to contribute towards salvation.   But publication of *The Laws of Ecclesiastical Polity* was held up, probably because he went too far in that direction, and the 1593 edition was not sold out until 1606 whereas William Perkins' *Golden Chain* was reprinted twelve times between 1591 and 1600.   The centrality in Elizabethan thought which modern Anglicans have accorded to Hooker's work is quite unjustified.

At the Hampton Court Conference which James I called in 1604 to settle the structure of the Church the quarrel was again hardly doctrinal; James was a Calvinist and so was George Abbott, Archbishop of Canterbury from 1611 to 1633.   The Arminian party, who believed in free will and a compromise with the Roman liturgy, were uninfluential until Charles I came to the throne in 1625 and promoted Laud, eventually to Canterbury in 1633. If anything, it was these Arminians, rather than the puritans, who disrupted the English Church and helped to cause the Civil War.   But even moderate protestants reflect the substantial force of Reformation doctrine.   Andrewes told King James in a sermon on Christmas Day, 1605, of the contrast between the glorious angels and our "vile bodies"—"And the mould is no better; the womb wherein we were conceived, vile, base, filthy, and unclean.   There is our quality" (*Works*, I, 4).   He was confident that the great majority will be damned: "the greatest part of the world by far are entered upon and held by the unholy spirit" (*Works*, VI, 191).

This doctrinal emphasis in the English Church has fascinating consequences for the study of literature of the period.   It obliges us to entertain the thought, for instance, that Marlowe's Faustus is not damned because he is wicked, but wicked because he is damned.   It invites us to regard Milton's assertion of free will not as a triumphant expression of orthodoxy, but as a hard-won rejection of authoritative teaching.   Writers accepted, modified and resisted Calvinism, but each individual position can be under-stood only in the light of this dominant theology.   In some cases it provoked an indirect critique, extending perhaps to the whole principle of a beneficent deity.

Reformation religion is remote from most modern experience. But if we are to comprehend the literature written during the period of its dominance we must attempt to see why many found it helpful and comforting at the time.

The basic protestant premise is a sense of human wretchedness. If one experiences genuine conviction of sin (and who would not when God is aware, for instance, of every repining at his arrange-ment of human affairs—of every wish that it should stop raining?), then to be told that one may be saved nevertheless, entirely through divine mercy, is relatively reassuring.   William Tyndale in *The Parable of the Wicked Mammon* (1527) invites the faithful to seize upon the slightest good impulse as evidence of election:

> So long as thou findest any consent in thine heart unto the
> law of God, that it is righteous and good, and also displeasure
> that thou canst not fulfil it, despair not, neither doubt but
> that God's Spirit is in thee, and that thou art chosen for
> Christ's sake to the inheritance of eternal life.
> (*Writings*, p. 18)

Disappointment at one's failure is a cheerful sign, only minimal
virtue is expected.   Upon this basis many must have felt that
they were "chosen for Christ's sake."

The protestant who believed that he or she had received
grace might rise above all the anxieties of this world and the
next.   Richard Sibbes explains that the faithful may eventually
be given "a sweet spiritual security, whereby the soul is freed
from slavish fears, and glorieth in God as ours in all conditions.
And this is termed by the Apostle, not only *assurance*, but *the
riches of assurance"* (*The Soul's Conflict*, 1635; p. 323).   Of
course, one was not to feel too secure—that would be pride—but
to trust the promise one had received from God.

George Herbert's assurance of election was apparently founded
upon an early experience, when God

> Vouchsaf'd ev'n in the midst of youth and night
> To look upon me, who before did lie
>   Weltring in sin.

He felt "delight . . . overrun my heart, / And take it in" ("The
Glance").   Some poems in *The Temple* express the contradictory
pressures of protestantism: "These contrarieties crush me: these
cross actions / Do wind a rope about, and cut my heart."   But
Herbert's sense that the crucifixion was intended for him in
particular wins through:

>   And yet since these thy contradictions
> Are properly a cross felt by thy son,
> With but four words, my words, *Thy will be done.*
>   ("The Cross")

In "The Glance" Herbert attributes this process to that initial
call:

>   But still thy sweet original joy
> Sprung from thine eye, did work within my soul,
> And surging griefs, when they grew bold, control,
>   And got the day.

Assurance of election could confer a great sense of well-being,
a trust in one's (that is, God's) powers, and an authority in dealing
with people and nature.

We must recognize also that most sixteenth-century people did not share the modern sociological and psychological perspective upon wrongdoing. They believed in the absolute existence of good and evil, and that evil is properly attended with harsh punishment. Hence the protestant respect for a stern, authoritarian deity who puts the universe back to rights by sending the wicked to hell. Damnation had little to do with deterrence, for the reprobate were created bad; it had little to do with reform, for there will be no further chance. It was simply that there are two categories, and the blessed belong in heaven and the wicked in hell. Thus the confusion we experience in life is eliminated and "right" made to prevail.

It was usual to explain earthly afflictions as divine punishment. Shakespeare's Henry IV is altogether in the spirit of protestantism when he envisages a God who avenges himself at the expense of succeeding generations:

> I know not whether God will have it so
> For some displeasing service I have done,
> That in his secret doom out of my blood
> He'll breed revengement and a scourge for me;
> But thou dost in thy passages of life
> Make me believe that thou art only mark'd
> For the hot vengeance and the rod of heaven,
> To punish my mistreadings.
>
> (I Henry IV, III.ii.4)

Apropos of the Second Commandment, where God promises to visit "the iniquity of the fathers upon the children unto the third and fourth generation" (Deuteronomy, 5: 9), William Lawne's objector interposes, "To punish an innocent for another man's fault is against right, and the word of God himself." But he is told that children are justly punished for the iniquity they themselves commit "when God taketh away grace and other helps of salvation from a family" (Abridgement, pp. 86-87). This seems to be the fate of the Lancastrian line in Shakespeare's Histories.

The authoritarian Reformation deity guaranteed this tidy means of rendering suffering explicable. Protestants did not believe that the Old Testament God of wrath had been superseded; they relied equally upon all parts of the Bible for illustrations of God's way with his people, and did not play down the violent and punitive elements in the New Testament. A stern but decisive deity seemed preferable to a universe without a manifest moral order, and was not thought incompatible with the principle of divine love. God's mercy appears in the fact that he saves some when all deserve condemnation. Carey, typically, regards Donne's concern with divine power as "a final and fully adequate expression of his power lust" (John Donne, pp. 122-3), but Donne's view is not extraordinary. George Herbert's evocation of "Love" at the end of The Temple is written from the perspective of one of the elect.   He has earlier proclaimed that his deity

$$\text{gives to man, as he sees fit} \begin{cases} \text{Salvation.} \\ \text{Damnation.} \end{cases}$$

("The Water-course")

Finally, we should appreciate that protestants did not expect divine judgements to be comprehensible to the human mind. Although they attempted to dispel the superstitions of the medieval church, they nevertheless insisted that there are spiritual forces operating upon mankind and that they are by definition mysterious. The Reformation was in part a reaction against the incipient rationalism of humanists like Erasmus.

Luther's early pronouncements provoked Erasmus' objections in *The Freedom of the Will* (1524):

> Pious ears can admit the benevolence of one who imputes his own good to us; but it is difficult to explain how it can be a mark of his justice (for I will not speak of mercy) to hand over others to eternal torments in whom he has not deigned to work good works, when they themselves are incapable of doing good, since they have no free choice or, if they have, it can do nothing but sin.
>
> *(Luther and Erasmus,* p. 88)

If this seems unanswerable to the modern reader then it is because he or she shares Erasmus' tendency towards a rational, ethical, and ultimately secular world view.   The whole aim of the reformers was to impose upon such natural human concerns a rigour more intense than they found in the Roman church.   Hence Luther's reply: "This is the highest degree of faith, to believe him merciful when he saves so few and damns so many, and to believe him righteous when by his own will he makes us necessarily damnable" *(Luther and Erasmus,* p. 138).   Rational, humanistic objections are more than irrelevant to the protestant; they actually illustrate the inadequacy of human reason. God's inscrutable will *should* be incomprehensible to the fallen intellect.

In a way, Reformation theology commands respect.   Compared with more genial religious doctrines, it does attempt to acknowledge the complexity of experience.   If there is a deity in charge of the universe then he cannot evade responsibility for human suffering and frustration.   Calvin does not try to shuffle off divine accountability; he positively insists upon it:

> When afflicted with disease, we shall groan and be disquieted, and long for health; pressed with poverty, we shall feel

17

> the stings of anxiety and sadness, feel the pain of ignominy,
> contempt and injury, and pay the tears due to nature at
> the death of our friends; but our conclusion will always
> be, The Lord so willed it, therefore let us follow his will.
> *(Institutes of the Christian Religion,* 1558; III.viii.10)

The reformers do not try to diminish God's responsibility by distancing him from his creation, and they make relatively little appeal
to the consolation of life after death.   Out of an unusually vivid
awareness of the trials that beset us, they declare that everything
is directly as God wills it.   The logical and emotional confusions
we observe derive mainly from an intense struggle to make the
divine beneficence posited generally in Christianity applicable
to the whole of life.
　　Yet, despite the confident tone of official doctrine, many
may have felt that election and reprobation, although scriptural
and logical, are somehow at odds with humane impulses and God's
proclaimed goodness.   Robert Burton in *The Anatomy of
Melancholy* (1621) evokes sympathetically the plight of those
who doubt their election:

> the more they search and read Scriptures, or divine treatises,
> the more they puzzle themselves, as a bird in a net, the
> more they are entangled and precipitated into this preposterous
> gulf.   "Many are called, but few are chosen."   (III, 419)

In his wish to give comfort Burton turns to just those texts which
Lawne's objector cited as promising general salvation, but the
result is confusing: "Now there cannot be contradictory wills
in God; he will have all saved, and not all; how can this stand
together?   be secure then, believe, trust in him, hope well,
and be saved" (III, 420-21).   But there *is* a contradiction: the
generous texts are at odds with those that signify election.
The humane Burton is drawn to general salvation but cannot
get round the Thirty-nine Articles.
　　He even expounds an alternative theology:

> our late Arminians have revived that plausible doctrine of
> universal grace, which many fathers, our late Lutherans
> and modern papists do still maintain, that we have free
> will of ourselves, and that grace is common to all that
> will believe.   Some again, though less orthodoxical, will
> have a far greater part saved than shall be damned (as
> Caelius Secundus stiffly maintains).   (III, 421)

The doctrine seems to have a lot of support; "plausible" may
mean either "specious" or "agreeable"; it is unclear how much
credit Burton intends here.   And he follows the Pelagian Caelius
through to his doubt about the beneficence of damning so many
for Adam's sin: "For how can he be merciful that shall condemn
any creature to eternal unspeakable punishment, for one small

temporary fault, all posterity, so many myriads for one and another man's offence?" (III, 423).

But Burton finally beats an abrupt and total retreat from such dangerous questioning: "these absurd paradoxes are exploded by our Church, we teach otherwise." He restates as clearly as he can the Calvinist belief in God's "immutable, eternal, just decree" by which "all are invited, but only the elect apprehended" (III, 423-24). Surely we have caught Burton in a mood of vacillation. He is moved by the problems but unwilling to deny the prevailing doctrine.

Sir Thomas Browne in *Religio Medici* (1636) admits to having been tempted by the heresy that damnation will not be eternal *(Selected Writings*, p. 12). He accepts predestination and declares, "That which is the cause of my election, I hold to be the cause of my salvation, which was the mercy and beneplacit of God, before I was, or the foundation of the world"; yet he will not grant the total inefficacy of works (pp. 64-65) and the second part of the book is mainly about charity.

Calvinism, then, was orthodox but controversial. The breakdown of censorship in the 1640s produced a flood of pamphlets questioning original sin and proposing universal salvation. The insistence of the English Church—or at least of most of its prominent members—upon a theory of divine justice which it could not render satisfactory created profound disjunctions, both in religious experience and in its relationships with contemporary literature.

I shall argue the complex interaction of protestantism and literature in five main areas. First, this religion tried to take seriously the demand of Christianity to dominate every aspect of life; this was specially problematic for secular literature, for the most respected models were pagan. Second, protestantism modified ways of thinking about love and marriage, and this stimulated innovation in the traditional modes of love poetry. Third, it confronted directly the humanist estimate of human potential; and fourth, it provoked alarm and scepticism by claiming as providential the control of its harsh God. Both these factors profoundly influenced tragedy. Finally, by the way it tried to contain these problems, protestantism actually assisted its own supersession and the development of a secularist approach to life.

3 Puritan humanists

Sidney, Spenser, Milton

> This word "damnation" terrifies not him,
> For he confounds hell in Elysium.
> His ghost be with the old philosophers.
>> (Marlowe, *Dr. Faustus*, I.iii.58)

In the Homily "Of the Salvation of Mankind" Elizabethans were exhorted to refer every aspect of life to their religion:

> these great and merciful benefits of God . . . move us to render ourselves unto God *wholly* with *all* our will, hearts, might, and power; to serve him in *all* good deeds, obeying his commandments during our lives; to seek *in all things* his glory and honour, not our sensual pleasures and vainglory.
> *(Homilies*, pp. 31-32; my italics)

What, then, was the role of literature and learning in this life of total service?   They were needed to help the faithful in their newly direct contact with Scripture, but they were dominated by classical letters, whose scope in ideas, imagination and expression immeasurably exceeded anything in English at 1580.   These supreme models were imbued with pagan values, not Christian, and much contemporary literature followed them, in tendency at least.

The extreme response to this split in values was to eschew secular literature altogether, as George Herbert did.   This reaction was not exclusive to protestants.   The Catholic Counter-Reformation produced in some people an equally intense determination that literature should serve a directly Christian purpose.   The Jesuit Robert Southwell complained in his preface to "Saint Peter's Complaint" that "In paynim toys the sweetest veins are spent: / To Christian works, few have their talents lent."   Like Herbert, he wrote only religious poetry, self-consciously adapting secular modes (like the complaint) to Christian themes.   The Catholic position was hardly developed in England because Southwell and others like him were tortured and killed by the government. Very many protestant writers sought to maintain classical literary traditions alongside or within an earnest religious involvement, and this produced a distinctive range of problems. This chapter is about the conflicting demands of literature and religious commitment in the thought and work of Sidney, Spenser and Milton.

Students of the period have traditionally smoothed over this issue with the term "Christian humanism", implying a harmonious co-operation between religion and literature founded upon a noble reciprocity between divine power and human dignity.

Some people experienced this happy balance. Neoplatonists like Ficino and Pico della Mirandola compared the Bible with the ideas of prechristian mystics and discovered an agreement about human capacity to ascend to the divine. But protestants insisted on the exclusive authority of Scripture and an anthropomorphic deity, and denied that one can, of oneself, ascend to God. Humanists like Erasmus proposed that Christians, with the additional inspiration of Jesus, should build on the classical programme of self-sufficient rational virtue. But protestants denied the congruity of pagan and Christian virtue, that people can achieve rational self-determination, and that moral achievement is relevant to salvation.

In brief, humanism values humanity for itself and finds the divine in it, usually in the exalted reason; it regards all poetry as a noble expression of the creative imagination. Protestantism insists upon human depravity and the gap between human and divine; it regards pagan and secular literature as inevitably fallible and insignificant. Luther used Erasmus' work on the Bible but declared in a letter of June 1524 that, "like Moses, he will die in the land of Moab, for he is powerless to guide men to those higher studies which lead to divine blessedness" (*Martin Luther*, pp. 112-13). Erasmus observed in a letter of March 1528: "Wherever Lutheranism is dominant the study of letters is extinguished" (*Opus Epistolarum*, VII, 366).

"Christian humanism" suggests a steady harmony and fulfilment; I use "puritan humanism" to indicate a persistent tension between religion and literature. The term is admittedly provocative, though I believe that Sidney, Spenser and Milton can be identified precisely as puritans and humanists in their respective theological, political and social contexts. But the aim is mainly to assert the conflicting imperatives in people who were deeply committed both to protestantism and literature. At a certain level of intensity no reconciliation was possible. So Tyndale declared: "The spirit of the world understands not the speaking of God; neither the spirit of the wise of this world, neither the spirit of philosphers, neither the spirit of Socrates, of Plato, or of Aristotle's ethics" (*Writings*, p. 66). And Donne warned in his sermon preached at the Hague (1619): "The Scriptures will be out of thy reach, and out of thy use, if thou cast and scatter them upon reason, upon philosophy, upon morality, to try how the Scriptures will fit all them" (*Sermons*, II, 308).

Calvin sought to systematize the issue (as he did everything else). He granted pagans a general idea about God but denied that it is sufficient for salvation. Their ignorance of the fall caused a presumptuous estimate of human dignity: "Hence the great darkness of philosophers who have looked for a complete building in a ruin, and fit arrangement in disorder" (*Institutes of the Christian Religion*, 1558; I.xv.8). Theologians should not try "to reconcile the doctrine of Scripture with the dogmas of philosophy" (II.ii.4). Sometimes Calvin seems to condemn all the works of pagans, but in a prominent passage he recognizes their achievements in the manual and liberal arts, and even in morals, which God enabled them to understand through merely human reason: "Nothing, indeed, is more common, than for man to be sufficiently instructed in a right course of conduct by natural law" (*Institutes*, II.ii.22). It is precisely the irrelevance of moral achievement to salvation which made this formula possible. We may even honour pagan thinkers: "the admirable light of truth displayed in them should remind us, that the human mind, however much fallen and perverted from its original integrity, is still adorned and invested with admirable gifts from its Creator" (II.ii.15).

This strategy—a version of rendering unto Caesar that which is Caesar's—allowed classical letters a role in moral and practical matters though they are irrelevant to salvation. All the good protestant had to do was to maintain the segregation and a sense of priorities. So Thomas Becon in his *Catechism* (1560):

> *Father.* After that the schoolmaster have diligently planted the religion of Christ in the tender breasts of the children, by teaching them the word of God, what is then his duty to do?
> *Son.* To teach them good letters, I mean poets, orators, historiographers, philosophers, &c.; not that they should be mates with God's word, but rather handmaids unto it, and serve to set forth the honour and glory thereof. (p. 382).

But it wasn't that simple. Becon went on quickly to reject writers who are in parts "wanton and unhonest" (Martial, the Latin elegiac poets) or "wicked and ungodly" (Lucian). In *The Nobles* (1563) Lawrence Humphrey lamented the lack of learning among the upper classes, but complained that too many read "human things, not divine; love toys, not fruitful lessons; Venus' games, not weighty studies tending to increase of godliness, dignity or true and sound commodity; as Ovid, *Of the Art of Love*" (sig. x). He rejected the *Aeneid* because it presents unchristian values too eloquently (sig. y). Roger Ascham in *The Schoolmaster* (1552) recommended many pagan and secular authors but condemned Italianate Englishmen who "have in more reverence the *Triumphs* of Petrarch than the Genesis of Moses; they make more account of Tully's *Offices* than St. Paul's Epistles" (*Whole Works*, III, 161). It is all a popish plot: "the readiest way to entangle the mind with false doctrine, is first to entice the will to wanton living", and that is what "papists abroad" and "subtle and secret papists at home" seek to do through "bawdy books" (III, 158-159).

These reservations created serious difficulties for men like Sidney, Spenser and Milton, who were deeply committed both to literature and to protestantism. There was a space for imaginative writing, but it was beset by cavilling and distrust. Thomas Nashe believed literature had been hindered by "the upstart discipline of our reformatory churchmen, who account wit vanity, and poetry impiety" ("Preface to Greene's *Menaphon*," 1589; *Works*, III,321). The puritan humanist who felt the force of protestant doctrine as well as the imaginative excitement of literature was sited at the crisis point of a sharp and persistent cultural dislocation.

Sidney's puritan allegiance is apparent in his role in Leicester's faction, his English and continental friends, his home and foreign policy, and his appointment as personal chaplains of the nonconformists James Stile and George Gifford. The *Defence of Poetry* (1580-81) is designed to justify literature to the ardent protestant; it is the most fully developed attempt to establish a puritan-humanist aesthetic. Sidney's strategies and difficulties are characteristic of puritan-humanist thought.

Three principal arguments in the *Defence* are designed to appeal to protestants. First, Sidney distinguishes three kinds of poet: the divine, who "imitate the unconceivable excellencies of God," the philosophical, who versify facts and arguments, and poets who invent their material, so teaching us not about "what is, hath been, or shall be" but about "what may be and should be" (*Defence*, pp. 25-26). The ultimate divine poems are biblical, and "against these none will speak that hath the Holy Ghost in due holy reverence" (p. 25). Having established this distinction and priority, Sidney can then allow natural understanding, in Calvin's manner, to the philosophical poet and the poet who shows what should be, for these are practical and ethical concerns. Sidney remarks, "in nature we know it is well to do well, and what is well, and what is evil, although not in the words of art which philosophers bestow upon us; for out of natural conceit the philosophers drew it" (p. 39). Classical literature is defended for the wisdom its authors derived from "natural conceit".

Second, Sidney insists upon the didactic function of poets of the third kind—the ones he mainly defends: "For these indeed do merely make to imitate, and imitate both to delight and teach; and delight, to move men to take that goodness in hand, which without delight they would fly as from a stranger" (*Defence*, p. 27). Many people in the period said that literature instructs and delights, though writers like Shakespeare, Marlowe and Donne in his love poems gave little heed to instruction. Sidney insists with unusual fervour upon the didactic purpose, to the extent even of positing a crude exemplary function for characters. This leads him to simplify the works he adduces: "If the poet do his part aright, he will show you in Tantalus, Atreus, and such like, nothing that is not to be shunned; in Cyrus, Aeneas, Ulysses, each thing to be followed" (pp. 35-36). What, then, of Aeneas' sexual involvement with Dido? Sir John Harington in his light-hearted defence of *Orlando Furioso* (1591) cites it to support the highly casual attitude to sex in Ariosto's poem (Smith, *Elizabethan Critical Essays*, II, 214). Again, when Sidney speaks of the elegy he treats it entirely as a mode of lament, ignoring the more prominent lascivious love elegies of Ovid, Tibullus, Propertius and modern imitations by poets like Joannes Secundus (*Defence*, pp. 43-44). Sidney bends the evidence to moralize poetry for the earnest protestant.

Third, Sidney appeals to the fall to validate his argument; it is this which sets him apart from the optimistic humanism of Erasmus. History and philosophy are inferior because they are less effective in moving the will of corrupt humanity. The former, "being captived to the truth of a foolish world, is many times a terror from well-doing, and an encouragement to unbridled wickedness" (pp. 37-38). Only poetry entices us to virtue—Sidney calls it "a medicine of cherries" (p. 41). And, as we shall see in a moment, he claims in his basic discussion of the validity of poetry that it offers "no small arguments to the credulous of that first accursed fall of Adam" (p. 25).

Sidney establishes a precise role for pagan and secular poetry: without presuming upon divine matters it moves the recalcitrant to virtue. Spenser and Milton adopt the essentials of this position. In the Letter to Raleigh about *The Fairy Queen* (1589) Spenser claims to be following the classical tradition and gives it Sidney's strong ethical interpretation: Homer, "in the persons of Agamemnon and Ulysses hath ensampled a good governor and a virtuous man, the one in his *Ilias*, the other in his *Odysseis:* then Virgil, whose like intention was to do in the person of Aeneas . . ." *(Poetical Works*, p. 407). Moreover, Spenser picks up a likely puritan objection ("good discipline" is the language of puritans and they valued above all the sermon):

> To some I know this method will seem displeasant, which had rather have good discipline delivered plainly in way of precepts or sermoned at large, as they use, than thus cloudily enwrapped in allegorical devices. But such, me seem, should be satisfied with the use of these days, seeing all things accounted by their shows, and nothing esteemed of that is not delightful and pleasing to common sense. (p. 407)

Spenser's distrust of humankind in "these days" seems even sharper than Sidney's.

In his early years Milton adopted enthusiastically Sidney's means of justifying poetry. He asserted in *The Reason of Church Government* (1641) that it teaches "over the whole book of sanctity and virtue through all the instances of example, with such delight to those especially of soft and delicious temper who will not so much as look upon truth herself unless they see her elegantly dressed" *(Complete Prose*, I, 817-18). Hence he could proclaim the power of poets "to imbreed and cherish in a great people the seeds of virtue and public civility, to allay the perturbations of the mind, and to set the affections in right tune" (pp. 816-17).

But these attempts to reconcile puritan and humanist attitudes left exposed several areas of strain and danger. Examination of three of them will show various forms taken by the disjunction between literature and Reformation thought.

One problem is that the puritan is bound to accord highest praise to divine poetry whilst the humanist is specially concerned to defend secular literature. Sidney calls divine poets "the chief, both in antiquity and excellency" *(Defence*, p. 25) but devotes almost all his attention to the ethical writer. Some puritans were prepared to sacrifice secular poetry in order to resolve this paradox, so upsetting the precarious balance Sidney laboured to establish. The Huguenot du Bartas became the spokesman of those who denied any validity to secular poetry. In *Urania* (1574; translated by James VI of Scotland in 1584) du Bartas nominated Urania the muse of divine poetry; she exhorts him:

> If ye be heavenly, how dare ye presume
> A verse profane, and mocking for to sing
> 'Gainst him that leads of starry heavens the ring?
> Will ye then so ingrately make your pen
> A slave to sin, and serve but fleshly men?
> (James VI, *Essayes of a Prentise*, p. 29)

So Herbert asked God, "Why are not sonnets made of thee? and lays / Upon thine altar burnt?" and resolved that his poetic abilities should be "ever consecrated to God's glory" *(English Poems*, p. 205).

Already in the *Defence* Sidney declared that sonnets might better be employed upon "the immortal goodness of that God who giveth us hands to write and wits to conceive" (p. 69). His attraction to this extreme view evidently increased, for we know that he translated du Bartas' long poem about the creation, *The First Week*. It seems that puritanism was gaining ground on humanism in Sidney's last months, for he began to translate also the Psalms and du Plessis-Mornay's treatise on *The Trueness of the Christian Religion*—which argues the radical inferiority of pagan religious thought (see further my article, "Sidney, du Plessis-Mornay and the Pagans," *Philological Quarterly*, LVIII [1979], 26-39). The revised *Arcadia* is more earnest than the first version, but Greville tells us that on his deathbed Sidney wished to destroy the book altogether, seeing that beauty, "in all earthly complexions, was more apt to allure men to evil than to fashion any goodness in them" (*Life of Sidney*, p. 13).   The whole argument of the *Defence* collapses if humanity is so far fallen that the delights of poetry can only mislead.

The tendency to move from secular literature, justified in ethical terms, to exclusively divine or severely instructive writing is apparent in other puritan humanists, for instance Fulke Greville and Joseph Hall.   This, in outline, was Milton's development. *Comus* (1634) is exactly the kind of poem Sidney meant to defend, but soon Milton was indicating that only divine poetry is acceptable. Despite his claim in *The Reason of Church Government* for the general moral validity of poetry, he himself contemplates

> a work not to be raised from the heat of youth or
> the vapours of wine, like that which flows at waste
> from the pen of some vulgar amorist or the trencher
> fury of a rhyming parasite, nor to be obtained by the
> invocation of Dame Memory and her siren daughters,
> but by devout prayer to that eternal Spirit.   (*Complete
> Prose*, I, 820-21)

This deprecation of secular and pagan literature led Milton to *Paradise Lost,* where he attempts to press the whole pagan tradition into the service of divine poetry.   What we have, as I shall demonstrate, is a massive struggle between the humanist and the puritan for dominance.

Yet a more radical position was already implicit in Milton's thought.   In *Of Reformation* (1641) he asserts that the individual's inner light is sufficient for the understanding of Scripture (I, 566); he makes the point more strongly (whilst allowing a role for languages and rhetorical and logical analysis) in *The Likeliest Means* (1659).   It would seem, from this, that secular imagery and allusion can contribute little to divine poetry: the biblical story should be adequate.   Eventually Milton was driven to accept the logic of this argument, and *Paradise Regained* (1671) eschews almost entirely the classical tradition.

Hence the insertion of a fourth temptation into the story of Jesus in the wilderness in *Paradise Regained*, the temptation to study pagan wisdom.   Critics whose Christianity is of a less abrasive cast than Milton's have tried to explain away Jesus' rejection of classical philosophy, but it is clear-cut and the austere tone of the poem shows Milton trying to write with it in mind. Satan is given arguments which puritan humanists had often advanced—that Jesus must converse with gentiles on their own terms (IV, 227-35); that tragedians instruct and delight in the manner proposed by Sidney (IV, 261-66).   But Jesus will have none of it.   His rejection is based both on the sufficiency of Scripture and the worthlessness of pagan thought:

> He who receives
> Light from above, from the Fountain of Light,
> No other doctrine needs, though granted true;
> But these are false, or little else but dreams,
> Conjectures, fancies, built on nothing firm.
>   (IV, 288)

It seems that there is no role for secular literature.

Even at this point, though, the humanist in Milton is not quite overcome. Jesus gives just two lines (out of 78) to Calvin's saving formula: there may be pagan writing "where moral virtue is expressed / By light of nature not in all quite lost" (IV, 351). And this concession is startlingly exploited when, with Satan finally abashed, Milton introduces the only two substantial classical allusions in the poem, to the triumphs of Hercules over Antaeus and Oedipus over the Sphinx (IV, 563-75). He tells us that he compares "Small things with greatest" (line 564), but the impact is huge and deeply disturbing. Milton's poetry shows a steady movement from Sidney's position in the *Defence* to du Bartas', but he managed no ultimate resolution of the puritan-humanist dilemma.

Spenser had experimented with divine poetry by 1591, for several titles are listed in the printer's note to the *Complaints.* But his attitude shows no smooth development for he continued to write secular poetry and *The Fairy Queen*, as I shall argue, moves towards a general disillusion with protestant values. Spenser's vacillation is epitomized by the *Four Hymns* (1596). The first two, to Love and Beauty, are entirely Petrarchan and Neoplatonic; they make no concession to a puritan anxiety about pagan doctrine and imagery. But in the dedication to the Countesses of Cumberland and Warwick (both puritans) he attributes those poems to "the greener times of my youth" and says that they "too much pleased those of like age and disposition, which being too vehemently carried with that kind of affection, do rather suck out poison to their strong passion, than honey to their honest delight" *(Poetical Works,* p. 586). This is the reason why, according to Greville, Sidney wished to destroy *Arcadia:* mankind is too far fallen for the delights of poetry to have a beneficial effect. So, Spenser says, he has made "instead of those two hymns of earthly or natural love and beauty, two others of heavenly and celestial." Such are the second two hymns, and they begin with a repudiation:

> Many lewd lays (ah woe is me the more)
> In praise of that mad fit, which fools call love,
> I have in th'heat of youth made heretofore,
> That in light wits did loose affection move.
> But all those follies now I do reprove,
> And turned have the tenor of my string,
> The heavenly praises of true love to sing.   (p. 593)

The paradox, of course, is that Spenser has published all four poems—the "lewd lays" as well as the "heavenly praises". We may assume that the latter supersede the former, but Spenser is plainly reluctant to discard his earlier work. The humanist will not submit to the puritan.

A second danger with the puritan-humanist aesthetic is the temptation to smuggle back in an exalted status for pagan letters by undermining the separation between divine and natural comprehension. Neoplatonic thought filtered generally into Renaissance culture and it became common to imply the consonance of Christian and pagan understanding through a cross-referencing of images. Pierre de Ronsard presents his hymn "Christian Hercules" (1555) as a song to please Christian ears; the greater part is a series of comparisons between the lives of Hercules and Jesus. Juno sent two serpents to kill the infant demi-god and Herod tried to murder Christ; Hercules put on the shirt sent him by his wife and Christ put on human form; Hercules' self-immolation on Etna parallels the crucifixion (*Oeuvres Complètes*, VIII). Earnest protestants strongly opposed such blurring of Christian and pagan. Du Plessis-Mornay in *The Trueness of the Christian Religion* (1581), which Sidney began to translate, explained that pagans understand just sufficient to know that they should serve and obey God and that they are fallen, but that this must bring them to a depth of despair which only the New Testament revelation can reach.

Sidney holds carefully to Mornay's principles. In *Arcadia* he goes to some trouble to attribute unobjectionable religious ideas to his pagan characters without allowing them Christian insight. When Pamela submits to God—"O Lord, I yield unto thy will, and joyfully embrace what sorrow thou wilt have me suffer" (*New Arcadia*, p. 464)—this could of course be Christian but it could also be an elaboration of the famous prayer by the Stoic, Cleanthes. Milton recognised as much when he complained at Charles I's use of it (*Complete Prose*, III, 366-67). When Pamela disputes with the atheistic Cecropia (pp. 488-92) Sidney gives her arguments drawn from Cicero's *Of the Nature of the Gods*. She says nothing of God's goodness in redeeming humanity from the fallen condition.

In Milton's poems the relationship between pagan imagery and Christian understanding is always interesting. In *Comus* we are told that ancient poets were "taught by th' heav'nly Muse" (line 515), but the theme is primarily ethical—the threat of sensuality to the rule of reason and temperance—and hence easily contained within the Sidneyan formula. In fact, the line between natural and divine is precisely drawn. In the *Odyssey* Ulysses overcomes Circe because he possesses the herb moly. The parallel in Milton's poem enables the Brothers safely to approach Comus with the

protection of reason, but they are unable to free the Lady.
The limitations of the Brothers' human power and of pagan myth
therefore coincide: neither Homer nor the Brothers, of themselves,
have a final answer to evil.   Grace is required, and it is represented by Sabrina, whose story is derived from Spenser, a Christian
poet (lines 814-23).

In *Paradise Lost* Milton places the classical gods—Saturn,
Jove and their peers—among the devils (I, 506-21).   The poem
is replete with pagan imagery but Milton frequently insists upon
its inferior status.   Yet the ultimate effect is to grant classical
literature a significance which is explicitly repudiated, for it
becomes apparent that Milton depends upon it for emotional
richness.   It is not just a matter of epic set pieces, like the
war in heaven.   The immediate penalty experienced by Satan
and the devils, transformation into snakes, is taken from Ovid
and Lucan (X, 504-09);   the story of Noah is elaborated with
details of the storm which, according to Ovid, caused Deucalion's
flood (XI, 738-45).   Milton avoids this technique in theologically
significant passages, but the impression gradually and inevitably
builds that the biblical account is inadequate, that its followers
may learn much from pagan myth.

Also, Milton allows certain allusions to escape the control
of derogatory comment and to bulk larger than subordinate illustration.   At the start of book VII he appeals to du Bartas' muse,
Urania, claiming to soar "Above the flight of Pegasean wing"
(VII, 4).   But almost at once he thinks of his own society and
a heathen image thrusts forward:

> But drive far off the barbarous dissonance
> Of Bacchus and his revelers, the race
> Of that wild rout that tore the Thracian bard
> In Rhodope, where woods and rocks had ears
> To rapture, till the savage clamour drowned
> Both harp and voice; nor could the Muse defend
> Her son.   So fail not thou who thee implores;
> For thou art heav'nly, she an empty dream.   (VII, 32)

Orpheus' muse was a delusion, Milton says, but Ovid's account
of the prophet's death at the hands of the profane mob
(*Metamorphoses*, XI) obviously moves him.   This comparison
is not presented so that we can see the inferiority of the pagan
imagination—contemporary Christians are the problem—but because
it speaks truth for Milton.

Explicitly Milton observes Sidney's segregation of Christian
and pagan; implicitly we observe his reluctance to discount classical
myth.   Spenser allows a happy confusion.   It is commonly asserted
that he maintains a distinction between the realms of grace
and nature, but his humanistic impulse tempts him beyond accepted
protestant principles.   At a crucial stage in the spiritual development of Redcross, Fidelia introduces him to the Bible—"heavenly
documents . . . That weaker wit of man could never reach, /

Of God, of grace, of justice, of free will" (I.x.19).   This seems
to establish the unique authority of the Bible and sometimes
Spenser purposefully subordinates myth.   But often he implies
a radical validity in pagan imagery.   The angel who restores
Guyon after his descent into the Cave of Mammon is compared,
in Neoplatonic fashion, to Cupid when he has laid aside his "cruel
bow" (II.viii.6); not only is the Mount of Contemplation compared
to Parnassus as well as Olivet, but the pagan image is placed
in the second, implicitly climactic half of the stanza (I.x.54).
The connotations run wild when Spenser evokes the garden around
the Bower of Bliss, the dwelling of the wicked seductress, Acrasia:

> More sweet and wholesome than the pleasant hill
>> Of Rhodope, on which the nymph that bore
>> A giant babe herself for grief did kill;
>> Or the Thessalian Tempe, where of yore
>> Fair Daphne Phoebus' heart with love did gore;
>> Or Ida, where the gods loved to repair,
>> Whenever they their heavenly bowers forlore;
>> Or sweet Parnass, the haunt of Muses fair;
> Or Eden 'self, if ought with Eden mote compare.   (II.xii.52)

Rhodope and Thessaly were the scenes of disasters, Ida and
Parnassus have mystical Neoplatonic associations, and it is left
unclear whether Acrasia has somehow managed to outdo Eden.
Compare Milton's firmer consistency when he invokes a sequence
of pagan gardens and uses their ominous implications but denies
that they compare with Eden *(Paradise Lost,* IV, 268-87, IX, 439-43).
Spenser does not maintain a protestant control of pagan imagery.

The third danger with Sidney's argument is that whilst the puritan
emphasizes the fall, the humanist is inclined to claim a lofty
insight for the poet.   This allows the strange inference that
readers are corrupt and in need of a "medicine of cherries" whilst
poets have a privileged access to the truth.   With the nineteenth-
century decline in religious belief this became an acceptable
proposition, but it is hard to align with protestantism around
1600.   The attribution of elevated status to the poetic imagination
exposes the division in the puritan-humanist aesthetic.
    Sidney cautiously denies that the poet is divinely inspired
(Defence, p. 60) but he declares that poetry penetrates beyond
other disciplines because they are obliged to follow fallen nature:

> Only the poet, disdaining to be tied to any such subjection,
> lifted up with the vigour of his own invention, doth grow
> in effect another nature, in making things either better
> than nature bringeth forth or, quite anew, forms such as

> never were in nature. . . . Her world is brazen, the poets
> only deliver a golden.   (pp. 23-24.)

This, Sidney adds, offers "no small arguments to the credulous
of that first accursed fall of Adam" (p.25): we can see that
people once lived in a perfect world because the poet is able
to intuit it.
    But how does the poet—and Sidney specifies pagans like
Xenophon and Virgil—achieve such an exalted vision?   How does
he see past the fall?   Sidney is in danger of sounding like Ficino,
who ignores the fall and argues man's immortality not from divine
grace and biblical authority but from his own power: man

> imitates all the works of the divine nature, and perfects,
> corrects and improves the works of the lower nature.   There-
> fore the power of man is almost similar to that of the divine
> nature, for man acts in this way through himself.   Through
> his own wit and art he governs himself, without being bound
> by any limits of corporeal nature.   *(Platonic Theology,* p. 233)

Sidney quickly tries to head off the hint of such presumption—we
must "rather give right honour to the heavenly Maker of that
maker" (p. 24).   But the humanist is pushing hard against the
puritan.
    The conflict is not relieved by the further explanation that
"our erected wit maketh us know what perfection is, and yet
our infected will keepeth us from reaching unto it" (p. 25).
This is often taken as a triumphant statement of "Christian humanism," but in fact it is a contradiction in sixteenth-century theological terms.   It epitomizes the disjunction in puritan humanism.
"Infected will" is Calvin's concept: he insists, contrary to Aristotle,
Aquinas and Hooker, that the will is depraved to the extent
that it is likely to refuse to obey the reason *(Institutes,* II.ii.2-4,
26-27).   "Erected wit," on the other hand, offered as a faculty
which can penetrate beyond the fall and which is available to
pagans, gives much more credit to unaided human nature than
most protestants would allow.   Infected will is a puritan concept,
erected wit a humanist.   Sidney's idea of humanity conflicts
with his idea of the poet.
    Spenser and Milton both use the fall as an argument for
poetry, but they too reflect a countervailing humanistic estimate
of the poet's insight.   Spenser appears with increasing authority
as Colin Clout.   In book VI of   *The Fairy Queen* when, as I
shall argue, other structures of value are breaking down, Colin
becomes the sole vehicle of ultimate truth.   He alone is visited
by the Graces whilst Calidore, the knight of the book, disrupts
the vision—"none can them bring in place, / But whom they of
themselves list so to grace" (VI.x.20).
    In the sonnet "How soon hath Time" (1632) Milton readily
attributes any poetic achievement he may make to "the will
of Heav'n"—"All is, if I have grace to use it so, / As ever in
my great Task-Master's eye."   Nevertheless, he often manifests

31

an exalted sense of his own talent and its noble humane standing.

"Lycidas" (1637) is at first sight the complete puritan-humanist poem. Milton establishes totally the genre of the pastoral elegy, initially lamenting Lycidas as a shepherd lost to an idealized rural scene. But then two movements shift the poem to a protestant mode of consciousness. One is Milton's attack on false pastors, which reminds the reader that we do not live in a remote or perfect world. The other is the supersession of pagan images by Christian. Traditional mourners are followed by "The Pilot of the Galilean lake" (line 109), though at first this perspective is not sustained:

> Return, Alpheus, the dread voice is past
> That shrunk thy streams; return, Sicilian Muse,
> And call the vales, and bid them hither cast
> Their bells and flow'rets of a thousand hues.   (line 132)

The pagan mode is recalled, the humanist poet is reluctant to let it go. But it will not do: we cannot strew Lycidas' hearse with flowers because he is washed far away beneath the seas. The reality of death requires a more powerful answer. This is afforded by Christian revelation: "So Lycidas sunk low, but mounted high, / Through the dear might of him that walked the waves" (line 173). We see Milton actually work his way through the pagan response to death, which the pastoral genre implies, to a Christian understanding. The puritan, it seems, controls and uses the humanist.

The flaw, I think, is our overwhelming sense of Milton himself. Near the beginning of the poem he envisages his own "destined urn" (line 20), then he laments how death cuts off the fame of those who "strictly meditate the thankless Muse" (line 66). This refers us inevitably to the present writer, and the poem becomes part of his attempt "to burst out into sudden blaze" of literary renown (line 74). We become aware of the exploration of pagan and Christian values as an achievement of Milton rather than a submission to divine will. The humanist protrudes. The last eight lines of the poem—"Thus sang the uncouth swain . . ."—distance Milton from his shepherd persona and hence, arguably, from the pagan pastoral tradition. But they also draw attention again to the poet himself.

The dignity of the poetic vocation is often asserted in Milton's writing. It may be assimilated to protestantism if it is presented as a divine calling—the basic Reformation rule for everyday life was that each person should labour in his or her calling. But this claim cannot be made for pagan writers. Nevertheless, in the passage we have considered in *The Reason of Church Government* Milton says, "These abilities, wheresoever they be found, are the inspired gift of God rarely bestowed, but yet to some (though most abuse) in every nation" (*Complete Prose*, I, 816). But why should God bestow his inspiration upon "every nation," including pagans who must abuse it? The humanist wants to grant true inspiration to the heathens he admires but the puritan recognizes that their products must be unsatisfactory. They have and do not have divine approval.

In *Paradise Lost* Milton may reasonably claim divine inspiration. But even at the start of Book III, where he apostrophizes "holy Light" and attributes his poetry to "the Heav'nly Muse," Milton admits to wandering on Helicon as well as Sion and compares himself to blind sages like Homer and Tiresias (III, 1, 19, 26-37). Indeed, he becomes one of the poem's heroes, for he too has made his descent into the underworld and returned, "Though hard and rare" (III, 21). The humanistic implications of the passage feed into Milton's evocation of the world he cannot see:

> but not to me returns
> Day, or the sweet approach of ev'n or morn,
> Or sight of vernal bloom, or summer's rose,
> Or flocks, or herds, or human face divine.
> (III, 41)

At the point of transition between the hell of the first two books and the heaven of the third, Milton thinks longingly of the mortal world between. From this perspective the climactic translation of light into poetic inspiration is profoundly inclusive : "So much the rather thou, celestial Light,/ Shine inward" (III, 51). In context with Homer and Tiresias, "celestial Light" may refer to the humanistic idea of the poet's imaginative insight as well as to God's guidance. Milton has invoked light as a divine effusion and as the illumination of the human world, and though the latter is literally denied to him·he draws inspiration from both.

Milton's commitment in *Paradise Lost* is to humanistic glory as much as to God. It can hardly be demonstrated either way, but many readers feel that Milton's ego is asserted as vigorously as "the ways of God to men." Milton perhaps recognised as much when he moved on to the austere and self-denying mode of *Paradise Regained.*

In summary, then, the puritan humanist experienced a divided allegiance and attempted to resolve it by claiming that secular and pagan literature, without infringing upon the divine, moves fallen men to virtue. One danger with the theory is that it is bound to accord pre-eminence to divine poetry, and in fact puritan humanists tend to move towards a rejection of secular literature. Second, there is the temptation to imply a religious validity to pagan imagery. Third, puritan humanists are inclined to hold the poet in a lofty esteem which it is difficult to reconcile with the fall. The second half of this chapter is about the conflict of values in *Arcadia, The Fairy Queen* and *Paradise Lost.*

* * * * * *

The concern of writers like Sidney, Spenser and Milton to meet puritan as well as humanistic criteria produced two typical modifications of existing literary genres. Sometimes they add a specially urgent moral direction. Sidney's *Arcadia* is recognizably a pastoral romance but it criticizes the evasion of responsibility; in *Comus* Milton added to the mask an exalted ethical theme, enforced partly through substantial intellectual dispute. Spenser sharpens the moral implications of the eclogue, the sonnet sequence, the epithalamion and the romantic epic. Alternatively, in du Bartas' manner, a secular form might be put to divine purpose— so Sidney in his versification of the Psalms, Spenser in *Fairy Queen*, book one, and Milton in *Paradise Lost, Samson Agonistes* and *Paradise Regained.*

The consequence of these strategies, however, is more often a manifestation of the puritan-humanist disjunction than a resolution of it. The characterisitic features of the genre which is being adapted exert a drag back towards its more usual values. This is in part a technical problem. If Sidney's *Old Arcadia* is to be a pastoral romance in the tradition of Sannazaro and Montemayor, it must include noble and virtuous lovers who are treated in a generally lyrical and sympathetic manner, an idealized rural setting, singing competitions between shepherds and a happy ending. And so it does, but these features are liable to distract from an earnest didactic purpose. Moreover, the humanist may be reluctant to enforce the moral the puritan requires. The ambivalent author may be unwilling to resist the drag back towards a more genial ethic.

Critical dispute about the purport of puritan-humanist writings mostly results from this kind of ambivalent positioning. Many readers have assumed Sidney to be in full sympathy with his major characters in the *Old Arcadia*, which they take to be a light-hearted diversion. Careful reading suggests that this is not a sufficient account and that Sidney insinuates a moral commentary upon the romantic action through the princes' lapse from virtue, the degradation of comparable characters, the disruption of Arcadia by beasts and rebels which symbolize the passions, and through the attitudes of the shepherds in the eclogues. A stern interpretation is encouraged by the judgement of Euarchus, and by occasional remarks of the narrator, as when he attributes the role of the foolish Dametas in discovering the lovers' recklessness to "the everlasting justice . . . using ourselves to be the punishers of our faults, and making our own actions the beginning of our chastisement, that our shame may be the more manifest, and our repentance follow the sooner" (*Old Arcadia*, p. 265). But just how seriously Sidney wants us to take these hints—how earnestly he wants to teach as well as delight—is difficult to determine.

When, for instance, Pyrocles gets into Philoclea's bedroom he must be expected to admire her physically. Indeed, he might use a catalogue of her beauty like Sannazaro's (*Arcadia*, p. 49) or Montemayor's (*Diana*, p. 171). So Pyrocles has in his mind

the song "What tongue can her perfections tell?" and each of
Philoclea's features is described with appropriate erotic detail:

> So good a say [foretaste] invites the eye
> A little downward to espy
> The lovely clusters of her breasts,
> Of Venus' babe the wanton nests,
> Like pommels round of marble clear,
> Where azured veins well mixed appear,
> With dearest tops of porphyry.
>
> *(Old Arcadia, p. 239)*

Throughout this poem we are invited to share Pyrocles' admiration;
that is the usual assumption of the genre about eroticism.
But from this perspective it is hard to maintain a sense that
we should perhaps disapprove of such frank sexuality and even
more of the circumstances—the lovers anticipate the marriage
contract.

Sidney might control the appeal of Pyrocles' song through
the narrator, but he is swept along by the mood and merely breaks
off the story, "lest my pen might seem to grudge at the due
bliss of these poor lovers whose loyalty had but small respite
of their fiery agonies" (p. 243). That Sidney wanted in part
to restrain commitment to Pyrocles is apparent, I think, in the
immediate juxtaposition of a wedding among the shepherds.
Now the narrator's comment is neatly barbed:

> And so, with consent of both parents (without which neither
> Lalus would ask nor Kala grant), their marriage day was
> appointed; which, because it fell out in this time, I think
> it shall not be impertinent to remember a little our shepherds
> while the other greater persons are either sleeping or otherwise
> occupied. (pp. 244-45)

Evidently the rural folk have conducted their love in a better
manner, but Sidney's reluctance to make the point initially leaves
us confused about how seriously he wants it to be taken.

It seems that Sidney became aware of the drag back towards
romance values in the *Old Arcadia,* for in his revision he makes
the ethical structure firmer and more explicit. The many additional characters and episodes often involve clear-cut villainy, and
this helps Sidney to sustain a more rigorous moral tone and
gives a more distinct shape to the range of human behaviour.
His sterner control is evident in the disposition of "What tongue
can her perfections tell?" In the *New Arcadia* it is sung by
Pyrocles whilst he is watching Philoclea bathing naked. The
erotic implications for Pyrocles are fully developed before the
song, but immediately afterwards Sidney invites us to meditate
upon Pyrocles' bad faith in taking advantage of his female disguise
to observe his honoured lady in circumstances which would em-
barrass her. Pyrocles discovers watching in the bushes another

noble lord, Amphialus, who is also in love with Philoclea.   We
recognize in Pyrocles' violent response a case which might be
moved equally against himself, and an excess which demonstrates
the danger of sexual passion (*New Arcadia*, pp. 291-94).

A similar tension between genre and protestant purpose
perhaps explains the disquiet of many readers about Acrasia's
Bower of Bliss (*Fairy Queen*, II, xii).   If this is a symbol of
intemperance which Guyon must destroy, why does Spenser allow
it so much beauty?   Partly, I think, because he is developing
an image which initially had less severe connotations.   Ariosto
in *Orlando Furioso* (1532) describes Alcina with a full catalogue
of her attractions without derogating from her or her island
(VII, 11-15; VI, 20-22).   He tells us that she is a wicked sorceress
but suggests that we forgive Ruggiero for being ensnared (VII,
18).   Ariosto is tolerant of his heroes' frequent sexual lapses
and does not grudge Alcina her beauty.   The humanist Spenser
wants to use Ariosto's image but the puritan must evaluate it:

> Upon a bed of roses she was laid,
>   As faint through heat, or dight [dressed] to pleasant sin,
>   And was arrayed, or rather disarrayed,
>   All in a veil of silk and silver thin,
>   That hid no whit her alablaster skin,
>   But rather showed more white, if more might be.
>   (II.xii.77)

The moral tone here is finely balanced: replace "sin" with a neutral
word like "dalliance," and we might not worry about the disarray
or the hint of excess and falsification in the last two lines.
Often Spenser qualifies the beauty of Acrasia's island in similar
manner, but some stanzas, like those describing the harmony
of birdsong and music, seem very attractive— "Th' angelical
soft trembling voices made / To th' instruments divine respondence
meet" (II.xii.71).   Spenser uses Ariosto's conventions and tries
to firm up their ethical import, but intimations of genial romance
morality filter through.

Compare also Spenser's other main source, Tasso's *Jerusalem
Delivered* (1575; books xv, xvi).   Tasso disapproved of Ariosto's
casual treatment of the Alcina episode (*Discourses on the Heroic
Poem*, pp. 11-12) and his parallel account of Armida and her
island is qualified by a moral commentary like Spenser's.   But
Tasso's Rinaldo is persuaded by his own reflection and by appeals
to his honour to abandon Armida (XVI, 30-34), suggesting a natural
propensity to virtue.   Guyon's triumph is fervent and violent:
he thrusts aside Acrasia's minions, binds her and smashes the
Bower:

> Their groves he felled, their gardens did deface,
>   Their arbours spoil, their cabinets suppress,
>   Their banquet houses burn, their buildings raze,
> And of the fairest late, now made the foulest place.   (II.xii.83)

Spenser, I think with puritan zeal, insists upon a more hard-won and decisive defeat of evil. The poet who demands a reversed evaluation of fair and foul in the last line quoted is an extremist. But unfortunately it sounds as if one kind of intemperance is overthrown by another—hence the feeling of many readers that Spenser has difficulty in controlling his response to sensuality, that he protests too much. This may be so; we may say with confidence that Spenser is placed at the crisis of a cultural dislocation.

The New Arcadia, The Fairy Queen and *Paradise Lost* all adapt the heroic poem (or its romantic derivation) to purposes consonant with protestantism. In Renaissance aesthetics the epic was the most prestigious genre because it presents the most noble characters and actions. Sidney asserted: "as the image of each action stirreth and instructeth the mind, so the lofty image of such worthies most inflameth the mind with desire to be worthy" (*Defence*, p. 47).

But the values characteristically implied in the heroic poem bear a complex relationship to protestantism. First, the hero is defined by his marvellous accomplishments, whereas protestantism stressed human incapacity. Sidney (*Defence*, p. 47) and Spenser (Letter to Raleigh) credit the hero with Aristotle's preeminent virtue, variously translated as pride, magnanimity or magnificence (*Nichomachean Ethics*, IV, 3). But William Perkins denied that this is a virtue at all:

> the scope and end of this virtue (as they term it) is to make men to attempt high and great matters above their reach, and so to go beyond their callings. Besides, it is directly opposite to the virtue of humility, which teacheth that a man ought always to be base, vile, and lowly in his own eyes. *(William Perkins, p. 165)*

Moreover, epic poetry had interpreted magnanimity principally in terms of martial valour. So Luther demanded, "what are Homer, Virgil and the other heroic poets but firebrands, glorifiers of homicide, of tyrants and of the enemies of mankind?"

As humanists, Sidney, Spenser and Milton were eager to adapt the heroic poem, but as puritans they experienced conflict. It takes a different form in each, indicating the range of negotiation possible within the constraints of this divided allegiance.

Sidney's treatment is the most orthodox. It is proper for his princes to attempt heroic virtue because as noblemen that is their calling in life. Musidorus' account of their dedication (*New Arcadia*), p. 110) is very like Sidney's advice to his brother Robert: "your purpose is, being a gentleman born, to furnish

yourself with the knowledge of such things as may be serviceable
to your country, and fit for your calling" *(Prose Works,* III, 125).
Indeed, the princes have been educated in the manner proposed
in the *Defence,* through heroic poetry—"all the stories of worthy
princes, both to move them to do nobly and teach them how
to do nobly" *(New Arcadia,* p. 258).   They set out on their adventures to excel the classical heroes, "thinking it not so worthy
to be brought to heroical effects by fortune or necessity, like
Ulysses and Aeneas, as by one's own choice and working" (p. 275).

But, after demonstrating very amply the heroism of Musidorus
and Pyrocles, Sidney shows it to be inadequate.   Pyrocles and
the princesses Pamela and Philoclea are captured by the noble
Amphialus and his wicked mother, Cecropia.   Pyrocles is rendered
impotent by the female disguise he adopted to further his wooing
of Philoclea; Musidorus tries to rescue his friends, but is unable
decisively to defeat Amphialus (pp. 534-44).   Even more problematic, Amphialus is truly noble, fights excellently and courteously,
and is moved by love not unlike Pyrocles'.   Sidney shows that
there may be heroism on both sides, that it is an unsatisfactory
criterion of virtue, and that it cannot transform a disordered
world.

The *New Arcadia* proposes to supersede the heroic ethos
in two respects.   First, Sidney requires his characters to develop
out of the experience of suffering, impotence and failure a more
inward and spiritual strength.   The magnanimous gesture of
the epic hero is replaced by a quiet determination.   But this
is not simply a matter of patience as it is manifested by Griselde
in Chaucer's "Clerk's Tale."   Puritans admired a more zealous
and vigorous stance—it is apparent in Sidney's violent utterances
against papal and Spanish power.   When Pamela raises her hands
in prayer it is "as if the right had been the picture of Zeal,
and the left of Humbleness" (p. 464).   She is vehement, even
vindictive, towards Cecropia and Amphialus (pp. 488, 572).
Sidney develops a distinctive protestant heroism which is active
as well as humble.   It involves an unremitting stand against
evil, though human action is liable to be unsuccessful and there
will be a role for sheer fortitude.

Second, Sidney indicates that worldly affairs are in the hands
of divine providence and that the virtuous should never despair.
Pyrocles attempts suicide when he believes Philoclea to be dead;
he exclaims, "O tyrant heaven, traitor earth, blind providence,
no justice, how is this done?   How is this suffered?   Hath this
world a government?" *(New Arcadia,* p. 563).   Even Pamela
proposes suicide—it is the heroic solution: "undoubtedly it becomes
our birth to think of dying nobly, while we have done or suffered
nothing which might make our soul ashamed at the parture from
these bodies" (p. 585).   But these alarms are countered by the
action.   Philoclea is not dead and their captors will be defeated;
their distrust of providence was mistaken.   The very failure of
Pyrocles to kill himself—an unaccustomed lapse in martial prowess—
is providential.   The heroic ethos is again shown to be wrong.

Through his pagan setting Sidney is demonstrating a benevolent controlling providence such as he himself believed in.

The relationship between human incapacity and divine power is precisely given in a letter from Sidney to Walsingham about the struggle against Spain: "methinks I see the great work indeed in hand, against the abusers of the world, wherein it is no greater fault to have confidence in man's power, than it is too hastily to despair of God's work" (*Prose Works*, III, 166). The truth will conquer not through human effort but through divine determination. Protestant activists must learn the same lesson as the Arcadian principals: heroic fortitude will be required but we cannot trust in our own capacity; God is working his purpose out and the good will triumph ultimately.

Milton's treatment of heroic virtue in *Paradise Lost* may be regarded as a development of Sidney's. It is ambitious and has led to confusion. The cause, I think, is his attempt at a special compromise between puritan and humanistic attitudes. He wants to maintain the sense of providential control which Sidney emphasized—that is why his God is so stern and commanding. (Modern Chistians tend to imagine that Milton meant to make God gentle and loving, as we understand the word, but somehow failed; but his deity is not surprising in seventeenth-century theology). At the same time, and in the face of the main thrust of protestantism, Milton wants to assert human freedom and even dignity.

Milton is not, like Sidney, a Calvinist writing about mere ethical achievement; he believes that "by degrees of merit raised" human beings may work their way to heaven (*Paradise Lost*, VIII, 157). The heroism he seeks to identify is a directly spiritual quality and to delimit it within God's overwhelming power requires precise discrimination. Milton asks us, therefore, to attribute full virtue and power to God and the Son only; heroic virtue, but not power, to the good angels; perverted heroism and no power to Satan; and a modified virtue and power to mankind. This complex analysis makes it difficult for the twentieth-century reader to get his or her bearings in the poem.

In books I and II Satan is granted traditional heroic stature; for instance, he wins his way through Chaos though even "harder beset" than Jason and Ulysses (II, 1016-20). Milton seeks to control our response by making apparent Satan's viciousness and deviousness, and by derogatory comments. This procedure, notoriously, involves the risk that the reader will empathize nevertheless with Satan's resistance. But there is also the opposite danger, that we will assume that Milton is simply condemning heroic endeavour. After all, he makes the fallen angels pass their time composing epics of "Their own heroic deeds and hapless fall / By doom of battle" (II, 549). But not all heroism is wrong.

The response of God's forces to Satan's rebellion is heroic: at
the divine command, the angel legions advance

> to the sound
> Of instrumental harmony that breathed
> Heroic ardour to advent'rous deeds
> Under their godlike leaders, in the cause
> Of God and his Messiah.
>
> (VI, 64)

God approves the heroism of the good angels; Milton does not
itemize their deeds because they are "contented with their fame
in heav'n" (VI, 375).

Satan's impotence is apparent. But notice also that the
good angels are unable to defeat him.   That is accomplished
by the Son alone.   The implication is that power is possessed
ultimately by none but the divinity.   The good angels have virtue
and it pleases God, but it is finally irrelevant.   The same inference may be drawn from the confrontation of Satan and Gabriel
at the end of book IV.   Satan flees because he sees that God's
scales in the heavens mean his defeat; it is unnecessary even
for the angels to fight (in the classical sources Zeus' scales are
not seen by the characters and are not felt to determine the
action in the same degree).   And this perhaps accounts for Raphael
fumbling explanation of why he was absent at the time of Adam's
creation.   He says he was busy patrolling hell, but then adds
that the effort was pointless :

> But us he sends upon his high behests
> For state, as sovran King, and to inure
> Our prompt obedience.
>
> (VIII, 238)

The useless tasks given to the angels have provoked critical de-
rision, but Milton's point, I think, is that the angels should be
virtuous although everything attempted by God's creatures is
as nothing in the perspective of divine power.   This is, of course,
a truism for Christians, but Milton makes it work forcefully,
even perplexingly, in *Paradise Lost.*   Heroic virtue like that
in pagan epics is disallowed in Satan's case, approved in Gabriel's,
but ultimately insignificant.

At the start of book IX Milton finally expounds a more positive
heroic ethos.   He declares that his argument is "Not less but
more heroic" than the classical epics and that knights in battle
are "tedious", and proposes instead "the better fortitude / Of
patience and heroic martyrdom" (IX, 14, 30).   What God requires
above all of his creatures is that they should *stand:*

> I made him just and right,
> Sufficient to have stood, though free to fall.
> Such I created all th' etherial Powers

> And Spirits, both them who stood and them who failed;
> Freely they stood who stood, and fell who fell.
>
> (III, 98)

Satan recognizes as much:

> other Powers as great
> Fell not, but stand unshaken, from within
> Or from without, to all temptations armed.
> Hadst thou the same free will and power to stand?
> Thou hadst.
>
> (IV, 63)

Of this Raphael warns Adam repeatedly: "Firm they might have stood, / Yet fell; remember, and fear to transgress"; "Stand fast; to stand or fall / Free in thine own arbitrement it lies" (VI, 911; VIII, 640). When the Son relieves the angels of the task of defeating Satan he commands, "Stand still in bright array, ye saints, here stand" (VI, 801). God expects of his creatures not the ambitious, tempestuous and outwardgoing heroism which pagans called "magnanimity," but a determined stand against evil.

Milton's revision of the heroic ethos derives partly from St. Paul: "Wherefore take unto you the whole armour of God, that ye may be able to withstand in the evil day, and having done all, to stand. Stand therefore . . ." (Ephesians, 6: 13-14). But Ephesians starts with one of Paul's classic statements about predestination and human depravity, whereas Milton means to fashion a more exalted image of human dignity within the divine dispensation. Adam's immediate instinct at his creation is to spring up and stand on his feet (VIII, 258-261); Satan sees "Two of far nobler shape erect and tall, / God-like erect" (IV, 288). Man's tendency to stand is indicative of his status in the universe. When God had made everything else,

> There wanted yet the master work, the end
> Of all yet done: a creature who not prone
> And brute as other creatures, but endued
> With sanctity of reason, might erect
> His stature, and upright with front serene
> Govern the rest, self-knowing, and from thence
> Magnanimous to correspond with heav'n,
> But grateful to acknowledge whence his good
> Descends .
>
> (VII, 505)

The humanistic implications of this passage are specific, for it alludes strongly to Ovid's account of the creation in the *Metamorphoses* (I, 76-86); Milton adds man's acknowledgement of divine beneficence. "Erect" recalls Sidney's provocative "erected wit"; "Magnanimous" is Aristotle's pre-eminent virtue

but it is oriented towards "heav'n." Milton seeks to identify
for the puritan humanist a heroic stance which is dignified but
does not presume upon divine power.

The ambivalence in this account of human stature concerns
how far it is applicable to fallen man (there is not much question
about woman). Explicity, it refers to created man, but it is
easy for the reader to take it as a general description of humanity.
But when Eve tells Adam she has eaten the apple he "Astonied
stood and blank, . . . Speechless he stood and pale" (IX, 890,
894), and this is the last time he stands in the virtue with which
he was created. Considered statements about fallen man allow
him less heroic grandeur. God declares:

> once more I will renew
> His lapsed powers, though forfeit and enthralled
> By sin to foul exorbitant desires;
> Upheld by me, yet once more he shall stand
> On even ground against his mortal foe.
>
> (III, 175)

Man's standing becomes dependent, conditional, insecure, tainted
with inevitable sin. Virtue becomes a matter of painstaking
accumulation:

> only add
> Deeds to thy knowledge answerable, add faith,
> Add virtue, patience, temperance, add love.
>
> (XII, 581)

Christians find this a humble and moving statement of the good
life which God has restored to us, and I would not quarrel with
them. But in the context of *Paradise Lost* we must detect
a scaling down of the heroic potential of humanity.

Logically Milton is consistent: active heroic virtue is denied
to man but at his creation he can stand nobly, whereas after
the fall he must struggle to retrieve himself. But poetically
the vast scope of *Paradise Lost* cries out for the grander conception of mankind. The heroic form which Milton has given to
his puritan rejection of heroism implies a humanistic wish to
reinstate it. His frustration at the limitations of the fallen world
is apparent in the sonnet "On his Blindness," where Milton forces
himself to recognize that "God doth not need / Either man's
work or his own gifts." The puritan notion of the cosmic irrelevance of human kind was, I think, hugely difficult for the humanist
in Milton to accept. The sonnet's climactic submission to divine
will is hard-won: "They also serve who only stand and wait."

In *Paradise Lost* Milton's yearning for the heroic opportunity
may be inferred from the emotional charge with which he reports
the stand of Abdiel, Enoch and Noah. Abdiel alone speaks out
against Satan:

> Among the faithless, faithful only he;

> Among innumerable false, unmoved,
> Unshaken, unseduced, unterrified,
> His loyalty he kept, his love, his zeal.
>
> (V, 897)

Enoch opposed the giants in days when "might only shall be admired, / And valour and heroic virtue called" (XI, 689); he was

> The only righteous in a world perverse,
> And therefore hated, therefore so beset
> With foes for daring single to be just.
>
> (XI, 701)

Noah admonished the wicked and was "Of them derided, but of God observed / The one just man alive" (XI, 817). These heroes stand not just with patience and humility, but with unique and significant virtue at a critical juncture.

Milton accepts in theory the meek virtue which Christianity usually requires of fallen men, but yearns for the more decisive role of the hero who stands alone and achieves a virtue beyond the ordinary. It is a reflection of his temperament, of his disappointment at the failure of the Commonwealth, and of the apocalyptic strain in seventeenth-century puritanism. It smuggles back in heroic virtue.

In *Samson Agonistes* Milton indulges the ideal of the hero who is able to act. Most often, the Chorus says, patience is "the exercise / Of saints," but sometimes

> God into the hands of their deliverer
> Puts invincible might
> To quell the mighty of the earth, . . .
> He all their ammunition
> And feats of war defeats
> With plain heroic magnitude of mind
> And celestial vigour armed.
>
> (lines 1270-88)

But in *Paradise Regained* Milton acknowledges that God rarely welcomes grand gestures, that the Christian life is essentially one of self-abasement. Jesus simply stands and obeys God:

> To whom thus Jesus : "Also it is written,
> 'Tempt not the Lord thy God.'" He said, and stood.
>
> (IV, 560)

This is Satan's final defeat and it implies very little scope for human initiative. Puritan notions of divine power and human impotence were always at odds in Milton's thought with his humanistic estimate of humankind. Finally, I think under the pressure of events, he was forced to admit the impotence in his society of even the protestant hero.

Spenser's treatment of heroic virtue also turns on the respective
spiritual powers and responsibilities of God and humanity.   In
book I of *The Fairy Queen*, as in *Paradise Lost*, the perspective
is divine, and Spenser represents the state of the soul through
martial imagery.   Already there his purpose is more difficult
to discern than Sidney's or Milton's.   By the end of *The Fairy
Queen*, I shall argue, Spenser becomes the boldest of the three
writers discussed in this chapter, for he throws into doubt both
protestant and humanist values.   Spenser is generally reputed
to be the most Christian of poets, but I think this view cannot
be maintained in the light of his works.

In the Letter to Raleigh Spenser alludes to Paul's imagery
of the armour of God, declaring that without it Redcross "could
not succeed" in killing the dragon.   It seems that knightly prowess
is therefore to be regarded as a metaphor for spiritual qualities
bestowed by God, and several attacks are made in book I on
heroic pride and the notion that people have power other than
from God (I.v.46-51; I.viii.1; I.x.1).   For the final battle with
the dragon Spenser repudiates the martial muse who "hearts
of great heroes dost enrage": "O gently come into my feeble
breast" (I.xi.6).   Redcross twice falls before the dragon, and
is saved first by the Well of Life then by the Tree of Life
(I.xi.29, 46).   His spiritual strength is not his own, the heroic
convention is given a protestant twist.

For all this, the knights are often praised for heroic virtue.
There is a close juxtaposition at the start of canto viii.   Spenser
declares,

> Ay me, how many perils do enfold
>   The righteous man, to make him daily fall?
>   Were not, that heavenly grace doth him uphold,
>   And steadfast truth acquit him out of all.
>
> (I.viii.1)

But then Arthur shapes up to fight Orgoglio:

> That when the knight beheld, his mighty shield
>   Upon his manly arm he soon addressed,
>   And at him fiercely flew, with courage filled,
> And eager greediness through every member thrilled.
>
> (I.viii.6)

This sounds simply heroic, as if Arthur faces Orgoglio with his
own resources.

One way round the problem is to insist upon the allegory.

Arthur is grace and Orgoglio is pride: their battle does not
involve human heroism at all. We have been told that many
knights tried to kill Orgoglio,

> But all still shrunk, and still he greater grew:
> All they for want of faith, or guilt of sin,
> The pitious prey of his fierce cruelty have been.
>
> (I.vii.45)

The knights' conflict with Orgoglio is determined by faith and
guilt, and we should translate Arthur's "manly arm" and "courage"
into such spiritual qualities. This may have been Spenser's
intention, but we find it difficult to manage because of the
kind of drag back to the romance genre which we observed
with Acrasia.

Even if we do not allegorize them, the martial efforts
of Arthur and Redcross need not be interpreted as a humanistic
revolt against the Calvinistic doctrine of grace. Although divine
determination seems to make human effort logically pointless,
protestants were always urging the faithful to fight the good
fight. Calvin refers to Ephesians 6, warns that the devil is
"most expert in the science of war," and enjoins: "let us not
allow ourselves to be overtaken by sloth or cowardice, but, on
the contrary, with minds aroused and ever on the alert, let us
stand ready to resist." He adds, "Above all, fully conscious
of our weakness and want of skill, let us invoke the help of God,
and attempt nothing without trusting in him, since it is his
alone to supply counsel, and strength, and courage, and arms"
(*Institutes*, I.xiv.13). That "Above all" is supposed, I think, to clarify
sufficiently the relationship between divine power and human
effort. Spenser too may have found the accommodation useful.

Spenser was writing before the Cambridge dispute about free
will in the 1590s, and probably did not feel a need for the careful
analysis of protestant heroism which Milton was to undertake.
I am inclined to credit his purpose in book I because the critique
of heroic pride is sustained in book II. But as *The Fairy Queen*
proceeds Spenser takes less trouble to attribute human achievement
to divine intervention, and the martial prowess of the knights
and ladies comes to seem simply their own. Consequently
the protestant sense of the overwhelming importance of grace evap-
orates. Yet there is no correspondent strengthening in Spenser's
estimate of human potential for virtue, either within a free-will
version of Christianity or as a sheerly human capacity. By book
VI he is disillusioned with both religion and humanism.

The sense that people are fallen remains. It is manifest
in the threat from the Blatant Beast and in the irruption of
brigands into the pastoral scene of the last four cantos. What
we miss is the sense of benign providential direction. Neither
the Beast nor the brigands are presented as a divine test; on
the contrary, the latter are attributed to the malicious intervention of "fortune fraught with malice, blind and brute, / That envies

lovers long prosperity" (VI.x.38). And Calidore's victories over
these evil forces seem to be his own achievement. He seeks
the brigands "(God before)" (in parentheses; VI.xi.36) but there
is no real indication that his triumph displays divine grace. The
book ends with the Blatant Beast loose again, and now there
is no prospect of restraining it. No divine pattern is discernible.

Calidore's victories are his own, but book VI manifests little
exuberance about humanistic potential. The battle imagery
seems particularly perverse in relation to courtesy, which is
represented centrally by the Graces who "always smoothly seem
to smile, / That we likewise should mild and gentle be" (VI.x.24).
Calidore's final deeds are violent and the capture of the Beast
is hardly knightly:

> His shield he on him threw, and fast down held,
> Like as a bullock, that in bloody stall
> Of butcher's baleful hand to ground is felled,
> Is forcibly kept down, till he be throughly quelled.
>
> (VI.xii.30)

The Blatant Beast may figure discourtesy, but courtesy does
not defeat it. The climactic events of the book demonstrate
neither the care of providence nor the virtue of the hero, but
that evil will submit only to brute force. And the last two
stanzas show that "Of late" matters are even worse.

I suspect that Spenser's disillusionment with God and humanity comes to the fore in book VI because the virtue of courtesy
implies the court. His ambivalent attitude towards Elizabeth's
court is apparent in the proem. In stanzas four and five he
derogates the courtesy of the "present age," in stanzas six and
seven he extols Elizabeth and her court as the most notable
pattern. Spenser wanted to believe, as he did when he wrote
The Shepherds' Calendar, that Elizabeth is an appropriate symbol
for all spiritual and mundane virtues, but experience had taught
him that Christian and heroic values alike were but weakly
represented at the English court. The same tension occurs
in "Colin Clout's Come Home Again" (1591), where after celebrat-
ing the court Colin explains that his reason for leaving was the
malice, slander, vanity and "fair dissembling courtesy" (line 700)
which prevail there.

Hence Spenser's uncertainty about Calidore's pause in his
pursuit of the Beast while he wooes Pastorella in an apparently
tranquil rural setting. Explicit comment seems designed to
prevent us from clearly evaluating the episode. Spenser observes
that Calidore is "Unmindful of his vow and high behest, / Which
by the Fairy Queen was on him laid" (VI.x.1.), but then adds
that Calidore cannot "greatly blamed be" for preferring "happy
peace" to the values of the court—

painted show

Of such false bliss, as there is set for stales ["snares"],
T' entrap unwary fools in their eternal bales.

(VI.x.3)

Spenser indulges Calidore's truancy because he suspects that
the active pursuit of virtue is a chimera, especially within the
context of the court.

The undercutting of value in *Fairy Queen* VI is completed
by Spenser's refusal to allow an unambiguous evaluation even
of Calidore's behaviour in the pastoral world.   A further objection to court life in "Colin Clout" is that people use love "But
as a complement for courting vain" (line 790).   Calidore's good
faith is undermined by his conscious manipulation to secure
Pastorella's love; for instance, when Coridon fails to fight a
tiger:

Yet Calidor did not despise him quite,
But used him friendly for further intent,
That by his fellowship, he colour might
Both his estate, and love from skill of any wight.

(V.x.37)

Calidore wins Pastorella and rescues her from the brigands, but
it is never said that he returns to marry her.

In this context of collapsing values Spenser locates truth
in Colin's vision of the Graces—a vision in which neither Calidore
nor the Queen has a proper part (VI.x.18-20, 28).   Colin's explanation to Calidore is itself an instance of courtesy, for the Graces
show "That good should from us go, then come in greater store"
(VI.x.24).   But the conversation is one-way, Calidore is distracted
by his love, and our principal recollection is of how he disrupted
the vision.   More remarkable, there is no sign that the appearance of the Graces makes any difference at all to Calidore or
to the world.   At this point the entire puritan-humanist
programme for the poet breaks down, for whilst Colin can perceive truth he has no way of making it effective in the world.
The "erected wit" is condemned to solipsism, the "medicine
of cherries" doesn't work.   Hence the bitterness of the concluding
stanzas, where Spenser presents himself as the victim of calumny
and misrepresentation at court.   He is unable to communicate
his courteous vision within that society.

This chapter has taken three main themes: the status of the
poet, the problems of subjecting secular forms to protestant
purposes, and the possibility of heroism.   They prove to be
key issues in the development of Sidney, Spenser and Milton.
Initially Sidney has difficulty in reconciling humanist and puritan
objectives.   The formula of the erected wit and infected will

raises more questions about the poet's vision than it settles, and in the *Old Arcadia* the love element tends to get out of hand.   In the *New Arcadia* we see Sidney determinedly humbling his heroes, and at the same time he moves towards the merging of his human creativity into divine poetry.

Spenser seems convinced by Sidney's analysis and he pursues it, broadly, in the early books of *The Fairy Queen*, but already there are signs of confusion about the hero and the superiority of Scripture.   By book VI Spenser's sense of the validity of the poet's vision has grown but he has little faith in God or humanity.   The erected wit of the poet splits apart from the infected wills of people at large.   Colin Clout is condemned to pipe alone to the Graces.

Milton's attitude moves from exuberant confidence in the instructional properties of secular poetry to an austere rejection of it.   In "Lycidas" and *Paradise Lost* he struggles to incorporate pagan imagery in a legitimate manner and to subdue the pretensions of himself as poet.   He develops a complex and restrained model of the Christian hero, but individual attainment breaks through and we recognize, implicitly, the image of Milton, the heroic poet.

We are liable to overlook the strain in the work of these writers because we do not allow that Reformation Christianity demanded of its adherents a commitment which we now associate mainly with extreme sects.   At the intensity with which Sidney, Spenser and Milton were working, protestantism and humane letters were ultimately irreconcilable.   The sequence of attempted closures indicates the importance of the issue; they bear witness to a fundamentally dislocated culture.

4 Who bids abstain?

Donne, Sidney, Spenser, Milton, Shakespeare

> *Socrates.*   What of love then? Is it to be classified
> as ambiguous or unambiguous?
> *Phaedrus.*   Ambiguous, obviously.   Otherwise, how would
> it have been possible for you to describe it as you did just
> now as a curse to lover and loved alike, and then to turn
> round and assert that it is the greatest of blessings?
> (Plato, Phaedrus, p. 77)

E.D. in *A Brief and Necessary Instruction* (1572) complained
that "we have multiplied for ourselves so many new delights
that we might justify the idolatrous superstition of the elder
world.   To this purpose we have printed us many bawdy songs,
. . . our songs and sonnets, our Palaces of Pleasure."   This
attitude formed a continuous pressure upon love poetry—a pressure
which, we have seen, was internalized by Sidney, Spenser and
Milton.   It produced ambivalence and radical modifications
of the European love tradition, though without affecting, of
course, the fundamentally patriarchal structure of that tradition.

Protestant hostility to passionate love was mainly, of course,
a continuation of the general Christian alarm about sexual expression.   The Reformation set up a further barrier against one
resolution which had seemed possible: the notion that one may
ascend through love of a person to love of God.   Dante fashioned
from his passion for Beatrice a means to union with the divine.
Neoplatonists held that one might ascend "step by step, first
to the body of the loved one, then to his soul, then to the Angelic
Mind, and finally to God, the first origin of this glow" (Ficino,
Commentary on Plato's Symposium, p. 199).   Petrarch convinced
himself even before Laura's death that her rejection of him
was for the best because it led him to seek heavenly bliss (e.g.
Rime 204).   The strategy justifies human love, but as a temporary stage.

Protestants found this accommodation unhelpful because it
proposes a continuity between human and divine—a series of
steps—where they insisted upon disjunction.   The whole argument of the Reformation was that one is either in the devil's

kingdom or in God's: there is no compromise.   Divine grace
may raise sinners from one to the other, but they cannot work
their way up.   The spiritual realm is absolutely distinct from
the human and there are no mediators—neither blessed virgins
nor priests nor Beatrices.
       Elizabethan and Jacobean literature alludes frequently to
neoplatonic notions, but rarely with any respect for the theory
of love as a whole.   The most important Platonizing poem of
the period is Spenser's *Four Hymns*, but it is not very precisely
neoplatonic.   In the hymn "Of Beauty" the lover moves on from
his beloved to envisage "A more refined form," but he does
not ascend beyond this point to the divine *(Poetical Works,* p. 592).
In "Heavenly Beauty" our inability to approach God is recognized
and we are referred to the beauty of this world as "The means
therefore which unto us is lent, / Him to behold" (p. 597).
But Calvin allows as much *(Institutes,* I.v.1) and loving a person
is not proposed.
       The Reformation disjunction between human and divine
is reflected in the all-or-nothing determination of many of the
zealous to replace love poetry with religious.   John Hall's
Court of Virtue (1565) was written as a counter to the miscellany
of love poems, *The Court of Venus.*   In the prologue Lady Virtue
complains of "Trim songs of love" and urges Hall "To make
a book of songs holy, / Godly and wise, blaming folly" (pp. 15, 16).
The Second Day of du Bartas' *First Week* opens with an attack
on love poets, who draw "their readers with themselves to hell"
(Sylvester, *Complete Works,* I, 27).   Even Sidney says he would
prefer "songs and sonnets" to be employed "in singing the praises
of the immortal beauty: the immortal goodness of that God
who giveth us hands to write and wits to conceive" *(Defence,*
p. 69).
       But the split between spiritual and worldly also gave a
distinct status to human affairs and hence encouraged new attention to the relation between love and marriage.   At the same
time, puritan humanists could not altogether discard the traditional
forms of love poetry, and religious strictures seem to have stimulated a self-consciously "immoral" reaction in the less earnest.
These are the discourses within which writing about love was
negotiated in the period.
       I propose to attempt an analysis of the two main conventions
of sexual love which the Elizabethans inherited and developed
(I call them the Ovidian and the romantic); then to discuss particularly *Astrophil and Stella;* then to explore the impact of
the protestant doctrine of marriage in the work of Spenser,
Milton, Shakespeare and Donne.

The Ovidian lover is so named out of respect for the completeness
with which Ovid represents him in the *Amores* and *Art of Love.*

We might now term him an extreme sexist.   His goal is sexual
conquest; he sees love as a battle, a skirmish of wits, an opportunity to exercise his powers, an "art."   Woman is objectified
as the means of his satisfaction.   She is perceived as flirtatious,
lustful and promiscuous, in fact as a suitable target for Ovidian
assault; her function is to flatter the man's crude notion of
masculinity.   The positive aspect of this lover, from the modern
point of view, is that he has a sense of humour and knows sex
is enjoyable; but when he meets resistance he is not above rape.
In the *Metamorphoses* Ovid developed a more lyrical and sympathetic tone, but the Elizabethans largely assimilated to the
basic type these stories of the amorous adventures of the classical
gods and heroes.
    For earnest protestants the name of Ovid was synonymous
with illicit sexuality in poetry.   Joshua Sylvester was moved
to augment du Bartas' condemnations in his translation of the
Second Week:

> O! furnish me with an unvulgar style,
> That I by this may wean our wanton isle
> From Ovid's heirs, and their unhallowed spell
> Here charming senses, chaining souls in hell.
>   (Sylvester, *Complete Works*, I, 99)

In the early part of the period puritan humanists like Thomas
Wilson in his *Art of Rhetoric* (1553; fol. 104) and Arthur Golding
in the preface and epistle to his translation of the *Metamorphoses*
(1567) tried to rescue Ovid for protestants by pretending that
his stories are moral allegories (Jupiter's assault on Danae shows
that women will be won with money; the adultery of Mars and
Venus shows that secret sins will come to light).   This may
have seemed satisfactory to those who wished to be convinced,
but the more light-hearted welcomed exuberantly a mode which
flouted official morality.   Sir John Harington in the preface
to his translation of *Orlando Furioso* seems purposefully to
revise Sidney's didactic emphasis:

> As for the pastoral with the sonnet or epigram, though many
> times they savour of wantonness and love and toying and
> now and then, breaking the rules of poetry, go into plain
> scurrility, yet even the worst of them may not be ill applied
> and are, I must confess, too delightful.
>   (Smith, *Elizabethan Critical Essays*, II, 209)

An Ovidian vogue in the last decade of the century produced
numbers of love elegies and sonnet sequences in which the lusty
male seeks union with his desirable mistress, and several erotic
romances in the manner of Marlowe's *Hero and Leander* and
Shakespeare's *Venus and Adonis* in which the same approach
is given a genial mythological veneer.

Donne is in some poems—the Elegies, "Woman's Constancy," "The Indifferent," "Community," "Love's Alchemy"—the most confident English Ovidian.

> Love, let my body reign, and let
> Me travel, sojourn, snatch, plot, have, forget,
> Resume my last year's relict: think that yet
> We had never met.
>
> ("Love's Usury")

He develops particularly the witty intellectual justification. Ovid used it much less, and as well as Donne's personal bent it manifests his awareness of the challenge which the Ovidian ethos posed to the moral norms of protestant society.

Donne is specially fond of the argument that humans have imposed arbitrary laws upon themselves whilst the rest of nature makes love at will.   It derives from the *Metamorphoses*, where Myrrha uses it to justify her love for her father:

> In happy case they are
> That may do so without offence.   But man's malicious care
> Hath made a bridle for itself, and spiteful laws restrain
> The things that nature setteth free.
>
> (trans. Golding, X, 364)

Donne offers this argument repeatedly in the Elegies; it occurs in words very like Golding's in the last stanza of "The Relic"; it is fully expounded in "Confined Love":

> Are sun, moon, or stars by law forbidden
> To smile where they list, or lend away their light?
> Are birds divorced, or are they chidden
> If they leave their mate, or lie abroad a-night?
> Beasts do no jointures lose
> Though they new lovers choose,
> But we are made worse than those.

This idea was rather daring in Ovid's society, where it was held that restrictions on sexual behaviour are, by and large, of human institution, designed to help men and women live in dignity and order, unlike the beasts.   Ovid undermines this human ideal with a countervailing human need.   But Donne's society claimed that its morality was divinely instituted, and the very assumption that these are simply matters of human ordinance was outrageous.   The "law" which Donne derogates was given by God.   The Homily "Against Adultery" observes that God punished Old Testament adulterers even "before the Law was given, the law of nature only reigning in the hearts of men" *(Homilies,* p. 135).   Donne wants to overthrow Moses' law and return to the law of nature—in "The Relic" he speaks of "nature, injured by late law."   Philip Stubbes in *The Anatomy of Abuses* (1583) attacks as blasphemy the argument that "nature" allows all other creatures to "engender together": "The devils themselves never sinned so horribly nor erred so grossly as these (not Christians, but dogs) do, that make whoredom a virtue and meritorious" (I, 90).

As so often, it is doubtful how seriously we should treat Donne's stance; probably he intends primarily a joke, a witty irreverence. But to the earnest protestant that very levity was sinful. Donne's Ovidian poems challenge the reader, not just with an unusually vivacious attitude to love, nor just with a witty and conceited argument. He makes explicit the irreligious basis of Ovidian love and hence challenges, outrageously, Christian thought about sexuality.

Generally, however, the aggressive masculinity of the Ovidian lover is complicit with patriarchy. Finally, Christian asceticism and Ovidian love belong together. Both subordinate women and both limit the role of sexuality in human life. Christianity claims the "higher" emotions and leaves to sexuality mainly those of which it disapproves. The Ovidian lover colludes with this assessment:

> Changed loves are but changed sorts of meat,
> And when he hath the kernel eat,
>> Who doth not fling away the shell?
>> (Donne, "Community")

He grants freely that there is little emotional substance in his loving and the church welcomes the admission so that it can denounce him. Conversely, religious condemnation helps him to generate a self-conscious naughtiness.

The prevailing modern response is to deny the dichotomy—to resist the identification of serious emotions with the other-worldly and of sexual experience with the merely physical. To some extent, as we shall see, the protestant doctrine of marriage began to do this. But the sixteenth century also inherited romantic love—the reaction developed by medieval poets to afford expression to officially despised emotions. In many ways romantic love is the opposite of Ovidian love and medieval marriage: it exalts the woman and, even more, the man's emotional commitment. It is essentially chaste and can therefore claim to be morally pure and ennobling. The romantic lover worships his lady from afar; the favour he pleads for is a gesture of acknowledgement, perhaps a kiss. He complains about his lady's tyranny, but we are not convinced that he really wants a change:

> Though I your thrall must evermore remain
> And for your sake my liberty restrain,
>> The greatest grace that I do crave
>> Is that ye would vouchsafe
>>> To rue upon my pain. (Wyatt, *Collected Poems*, p. 44)

Montaigne in his essay "Upon some Verses of Virgil" (1588) admits that romantic love thrives upon frustration: "A gallant undaunted spirit leaveth not his pursuits for a bare refusal, so it be a refusal of chastity, and not of choice.   We may swear, threaten and wailingly complain; we lie, for we love them the better" *(Essays,* III, 87).

Romantic love is really in collusion with Ovidian and Christian notions.   It agrees with them that sex and virtue are hardly compatible outside marriage, for its claim to be pure and ennobling depends on chastity.   Therefore it does not threaten property relations.   Moreover, although it seems to exalt and privilege the woman, the poets are men and the poems deal mainly with their "suffering."   It seems that the lady has her lover at her mercy, but she equally is trapped in a static relationship which denies her individuality and assumes that sexual contact with her is sinful except in limited circumstances.

In matters of love, literature of the period manifests a dislocation deriving from the co-presence of these three discourses: the romantic, Ovidian and Christian.   Such confusion is not entirely new—in Chaucer's *Troilus and Criseyde* Troilus is the complete romantic but Pandarus performs the Ovidian manipulations necessary to get Cressida to bed; their relationship then takes on a permanence associated more with marriage. That is why it is so difficult to define "courtly love."   The configurations in protestant England are nevertheless distinctive.

Some protestants condemned romantic love because of its emotional excess.   Joseph Hall declared, in the seventh of his satires (1597),

> Great is the folly of a feeble brain,
> O'erruled with love and tyrannous disdain:
> For love, however in the basest breast
> It breeds high thoughts that feed the fancy best,
> Yet is he blind, and leads poor fools awry,
> While they hang gazing on their mistress' eye.
>
> *(Collected Poems,* p. 18)

Hall recognizes the ennobling case for love but still thinks it foolish.   Sidney, I shall demonstrate, was inclined to believe that fallen humanity is unable to sustain the lofty chastity of romantic love.   He shows it degenerating steadily to the Ovidian.

But many protestants sought to reconcile romantic love with marriage, mainly by accepting it as appropriate to the courtship period (this formula is still with us).   In *As You Like It* Silvius expounds in fully romantic terms the emotion experienced by all the young lovers, who intend marriage:

> It is to be all made of fantasy,
> All made of passion and all made of wishes,
> All adoration, duty and observance,
> All humbleness, all patience and impatience,

> All purity, all trial, all observance.   (V.ii.93)

But this is now a temporary stage, fulfilment in marriage is
the goal.   Rosalind is severe on Phebe, who persists in the proud
indifference of the romantic love lady (III.v.35-63).
    The religious implications of the assimilation of romantic
love to courtship are apparent in the dedication and preface
which Giles Fletcher added to his sonnet sequence, *Licia* (1593).
He recognizes that love poetry has become "a thing foolishly
odious in this age," partly because "our English Genevan purity
hath quite debarred us of honest recreation" (Lee, *Elizabethan
Sonnets*, II, 27).   He defends his sonnets by repudiating Ovidian
passion as "not love" and invoking instead the romantic attachment,
loving "but the virtues of the beloved, satisfied with wondering,
fed with admiration, respecting nothing but his lady's worthiness,
made as happy by love as by all favours, chaste by honour, far
from violence: respecting but one" (II, 31, 32).   And he asks,
"if our purest divines have not been [in love], why are so many
married?" (II, 28-29).   Ovidian love is repudiated but even severe
protestants should accept chaste romantic love as a proper prelude
to marriage.
    We have now the context and concepts to discuss Astrophil's
sonnets to Stella.

Astrophil and Stella (1581-82) poses the most fascinating problem
in the love poetry of the period.   It falls quite outside Fletcher's
defence, for Stella is married and Astrophil turns out to be primarily an Ovidian.   Does Sidney mean us to endorse his passion,
or is the sequence contrived as a warning against the dire effects
of improper love?   I propose to discuss it with the latter reading
in view.
    Personal allusions in the sonnets suggest that Sidney and
Astrophil are the same and that Stella is to be identified with
Lady Penelope Rich.   But these could be casual signatures and
compliments, rather than signs of a substantial personal involvement
implying endorsement of Astrophil.   Against them we must
set the manifestly contrived structure of the sequence and Sidney's
determination to use secular forms with an ethical slant consistent
with protestant values.   Also Astrophil is, I believe, the first
male speaker in a series of love poems to have a name distinct
from the poet's.   It seems impossible to decide absolutely that
Sidney is or is not Astrophil; we should consider why he cultivated
this ambivalence.   It may be that he wanted to unsettle the
reader by resisting attempts to bring the poem into focus as
either fiction or fact—notice also inconsistencies in point of
view (poems set in an impossible present, in dialogue and in narra-
tive form) and the many references to the process of writing.
I shall suggest shortly a reason why Sidney may have chosen

to exercise his reader with shifting levels of reality.

The strongest ground for taking *Astrophil and Stella* as a critique of ungoverned sexual passion is the unprecedented manner in which Sidney deploys Christian objections to love.

> It is most true, that eyes are form'd to serve
> The inward light: and that the heavenly part
> Ought to be king, from whose rules who do swerve,
> Rebels to Nature, strive for their own smart.
>   It is most true, what we call Cupid's dart
> An image is, which for ourselves we carve;
> And, fools, adore in temple of our heart,
> Till that good god make church and churchman starve.
>   True, that true Beauty Virtue is indeed,
> Whereof this beauty can be but a shade,
> Which elements with mortal mixture breed:
> True, that on earth we are but pilgrims made,
>   And should in soul up to our country move:
>   True, and yet true that I must Stella love.
>   (Sonnet 5; *Selected Poetry and Prose*)

This is a thorough account opf protestant objections to passionate love of all kinds.   The functions Astrophil gives for the eyes—informing the reason of godly matters and recognising true beauty— are those offered by Sidney's friend du Plessis-Mornay in *The True Knowledge of a Man's own Self*:

> The commodities of this sense are evident, as well for the
> knowledge of God, our search for safety and assurance,
> our willing prevention of perils and inconveniences; as also
> for our choice and election of those things which are beautiful
> and fair, and leaving them which in themselves appear
> to be ill-shaped and counterfeit.   (pp. 81-82)

Astrophil admits to being distracted from these goals.

The second quatrain, about the image in the temple of Astrophil's heart, is very provocative.   Protestants were, of course, particularly sensitive about images, and they often used St. Paul's idea that the body is the temple of the Holy Ghost. Astrophil is not an innovator when he conjoins these themes in the context of adulterous passion.   The Homily "Against Adultery" warns: "If we be the temple of the Holy Ghost, how unfitting then is it to drive that Holy Spirit from us through whoredom, and in his place to set the wicked spirits of un-cleanness and fornication, and to be joined and do service to them!" *(Homilies*, p. 129).   Astrophil is violating fundamental beliefs.

The third quatrain has a Platonic base, but it is used to express disjunction between human and divine; there is no suggestion that love for Stella might afford a route to "true Beauty." For many modern readers, very likely, the conclusion, "True,

and yet true that I must Stella love," outweighs the preceding
thirteen lines, for we commonly credit experiential demands above
abstract morality.   Perhaps Elizabethans did this in practice,
but they did not normally countenance it as a theoretical principle.
The period did in fact see a considerable questioning of ethical
orthodoxies, but in obscure and indirect ways.

Thus Sidney brings into the reader's immediate awareness
Christian objections which Astrophil wants to ignore.   Several
sonnets near the beginning of the sequence force the same confrontation upon the reader—4, 10, 14, 18, 19, 21.   Either truculent-
ly or regretfully, Astrophil rejects all the assumptions of contemporary religion.   This was quite new.   Previously love poetry
either conveniently forgot such reservations (in Chaucer's *Troilus
and Criseyde* the pagan setting allows the reader to sympathize
with the lovers and Christian values appear with tantalising independence at the end); or, like Petrarch, it admitted and accepted
them.   By making Astrophil openly repudiate standard morality
Sidney invites criticism of him.

Astrophil's revelation of the principles by which he is condemned is made plausible and significant by his main characteristic:
self-deception.   He admits it in sonnet 2:

I call it praise to suffer tyranny;
And now employ the remnant of my wit,
    To make myself believe, that all is well,
    While with a feeling skill I paint my hell.

When he sees Stella looking at him he takes it as a good sign
and tells Hope,

Well, how so thou interpret the contents,
    I am resolv'd thy error to maintain,
    Rather than by more truth to get more pain.

(67)

Hopeful self-deception makes him think that Stella will eventually
say Yes, but she doesn't.

Self-deception allows Astrophil to believe that he has wittily
answered Christian objections, but we perceive the flaw.   In
sonnet 4 he repudiates virtue and warns,

I swear, my heart such one shall show to thee,
    That shrines in flesh so true a deity,
That Virtue, thou thyself shalt be in love.

Virtue would indeed love the deity, but not the love-god whom
Astrophil has in mind.   In the context of this sonnet, where we
hear of "will and wit," "vain love," "Churches or schools" and
"a fault confest," the sleight of hand is apparent.   Indeed, by
offering a substitute for Christ's incarnation (which enshrined
a deity in flesh) Astrophil manages a notable blasphemy.   Like

57

Musidorus in the *Old Arcadia*, he uses upon himself "all force of such arguments of which affectionated brains are never un-provided" (p.185).   He has a show of reason, but not such as would·convince an Elizabethan trained in grammar-school logic and rhetoric.   The tricksy language shows that we should not take him seriously: "Reason thou kneel'dst, and offeredst straight to prove / By reason good, good reason her to love" (10).

Astrophil's self-deceptive and irreligious arguments are not incidental. To protestants they were a natural concomitant of his passion.   Du Plessis-Mornay said that sensual desire produces

> a privation and defect of light in the understanding, whereof ensueth ignorance of God and his will, untruths, boldness to encounter with any of his inhibitions. . . . In these obscurities, our understanding loveth and conceiveth great admiration of himself and of his own wisdom, waxing bold to feign opinions of God and to apprehend them after his own pleasure.   (*True Knowledge of a Man's Own Self*, pp. 173-74)

Astrophil is bold to encounter with divine inhibitions; he has so high an opinion of his own wit that he challenges the common-places of protestant doctrine, apprehending them according to his own wishes.

Astrophil's error is further apparent in the way his love degener-ates towards a cynical Ovidian sexual quest.   Sometimes in the early sonnets he admires Stella's virtue like a romantic lover, but already in sonnet 5 he cannot accept that "true Beauty Virtue is indeed." In 52 he admits, unrepentantly, that "A strife is grown between Virtue and Love" and declares,

> Well, Love, since this demur our suit doth stay,
>   Let Virtue have that Stella's self; yet thus,
>   That Virtue but that body grant to us.

The virtue which the chaste romantic lover admires is separated off from Stella's body, leaving Astrophil exposed as a lustful Ovidian who will use any argument to get her to bed.   In 68 he affects to praise her qualities but concludes with a sexual innuendo: "O think I then, what paradise of joy / It is, so fair a Virtue to enjoy."   In sonnet 63 he proves to his own satisfaction that when Stella says No she means Yes.

A similar Ovidian degeneration occurs with the princes in the *Old Arcadia*.   Pyrocles begins by asking, perhaps tongue in cheek, "if we love virtue, in whom shall we love it but in virtuous creatures?" (p. 22), but ends by sleeping with Philoclea and, in the song "What tongue can her perfections tell?" admiring her "thighs (for Ovid's song more fit)" (p. 240).   Musidorus runs away with Pamela, insisting that she is in no danger: "You do wrong to yourself to make any doubt that a base estate could ever undertake so high an enterprise, or a spotted mind be able to behold your virtues" (p. 197).   But this romantic assertion of chastity proves inadequate.   When Pamela falls asleep Musidorus is "overmastered with the fury of delight" and reaches the point of raping her (p. 202).   Sidney's thought seems to be that romantic love slides inevitably towards the Ovidian.

Notice also that the princes' error is in part, like Astrophil's, a failure to respect marriage.   The Third Eclogues celebrate, in contrast, the wedding of Lalus and Kala—the epithalamion "Let mother earth now deck herself in flowers" sets aside "Foul Cupid, sire to lawless lust" and the Ovidian "art" *(Old Arcadia,* p. 247).   Euarchus judges the princes as violators of wedlock (pp. 406-07).

Astrophil argues himself out of virtue, but Stella keeps it before the reader by her refusals to countenance an unchaste love.   Sonnet 71 invokes her virtue in fulsome terms:

> Who will in fairest book of Nature know
>> How Virtue may best lodged in beauty be,
>> Let him but learn of Love to read in thee,
> Stella, those fair lines, which true goodness show.

For the modern reader all this is perhaps countered by the last line: "But ah, Desire still cries, give me some food."   But it is doubtful whether Elizabethan readers could dismiss virtue outright. And it is doubtful whether Sidney would wish them to, for he images Stella as a virtuous book, striving "all minds that way to move": she has the didactic purpose of the books Sidney justifies in *A Defence of Poetry.*   By refusing to be persuaded by the "inward sun" of Stella's "reason" Astrophil aligns himself with the "hard-hearted evil men" who "think virtue a school name, and know no other good but *indulgero genio* [following their inclinations], and therefore despise the austere admonitions of the philospher, and feel not the inward reason they stand upon" *(Defence,* p. 41).

Astrophil's Ovidian impulses spur him in the Second Song to steal a kiss while Stella is asleep, then to a passionate kiss for which he has to apologize ("I will but kiss, I never more will bite"—82).   At this point we should realize that he is following Ovid very closely:

> Though she give them not, yet take the kisses she does not give.   Perhaps she will struggle at first, and cry "You Villain!" yet she will wish to be beaten in the struggle.   Only beware lest snatching them rudely you hurt her tender lips, and she be able to complain of your roughness.   He who has taken kisses, if he take not the rest beside, will deserve to lose even what was granted.   *(Art of Love,* p. 59)

Astrophil chooses to interpret Stella as the Ovidian lady who
only pretends reluctance.   So in the Fourth Song, full of anticipation, he makes a physical assault, but Stella fends him off by
"force of hands."   He has misread her entirely, but even after
her moving rejection in Song 8 he hardly accepts that it is all
over.   The sequence ends with Astrophil neither comprehending
nor repenting, and that fits the unremitting view of the psychology
of sin held by most protestants: "custom in sinning brings hardness
of heart; hardness of heart, impenitency; and impenitency, condemnation" *(William Perkins,* p. 98).

This admonitory reading of *Astrophil and Stella* credits Sidney
with considerable innovation and subtlety in the handling of irony,
for Astrophil is required to give himself away almost entirely
through his own words.   This may be the function of the uncertainty
about levels of reality and fiction to which I have referred: the
predominantly first-person presentation draws us into Astrophil's
point of view sufficiently for us to feel with him, but we are
unsettled and discouraged from full identification by doubt about
how far real persons are involved, allusions to the process of
writing, and manifest signs that the sequence has been planned.
We are with Astrophil and share his predicament, but retain a
perspective from which to judge him.   Thus *Astrophil and Stella*
is a notable puritan-humanist poem, taking the sonnet sequence,
which often fudged the problem of sexual passion, and giving
it an ethical implication consonant with protestantism.

Such a complex reading is not too much to demand of
Elizabethans, for it is how they were exhorted to read the Psalms,
several of which express despair and resentment at divine providence.   Calvin proposed that we should read them as aids to self-
examination, setting vividly before us "all the griefs, sorrows,
fears, doubts, hopes, cares, anguishes" which trouble the mind.
This will   "draw every one of us to the peculiar examination
of himself, so as no whit of all the infirmities to which we are
subject, and of so many vices wherewith we are fraughted, may
abide hidden" *(Commentaries on the Psalms,* trans. Golding, 1571;
To the Reader). Most of the Bible consists of God's direct command-
ments, but we share David's thoughts, good and bad, and this
helps us to appreciate our own inadequacies.   Herbert's *Temple*
perhaps has this kind of design upon us; *Astrophil and Stella* may
be intended to draw the reader into an examination of his or
her own tendency to self-deception and passionate excess.

Astrophil and Stella does not represent Sidney's final thoughts
on love and marriage.   In the *New Arcadia* the critique of romantic
and Ovidian love is made firmer and more specific by the introduction of Amphialus and Cecropia.   Amphialus is romantically in
love with Philoclea but his mother is starkly Ovidian:

"No" is no negative in a woman's mouth.   My son, believe me,
a woman speaking of women.   A lover's modesty among
us is much more praised than liked. . . . Each virtue hath
his time. . . . Let examples serve.   Do you think Theseus

should ever have gotten Antiope with sighing and crossing
his arms?   He ravished her.   (p. 533)

This vicious version of Astrophil's reluctance to believe Stella's
denials is pure *Art of Love* (see pp. 59, 61).   Cecropia captures
Philoclea to enforce her will, and Amphialus cannot bear to release
her; the romantic colludes with the Ovidian.   His response to
Philoclea's complaint is a ridiculous parody of romantic commitment:

What then shall I say, but that I, who am ready to lie under
your feet, to venture, nay to lose my life at your least
commandment, I am not the stay of your freedom, but love,
love, which ties you in your own knots.   It is yourself that
imprison yourself.   (p. 451)

Here, manifestly, Amphialus is selfish (he removes Philoclea's
freedom), self-deceiving (he tries to divert responsibility to "love")
and self-defeating (his actions are hardly likely to win love).
It is a devastating analysis of the romantic sensibility.
     At the same time Sidney adds, in Argalus and Parthenia,
a highly positive instance of romantic courtship and marriage.
And whilst sustaining the reader's doubts about the princes, he
suggests that they will, through the firmness of the princesses
and the humbling of their heroic pretensions, be saved from the
worst consequences of their passion to arrive substantially unstained
at marriage.   The *New Arcadia* is both more severe and more
optimistic than Sidney's earlier work.   Passionate love may cause
total disaster or, if it can issue in an appropriate marriage, salvation.   Sidney's developing emphasis on the value and relevance
of marriage is characteristic of protestant thought.

The church's attitude to love and sexuality was shifted decisively
(though not, we shall see, straightforwardly) by the Reformation,
for it made a positive ideal of mutual love between man and
woman in marriage.   The Roman church held that the three reasons
for matrimony are first to get children, second to avoid carnal
sin, third for mutual help and comfort.   The reformers stressed
the third objective, often promoting it to first place; the Homily
"Of the State of Matrimony" says it "is instituted of God, to the
intent that man and woman should live lawfully in a perpetual
friendly fellowship, to bring forth fruit, and to avoid fornication"
(Homilies, p. 534).
     "Friendly fellowship"—a lasting, sexual and broadly reciprocal
relationship—has probably always occurred, but protestants gave
it new emphasis.   The standard treatment, Coverdale's translation
of Bullinger's *Christian State of Matrimony* (1541), defines wedlock
as

>the yoking together of one man and one woman, whom God
>hath coupled according to his word, with the consent of them
>both, from henceforth to dwell together, and to spend their
>life in the equal partaking of all such things as God sendeth,
>to the intent that they may bring forth children in the fear
>of him, that they may avoid whoredom, and that (according
>to God's good pleasure) the one may help and comfort the
>other. (ch. 2)

The quality of the relationship—"yoking together . . . consent
of them both . . . equal partaking"—is fulsomely evoked before
the other two purposes, and the definition closes with a re-
affirmation of mutual help and comfort.

Protestants legitimized sexual expression but without the
male bravura of Ovidian love, and promoted idealism but without
the frustration of romantic love. They discarded the Roman
church's preference for the single life—Perkins declared marriage
"far more excellent." Nor did they slight the sexual aspect:
Perkins said it signifies "that solitary and secret society which
is between man and wife alone" (*Christian Economy*, 1609; *Work*,
419, 424). Protestants defined chastity not as abstinence but
as fidelity to one partner; Stubbes termed "mutual copulation"
in marriage "pure virginity" (*Anatomy of Abuses*, I, 91). The
sex was not to be too passionate (Perkins called it "an essential
duty"), but it involved the whole personality and it was legitimate.

Thus protestants made of married sexuality a fulfilling and
desirable condition rather than a second-best compromise.
We may trace to this point the emergence of sexual love from
ascetic Christian restrictions which has continued, very unevenly,
until the present day. Protestant matrimony pointed beyond
Ovidian and romantic love. The assumptions and imagery of
those modes were totally readjusted in the more adventurous
writing of the period.

Puritan humanists seized eagerly upon this acceptable form
of love. In du Bartas' *First Week* disapproval of Ovidian love
poets is balanced by an enraptured celebration of the union of
Adam and Eve:

>Source of all joys! sweet He-She-Coupled-One!
>Thy sacred birth I never think upon,
>But (ravished) I admire how God did then
>Make two of one, and one of two again.
>O blessed bond! O happy marriage!
>Which dost the match 'twixt Christ and us presage!
>O chastest friendship, whose pure flames impart
>Two souls in one, two hearts into one heart!
>(Sylvester, *Complete Works*, I, 81)

Euarchus in the *Old Arcadia* speaks of marriage as "the most
holy conjunction that falls to mankind, out of which all families,
and so consequently all societies, do proceed, which not only by

community of goods but community of children is to knit the
minds in a most perfect union" (p. 383).   In the *New Arcadia*
Sidney depicts Argalus and Parthenia as an ideal marriage: "A
happy couple: he joying in her, she joying in herself, but in herself, because she enjoyed him: both increasing their riches by
giving to each other; each making one life double, because they
made a double life one" (p. 501).   This is the goal towards which
Sidney was guiding his enamoured princes and princesses.

Romantic love traditionally inspires paradoxes concerned
with the passion of the lover and the reserve of the lady—Petrarch's
"icy fires."   The Ovidian's typical figures are of delightful conquest.   Sidney and du Bartas develop new paradoxes of reciprocity and union— "He-She-Coupled-One," "each making one life
double, because they made a double life one."

The Fairy Queen book III is about Chastity but gives most
of its attention to the Reformation ideal of chaste marriage;
in book IV Friendship is very often friendly married love.
Belphoebe represents virginity but she is twin-born with Amoret,
who is married chastity: "and 'twixt them two did share / The
heritage of all celestial grace" (III.vi.4).   Despite this declared
equality, Belphoebe is relatively neglected whilst Amoret is "trained
up in true femininity . . . To be th'ensample of true love alone, /
And lodestar of all chaste affection" (III.vi.51-52).

Procreative love is symbolized in Venus' Garden of Adonis.
Here the legend has not the lustful and slightly fetid atmosphere
which Shakespeare gives it in his Ovidian poem, nor Golding's
anxious moral that "manhood strives / Against forewarning though
men see the peril of their lives" *(Metamorphoses*, p. 411).
Traditionally there were two kinds of Venus: the heavenly and
the procreative.   Usually their relative status was clearcut. Burton
follows Ficino who follows Plato:

> The one rears to heaven, the other depresseth us to hell;
> the one good, which stirs us up to the contemplation of
> that divine beauty for whose sake we perform justice and
> all godly offices, study philosophy, etc.; the other base . . .
> because it is abused, and withdraws our soul from the speculat-
> ion of that other to viler objects. *(Anatomy of Melancholy,*
> III, 13-14)

But the procreative Venus in book III, canto vi is not "base" or
concerned with "viler objects."

Spenser takes from protestant theory a revision of the usual
significance of chastity and the earthly Venus.   The Garden of
Adonis is

the first seminary

Of all things that are born to live and die,
According to their kinds.   (III.vi.30)

"Seminary" meant primarily "seed-bed"; it was just beginning to mean "college," mainly in the context of Catholic priests being trained to reconvert England.   Protestant preachers had this in mind when they referred to marriage as "appointed by God himself to be the foundation and seminary of all other sorts and kinds of life in the commonwealth and in the church" (Perkins, *Work*, p. 419; William Gouge and Daniel Rogers also refer to marriage as a seminary).   The family, with its procreative function, took for protestants the place of the priest, and that is Spenser's implication.

At the same time, he criticizes the coarseness of Ovidian and the frustration of romantic love.   In the House of Busyrane the triumphs of the gods in the *Metamorphoses* are depicted as bestial and unsatisfying rapes (III.xi.29-44); Cupid's altar draws the kind of disapproval I was envisaging for *Astrophil and Stella* 5:

> And all the people in that ample house
> Did to that image bow their humble knee,
> And oft committed foul idolatry.   (III.xi.49)

When Arthur comes upon proud and cruel Poena, the lady of romantic love, he persuades her to accommodate herself to "friendly love" and she and her squire live "From that day forth in peace and joyous bliss" (IV.ix.14-16).

I have argued that Spenser was disillusioned both with the protestant doctrine of grace and with human potential by the time he came to write book VI of *The Fairy Queen*.   In the central books, though, he picked out the most humanly positive aspect of Reformation thought.   He directs love poetry away from sexual conquest and romantic yearning, and religious opinion away from other-worldly virginity and distrust of sexuality, and suggests that a mutually fulfilling sexual relationship is a prime human good.

This attitude to love appears strongly in Milton's work. He went further than his contemporaries when he recommended divorce on the grounds that it is wrong to hold together two people who do not get on.   He stressed the origin of marriage in God's words at the creation of Eve: "It is not good that the man should be alone; I will make an help meet for him" (Genesis, 2: 18) and asserted that the burning which St Paul says justifies marriage is not sexual lust, as is usually assumed, but "the desire and longing to put off an unkindly solitariness by uniting another body, but not without a fit soul, to his" *(The Doctrine and Discipline of Divorce*, 1643; *Complete Prose*, II, 251).

In *Paradise Lost* Adam and Eve exhibit a harmonious inter-dependence and mutual respect.   They work together, share their experience, discuss the issues that arise.   Their "unanimous" evening prayer features "our mutual help / And mutual love" (IV, 736, 727).   And Milton insists that they enjoyed fulfilling sexual relations: "Our Maker bids increase; who bids abstain / But our destroyer, foe to God and man?" (IV, 748).   Hence Milton hails "wedded Love, mysterious law" and despises both Ovidian love—"Casual fruition"—and romantic love—"court amours," the

"serenade, which the starved lover sings / To his proud fair, best
quitted with distain" (IV, 750-70).   Part of Satan's torment is
to experience "neither joy nor love, but fierce desire" (IV, 509).
Moreover, the conclusion of the poem offers married love as
the principal consolation for the exclusion from Eden.   Eve declares,

> with thee to go,
> Is to stay here; without thee here to stay,
> Is to go hence unwilling.   (XII, 615)

Married love can be a renewal of paradise on earth.   In *The
Doctrine and Discipline of Divorce* Milton asks, "if it were so
needful before the fall, when man was much more perfect in
himself, how much more is it needful now against all the sorrows
and casualties of this life to have an intimate and speaking help,
a ready and reviving associate in marriage?" *(Complete Prose,*
II, 251).

The Reformation ideal of marriage gave writers a newly positive
model of sexual love, but it brought with it particular contradictions.   Husband and wife were supposed to love each other
equally, but not in the same way.   Briefly, the man was in charge.
Perkins declares: "A couple is that whereby two persons standing
in mutual relation to each other are combined together, as it
were, into one.   And of these two the one is always higher
and beareth rule: the other is lower and yieldeth subjection" *(Work,*
pp. 418-19).   This sounds clear but it builds in conflict.   The
wife is to receive the respect due to an equal partner, but also
to be subordinate.   It was difficult in practice to decide where
affectionate trust and shared responsibility should give way to
male authority—consider the awkward bullying and wheedling
in the disagreements between Shakespeare's Portia and Bassanio,
Caesar and Portia, Othello and Desdemona, Macbeth and Lady
Macbeth, Leontes and Hermione; and above all, Milton's Adam
and Eve.   When Petruchio is taming Katherina she wails, "And
that which spites me more than all these wants— / He does it
under name of perfect love" *(The Taming of the Shrew,* IV.iii.11).
    Basically, the period saw a gradual shift in the family structure
of the nobility and gentry, from the wide kinship network deriving
from feudal times to the nuclear family (see Lawrence Stone,
(The Family, Sex and Marriage, London, 1977).   The forces which
made for the idealization of marital love also gave a new status
to the husband as head of household.   The consequence was a
strengthening of patriarchy—the legal rights of women actually
diminished.
    Protestantism provided crucial theoretical justification for
patriarchy.   The removal of the mediatory priest threw upon
the head of household responsibility for the spiritual life and devout

conduct of the family. At the same time, there was a decline
in the significance of great magnates who might stand between
subject and monarch. From these developments protestants
devised a comprehensive doctrine of social hierarchy, with a double
chain of authority running from God to the husband to the individual,
and from God to the monarch to the subject. The Homily "Against
Disobedience and Wilful Rebellion" derives earthly rule from God
and parallels the responsibilities of the monarch and the head
of household (Homilies, p. 589). Indeed, the latter has the more
significant religious role: Henry Smith explains in "A Preparative
to Marriage" (1591), "a master in his family hath all the offices
of Christ, for he must rule, and teach, and pray; rule like a king,
and teach like a prophet, and pray like a priest" (Works, I, 32).

Patriarchy was ultimately inconsistent with the ideal of mutual
affection in marriage. This does not mean that the protestant
advocacy of mutuality should be perceived as part of an oppressive
conspiracy. That would be to envisage the constitution of ideology
as single and totalising rather than (as I argued in chapter I) a
piecemeal and shifting process. It is quite feasible to see the
idea of mutuality in sexual relations both as a progressive break,
at least in the long term, and as involved, perhaps contradictorily,
in an immediate regressive tendency. This analysis is supported
by the fact that mutuality and authority are often opposed in
literature of the period. Two main kinds of conflict occurred:
between parents and children over choice of partner (I will come
to this in a moment); and over authority within marriage.

Of course, protestants did not admit the divergent tendencies
in their doctrine. But the way they write about it often manifests
a strain. Sidney concludes his celebration of the mutual love
of Argalus and Parthenia with a statement about authority which
he strives to make consistent: "he ruling, because she would obey,
or rather because she would obey, she therein ruling" (New Arcadia,
p. 501). Does he mean that Parthenia was fulfilled in her subordinate role; or that by appearing submissive she managed to
insinuate her own way? Neither seems very satisfactory. Burton
in The Anatomy of Melancholy declares, "The husband rules her
as head, but she again commands his heart, he is her servant,
she his only joy and content" (III, 53). The opening clause sounds
definitive; the second is perhaps only mildly confusing because
we know that the head should rule the heart; but then the strong
phrasing of "servant" and "only joy and content" reverses altogether
the initial idea with attitudes more appropriate to romantic love.
Burton is in difficulty.

Spenser in the Amoretti (1595) undertakes an unprecedented
puritan humanist adaption of the sonnet sequence to a relationship
which ends in marriage. He announces in sonnet 6 that his goal
is "To knit the knot that ever shall remain"—wedlock; eventually
Elizabeth is persuaded and they agree to marry. Thus Spenser
commits himself to complex changes in role. His courting is
conducted in the usual romantic manner, but marriage must involve
a recognition of Elizabeth as more than fair and cruel (49, 56)

and the development of a different kind of relationship.   He
manages most of the transition with psychological and theological
accuracy, but cannot ultimately reconcile mutuality and rule in
marriage.   The crucial step occurs in the paired sonnets 58 and
59, which are introduced, uniquely, by a title: "By [i.e. concerning]
her that is most assured to herself."   At this point Spenser's
lengthy romantic complaints about Elizabeth's pride are brought
to an unexpected resolution.   In 58 he observes that all flesh
is frail and not to be trusted, but in 59 he celebrates Elizabeth's
assurance:

> Thrice happy she, that is so well assured
>   Unto herself and settled so in heart:
>   That neither will for better be allured,
>   Ne feared with worse to any chance to start.

Spenser breaks through to a realization that Elizabeth is not
arbitrarily cruel and arrogant, but properly confident in her own
virtue.
    The ground for this can only be assurance of election—that
is what "assurance" meant to protestants.   Thomas Norton's
translation of Calvin's *Institutes* (1561) is close to Spenser's wording
when he speaks of "that affiance of heart with which I say that
the assuredness of our election is established" (III.xxiv.7).   Perkins
declares, "God then according to his merciful promise lets the
poor sinner feel the assurance of his love wherewith he loveth
him in Christ, which assurance is a lively faith" *(The Foundation
of the Christian Religion*, 1590; *Work*, p. 158).   *Willobie His
Avisa* (1594) purports to chronicle the resistance of a chaste wife
to a sequence of lustful advances.   It affords a complete confrontation of married chastity with Ovidian love, and the lady is credited
with "full assurance of her faith" (p. 28).
    Elizabeth's assurance, which Spenser recognizes in sonnet
59, breaks up the traditional relationship with the sonnet lady.
It replaces the accusation of pride, which in most sequences
indicates the poet's resentment at her refusal to be seduced.
And it forms an appropriate basis for marriage, for protestants
were advised that their wife should be godly—"graced with gifts
and embroidered with virtues, as if we married holiness itself"
(Henry Smith, *Works*, I, 13).   Astrophil's whole problem was
Stella's virtue, but Spenser is delighted to find that Elizabeth
is "holiness itself"; it inspires him to new depths of self-abasement.
In sonnet 61 he terms her "The glorious image of the maker's
beauty" (alluding to the Calvinist belief that the elect regain some
of the divine image as it was originally created in Eden—*Institutes*,
I.xv.4), and declares, "Such heavenly forms ought rather worshipped
be, / Than dare be lov'd by men of mean degree."   The hyperbole
of the romantic lover gains new precision from protestant doctrine.
    But if we are to take seriously the idea of their marriage,
Spenser and Elizabeth must move on from the romantic relationship
of courtship to one appropriate to wedlock.   Most books in the

period flinch from this transition; Spenser attempts it in sonnet 65:

> The doubt which ye misdeem, fair love, is vain,
>   That fondly fear to lose your liberty,
>   When losing one, two liberties ye gain,
>   And make him bound that bondage erst did fly.
> Sweet be the bands the which true love doth tie,
>   Without constraint or dread of any ill:
>   The gentle bird feels no captivity
>   Within her cage, but sings and feeds her fill.
> There pride dare not approach, nor discord spill
>   The league 'twixt them, that loyal love hath bound:
>   But simple truth and mutual good will
>   Seeks with sweet peace to salve each other's wound:
> There faith doth fearless dwell in brazen tower,
>   And spotless pleasure builds her sacred bower.

Notice the usual protestant features: the paradox of gaining "two liberties," the absence of "discord," the "mutual good will," the "spotless pleasure." Such mutual and fulfilled love had not appeared in sonnets before.

But notice also Elizabeth's fear that Spenser is going to dominate her: she knows that protestant doctrine stresses the husband's rule as well as mutuality. He says that he is in bondage equally, but how does the image of the caged bird work? It is *"her* cage": Elizabeth is in the cage, and where is Spenser? I fear that he allows us to see that he has got her trapped.

This impression is confirmed by sonnet 67, where Spenser compares himself to a huntsman who rests from an exhausting chase only to find the deer returning "the self-same way":

> There she beholding me with milder look,
>   Sought not to fly, but fearless still did bide:
>   Till I in hand her yet half trembling took,
>   And with her own goodwill her firmly tied.

It is a tender image and we may feel sure that Spenser will not ill-treat the gentle creature he has captured, but it represents a distinct shift from the romantic admiration for her "heavenly form" and the marital ideal of "mutual good will." But then again, in sonnet 73, Spenser presents himself as encaged in Elizabeth's bosom. He juggles with three kinds of relationship—romantic, mutual and patriarchal—and cannot quite reconcile them.

The split between reciprocity and authority in marriage leads straight to the unease which very many readers experience with the fall in *Paradise Lost*. Milton believes in mutual love: when Adam asks for a mate equality is a prime consideration. The animals are "far beneath me set";

> Among unequals what society
> Can sort, what harmony or true delight?
> Which must be mutual, in proportion due
> Giv'n and received. . . .
> > Of fellowship I speak
> Such as I seek, fit to participate
> All rational delight. (VIII, 382)

Adam needs "Collateral love, and dearest amity" (VIII, 426).
But Milton also believes in male supremacy—he blames its failure
when Michael shows Adam the lascivious women descended from
Cain:

> "From man's effeminate slackness it begins,"
> Said th'Angel, "who should better hold his place
> By wisdom, and superior gifts received." (XI, 634)

I shall argue in chapter VII that the conjunction of libertarian
and authoritarian impulses is characteristic of Milton (see further
Jean H. Hagstrum, *Sex and Sensibility* [University of Chicago
Press, 1980], ch. 2). He tries to reconcile the two here by having
God provide Eve, who is nearly but not quite Adam's equal:

> Not equal, as their sex not equal seemed;
> For contemplation he and valour formed,
> For softness she and sweet attractive grace;
> He for God only, she for God in him. (IV, 296)

This is not what Adam wanted. His wish to "participate / All
rational delight" is not quite answered; he gets most out of talking
to Raphael. We may still ask, "Among unequals what society /
Can sort?" (VIII, 390, 383).
     This is the problem Adam presents to the angel. He finds
Eve persuasive although he knows her "th'inferior, in the mind /
And inward faculties which most excel" (VIII, 541). Raphael
tells him, "What higher in her society thou find'st / Attractive,
human, rational, love still" (VIII, 586), but that is just what he
wants to do—he enjoys most

> > unfeigned
> Union of mind, or in us both one soul;
> Harmony to behold in wedded pair
> More grateful than harmonious sound to the ear.
> > (VIII, 603)

But Milton and God have given him aspirations which Eve is not
created to meet.
     The difficulty emerges as soon as they form differing preferen-
ces—on the morning of the fall. When Eve proposes some independent gardening Adam begins his response with an acknowledgement
of their mutual relationship: "Sole Eve, associate sole" (IX, 227).

From this basis it is difficult to assert authority, and Eve's resentment at his distrust is understandable (IX, 273-89).   Adam falls not through the sexual passion of which Raphael warned, but because he needs a companion:

> How can I live without thee, how forgo
> Thy sweet converse and love so dearly joined,
> To live again in these wild woods forlorn?   (IX, 908)

Adam acts on his innate need for mutual love and forgets that he is supposed also to rule.   But what should he have done with the errant Eve?   C.S. Lewis suggested that he might have chastized her and asked God for mercy *(A Preface to Paradise Lost*, Oxford, 1960, p. 127).   That would have asserted patriarchal authority and might have pleased God, but how would they then have reestablished a "fellowship" of "All rational delight"? Eve's position seems unfair to most modern readers; Adam's is impossible.

By stressing mutual affection and male domination in marriage protestantism set up a tension.   It proved fatal in paradise and must have been difficult for many in the seventeenth century.

The other disjunction in the Reformation doctrine of marriage occurred because theorists wanted to maintain, as well as the husband's authority, the father's.   They did not mean to let their young folk get out of hand, or to let human feeling supplant the other important things in life.   The ideal of affectionate marriage was held alongside a continuing belief in parental control, mainly in the interests of social standing and financial security.   Henry Smith asked, "If children may not make other contracts without [parents'] good will, shall they contract marriage, which have nothing to maintain it after, unless they return to beg of them whom they scorned before?" *(Works*, I, 19).   Finance and contract law jostle with human feeling.

Many young people therefore experienced conflicting demands. They were encouraged to expect love in marriage, and poems and plays suggested that courtship might involve a romantic attachment; but they were also told to obey parental wishes.   It was argued that the issue would be resolved by the growth of love after marriage but this was, of course, optimistic.   Only a few extreme radicals like the digger Gerrard Winstanley proposed that "every man and woman shall have the free liberty to marry whom they love" *(Works*, p. 599).

The theme of lovers oppressed by authority recurs throughout the literature of the period.   The requirement in *Paradise Lost* that Adam place his (heavenly) father above his wife is perhaps an indirect reflection of it.   The consequences are tragic in *Romeo and Juliet, Hamlet, The Changeling, The Duchess of Malfi* and

The Broken Heart.   In comedy and romance love occasionally
wins and the parent is overruled, but only in exceptional circumstances.   In *A Midsummer Night's Dream* Egeus' preferred candidate
for his daughter's hand withdraws—with supernatural prompting.
In *The Merchant of Venice* Jessica is justified in abandoning her
father, or almost, by his character and religion..   More often
the issue is resolved by an optimistic shuffle.   *As You Like It*
toys with unauthorized marriage (III.iii; IV.i), but we sense little
danger and Oliver and Duke Frederick experience conversions
which enable the lovers to have their wealth, their social standing
and each other.   In *The Winter's Tale* Polixenes' argument about
marrying "A gentler scion to the wildest stock" (IV.iv.93) seems
proven for flowers but it won't do for people.   Perdita says she
was about to tell him that "The selfsame sun that shines upon
his court / Hides not his visage from our cottage" (IV.iv.445)
but she is in fact royal and this democratic sentiment need not
be tested.
      The *Old Arcadia* conducts an elaborate game with the rival
claims of children and parents.   Basilius is wrong to keep his
daughters from marriage and the princes' unauthorized wooing
is understandable.   But they lose control of themselves: Musidorus
admits as much when he announces his plan to elope with Pamela
(p. 173).   At this point he upsets the delicate balance between
love and authority, and his promise to return with an army to
force Basilius to let Pyrocles and Philoclea marry only compounds
the offence (p. 173).   His inability to restrain his passion when
they are outside society's control makes clear the dangers.
      Euarchus in his judgement adopts totally the parental view
of children as property to be disposed of.   Elopement is "a most
execrable theft; for if they must die who steal from us our goods,
how much more they who steal from us that for which we gather
our goods?" (p. 406).   We may think this harsh, materialistic
and one-sided but we are deprived of an alternative ideal, for
Euarchus points out that love, properly understood, is not in question:
"That sweet and heavenly uniting of the minds, which properly
is called love, hath no other knot but virtue; and therefore if
it be a right love, it can never slide into any action that is not
virtuous" (p. 407).   By their precipitate action, it seems, the
young people have forfeited their claim to virtuous love.   Euarchus
can reasonably invoke the Ovidian precedents, Helen and Europa
(p. 406).
      Sidney has driven his reader into an impasse.   The ideal
of love in marriage is thwarted by the principle of parental authority.   And the case is rendered more absurd by our knowledge
that Euarchus was coming to Arcadia to arrange just such marriages
(p. 359).   The final twist is his realization that another "theft"
of a child from its father is occurring, for he has condemned
his own son to death: "you have forced a father to rob himself
of his children" (p. 412).   Only a miracle can resolve the issue,
and because it is a comedy Sidney makes one happen.
      This is generally the way with comedy, but sometimes the

cynical reader wonders how the fortunate couple will manage
the transition from romantic courtship to domestic harmony.
Will the shallow Orsino prove any match for the resourceful Viola
of *Twelfth Night*? And the only reassurance offered Olivia,
who has married a total stranger, is the Duke's "Be not amaz'd,
right noble is his blood" (V.i.262). It seems that the spirit of
comedy will make satisfactory an arrangement which sorely afflicted
people in real life.

The marriages at the end of *Measure for Measure* (1604) are
particularly provocative. The action was instigated by the urgency
of Claudio and Juliet in the face of delaying "friends" (i.e. kinsmen;
I.ii.140). That is one extreme: love flouts authority. Notice
that it is not only Angelo who disapproves. The Duke asks, "So
then it seems your most offenceful act / Was mutually committed?"
(II.iii.26). Without permission, mutuality (upon which marriage
was supposed to be founded) is "most offenceful." Eventually,
at the end of the play, authority sanctions the love of Claudio
and Juliet, but at the same time we are given instances of the
opposite extreme, forced marriage where there is little liking.
Angelo is compelled to wed Mariana: "Look that you love your
wife," the Duke tells him (V.i.495). Should we assume, with
the handbooks, that affection will develop in time; or will they
be obliged, in Milton's words, "spite of antipathy, to fadge together"?
(Complete Prose, II, 236). The further instance of Lucio and
his punk suggests the latter. And does Isabella love the Duke
and could she, if she wished, refuse his proposal? The play offers
no clear prospect of reconciling love and authority in marriage.

I believe Shakespeare means us to reflect generally upon
the difficulty of transcending the dichotomy of license and legalism—
Lucio, speaking to Claudio, opposes "the foppery of freedom"
to "the morality of imprisonment" (I.ii.125). Throughout the
play these principles are locked in a destructive pattern of stultificat-
ion and defiance: sexual expression is stifled by the law and reacts
with sheer rebellion. In the last scene the Duke merely re-enacts
the dichotomy on a massive scale. First he awards strict penalties,
then he swings round completely and lets everyone off.

For some critics the Duke's clemency resolves the issues
of the play in a triumph of Christian forgiveness, with marriage
in particular as the agency by which sexuality is transformed
to love and reconciled to society. But the problem is surely
not so tractable. The Duke exaggerates only somewhat when
he says "I have seen corruption boil and bubble / Till it o'errun
the stew" (V.i.316). The policy of leniency has been tried already—
Escalus has used it consistently, but without achieving any reform.
Moreover, the Duke's final dispensation is not welcomed joyfully
by many of his subjects, and he is hardly generous in tone—"Well,
Angelo, your evil quits you well. . . . I find an apt remission in
myself"; "Take him to prison, / And see our pleasure herein
executed" (V.i.494, 518). I perceive him as steering with the
skid, swinging with the drift of the society in the hope of regaining
control.

Even Isabella's plea for the life of Angelo is legalistic: her brother "did the thing for which he died" whereas Angelo's "act did not o'ertake his bad intent" (V.i.447).   There is little transcendence here.

The persistence into the denouement of the typical Reformation confusion of love and compulsion in marriage further exemplifies the obduracy of the problem.   Only in the case of Claudio and Juliet does spontaneous mutual love coincide with official approbation.   The other marriages are imposed by the Duke.   He is more humane than Angelo, but nevertheless obliged to work upon the mere hope that mutual affection will grow to ratify his tidy coupling arrangements.   The elegant pairing off which concludes relatively untroubled comedies occurs here in circumstances which imply its hollowness.   Whereas in earlier plays Shakespeare was happy to indulge in genial adjustments to secure the coincidence of love and social approval, in *Measure for Measure* he allows us to perceive that the celebratory betrothal procession may mask an uneasy compromise, an instrument of social control. We are left to envisage for ourselves a more humane way of organizing society.

Writers analyzed but could not resolve the contradictions in the doctrine of marriage.   This may be observed even in Donne's poetry of mutual love.

Donne's poems of reciprocated, fulfilling and enduring sexual love are generally his most popular and they are without precedent. They are idealistic but despise the frustrations of the romantic lover; they eschew the exploitation of the Ovidian.   I shall argue that the pattern of feeling in them derives from the protestant conception of matrimonial harmony.   When Donne became an avowed authority on such matters he placed a distinct emphasis upon equality in marriage.   In his sermon "Preached at a Marriage" (1621) he glosses God's words: "I will make thee a help like thyself: not always like in complexion, nor like in years, nor like in fortune, nor like in birth, but like in mind, like in disposition, like in the love of God, and of one another, or else there is no helper" (*Sermons*, III, 247).   Unlike Milton, Donne believed that the wife may be "like in mind" to her husband and that they share the same kind of relationship to God.   For him mutuality meant equality—though we will still discern underlying patriarchal assumptions.

The pressure of the protestant stress on marriage is evident even in some of Donne's Ovidian poems.   Several include incidental remarks strangely respectful of marriage.   In "Woman's Constancy" it has the status of real experience as opposed to the chimera of Ovidian pursuit:

> Or, as true deaths true marriages untie,
> So lovers' contracts, images of those,
> Bind but till sleep, death's image, them unloose.

At the climax of "Break of Day" the man who leaves his lady
because he has "business" does "Such wrong, as when a married
man doth woo." The priority of marriage is implied also in "The
Flea": "We almost, nay more than married are"—only as a second
thought does Donne claim that their union (in the flea) is superior
to wedlock. These hints suggest that the matrimonial ideal helped,
to stimulate Donne's development, in other poems, of a love which
has not the limitations of the Ovidian and romantic modes.

Several commentators have believed that "The Canonization"
is about Donne and his wife. This seems likely (though it is
not necessary to my argument), if only because it gives body
to the extended repudiation of opponents in the first two stanzas.
Donne's marriage caused his "ruined fortune," stopped him getting
a "place," involved him with "Litigious men." The third stanza
offers a series of equivalents for the reciprocity and completeness
of their love:

> We are tapers too, and at our own cost die,
> And we in us find the eagle and the dove,
> The phoenix riddle hath more wit
> By us; we two being one, are it.

Donne used the same cluster of images in "An Epithalamion on
the Lady Elizabeth and Count Palatine" (1613): he tells St Valentine,

> Till now, thou warmed'st with multiplying loves
> Two larks, two sparrows, or two doves;
> All that is nothing unto this,
> For thou this day couplest two phoenixes;
> Thou mak'st a taper see . . .
> Two phoenixes, whose joined breasts
> Are unto one another mutual nests.

The ideas are not quite the same, but we see that Donne found
the imagery altogether congruous with marriage.

The translation of the lovers to saints in the last part of
"The Canonization"—"We . . . prove / Mysterious by this love"
and "all shall approve / Us canonized for love"—is bold but appropriate if it reflects the protestant sanctification of marriage and
derogation of the Romanist apparatus of intermediary saints.
Donne himself declared in a sermon "At the Marriage of the
Daughter of the Earl of Bridgewater" (1627), "by this sacramental,
this mysterious union, these two, thus made one between themselves,
are also made one with Christ himself" (Sermons, VIII, 104).
"The Canonization," despite the change in style, picks up the
theme of the holiness of love which Spenser explored in the
Amoretti.

In the last stanza Donne envisages that admirers will invoke his lady and himself as "You, whom reverend love / Made one another's hermitage" and ask them to "beg from above / A pattern of your love." The adaptation of Roman Catholic saints in their hermitage to a love relationship was anticipated by protestant preachers. (In Carey's view it shows that Donne's "habits of thought remain Catholic when he feels himself threatened"—*John Donne*, p. 43.) Latimer in a sermon on "Our Daily Bread" (1552) countered the complaint that "All religious houses are pulled down" with the reply, "That man and that woman that live together godly and quietly, doing the works of their vocation, and fear God, hear his word and keep it; that same is a religious house, that is, that house that pleaseth God" (*Selected Sermons*, p. 148). Latimer prefers to the papist monastic institution the household sanctified in married love. Donne made the same point in "Preached at a Marriage": "They that build walls and cloisters to frustrate God's institution of marriage, advance the doctrine of devils in forbidding marriage" (*Sermons*, III, 242). And so in "The Canonization" he represents mutual love as a holy way of life in which each is the other's "hermitage" and says that the lovers, like Catholic saints, may afford to others a "pattern." Du Bartas says that God gave Eve to Adam "For perfect pattern of a holy love" (Sylvester, *Complete Works*, I, 81).

The reader may fear that I am trying to domesticate "The Canonization." It is important to establish protestant marriage as a frame of reference in the poem, but I perceive also a characteristic audacity and a particular ambivalence. Protestants parallelled married love and Christ's love for his people: "the scripture describeth us in matrimony the mysteries and secret benefits which God the Father hath hid in Christ" (Tyndale, *Answer to More*, 1531; p. 153). Spenser uses the idea quite boldly in *Amoretti* 68, when he commemorates Easter Day and concludes, "So let us love, dear love, like as we ought, / Love is the lesson which the Lord us taught." Christ's sacrifice is an example for man and wife. But Donne pushes the comparison to the extraordinary length of a sexual pun upon the death of Jesus:

> We die and rise the same, and prove
> Mysterious by this love.

"Die and rise the same" means that desire is satisfied but then aroused again with equal strength. But we should think also of Jesus, who is said to have risen from the dead. Donne presses the analogy between divine and human love to the point of identifying the mysteries of intercourse and the crucifixion. You can still be prosecuted in England for printing poems containing adventurous ideas about Jesus and sexual love.

This pun affords the clinching indication of a note of hyperbolic insistence which runs through "The Canonization," quite unlike the complacency of contemporary writing on marriage. This may represent either insecurity or confidence—the pun is either

over-compensation or steady defiance (Carey calls it "smut"—p. 43).
Plainly there is something illicit about the relationship.
The poem rhymes throughout on "love," and with it Donne twice
couples "approve" and twice "prove." He lacks the usual approbation, presumably the legal and social sanctions which ratified
even mutual friendly love for protestants. If Donne is insecure
about the validity of the relationship, his insistence on its holiness
and emotional intensity may be designed to compensate for the
lack of official approval. He proclaims the virtue and fulfilment
in their love because he has to justify it by that alone. Alternatively, Donne perhaps seizes upon the aspect of protestant thought
which impressed and delighted him—mutual love—and rejects
the confused compromise with authority and property which was
usually demanded in marriage. In this interpretation the religious
imagery is sheerly defiant, it asserts that the quality of the relationship is a sufficient justification.

"The Canonization" may be about Donne's marriage. Isaac
Walton says it lacked "the allowance of those friends, whose approbation always was, and ever will be necessary, to make even a
virtuous love became lawful" (Lives, p. 15). Donne repudiates
Walton's expedient scruples. Or it may be about a relationship
with no legal status at all.

The latter is the case in "The Anniversary," where Donne
laments that "Two graves must hide thine and my corse." A
married couple would be buried together—observe the implication
that this is the kind of relationship appropriate to marriage.
Indeed, the poem claims for it all the qualities protestants usually
located in matrimony. Donne rejects the traditional structures
of courtly wooing—"All glory of honours, beauties, wits"; he says
their love is absolute ("truly keeps his first, last, everlasting day")
and will endure "till we attain / To write threescore." They
have mutual responsibility ("none can do / Treason to us, except
one of us two") and only death can part them. All this might
be coincidence of thought in Donne and the marriage treatises,
but the inference is definite when he anticipates after death "This,
or a love increased there above." In his sermon "At the Marriage
of the Daughter of the Earl of Bridgewater" Donne declared that
although there is no marrying in heaven, we will know each other
there (Sermons, VIII, 99); in "The Anniversary" he claims a heavenly
continuation for an illicit relationship. It is a marriage, he believes,
in everything but name.

It is impossible to determine whether Donne's attention to
the configuration of language and feeling associated with protestant
marriage signifies independence of official opinion or lurking respect
for it. I am temperamentally inclined to the former reading.
Like Claudio (though not quite the same, for Claudio is technically
married), Donne lacks "the denunciation . . . Of outward order"
for their "most mutual entertainment," but believes nevertheless
that they have "a true contract" (Measure for Measure, I.ii. 134-44).
But whereas Claudio only hesitantly repudiates the Duke's strictures
and advice, "Be absolute for death" (III.i.5), Donne is unrepentant

and absolute for life: "True and false fears let us refrain, / Let us love nobly, and live" ("The Anniversary").

Donne's original attitude to sexual love in these poems is responsible for major features of his style. His conceits, paradoxes and puns express the new and special complexities of reciprocal, sexual, continuing and sanctified love. Consider the oppositions which usually distinguish the Ovidian, romantic and married approaches to love: one stresses the man, another the woman; one the body, another the soul; one the absolute, another the changing; one the human, another the divine. Donne's conceits characteristically compress these oppositions into a tense conjunction.

The strain of adapting traditional concepts to this transformed model of sexual relations is apparent in examples we have considered already—the identification of intercourse and crucifixion, the claim that Donne and his mistress will be blessed in heaven. Donne brings together areas of experience which other analyses of love kept distinct. I mean to look finally at one dichotomy: body and soul, sexual and idealistic love. They were often thought almost incompatible—"it is not love when the appetite of the other senses drives us rather towards matter, mass, weight and deformity that is the opposite of beauty or love, but a stupid, gross and ugly lust" (Ficino, *Letters* I, 91). Protestant matrimony brought them together in certain circumstances and with certain reservations about tone and purpose; "the chaste womb inform with timely seed," Spenser writes in *Epithalamion* (line 386), with more spiritual dignity than sexual vigour. Explicit sexual reference in Elizabethan literature very often occurs as bawdy joke, indicating an embarrassment not unlike our own. Donne argues in several poems that sexual and spiritual love go together. It is often observed that his approach is in fact dualistic—that he assumes a body-soul dichotomy in his attempts to deny it. But this was inevitable, for the language did not afford the concepts to by-pass it. In a few poems Donne interlaces the connotations of divers kinds of love and creates a language.

Commentators on "The Good Morrow" point out that the first stanza ends with the notion that the lady is a Platonic arche-type—which implies an ideal, chaste relationship (compare Shakespeare's sonnet 31) and perhaps the first step in an ascent to the divine: "If any beauty I did see, / Which I desired, and got, 'twas but a dream of thee." But Donne "got" these beauties and he begins with "thou, and I" and moves at once to "we." He uses the idealistic emotional heightening of the Platonic model but adapts it to a mutual and sexually fulfilling relationship. In the second stanza he bids "good morrow to our waking souls," but the image suggests waking up in bed together, he is concerned with bodies as well as souls. His frame of reference is apparent in the adventurers he dismisses: like them, the lovers discover "new worlds" on this physical earth. Donne does not mean to transcend the world, but to concentrate it, to make "one little room an every where." The poem is committed to two kinds of harmony: "thou, and I" and soul and body.

The image of the two hemispheres, in the third stanza, claims
the dignity of Platonic provenance, but not from the climax of the
Symposium where the ladder of ascent is propounded.   It alludes
instead to Aristophanes' cheerful explanation, earlier in the book,
of why people form sexual couples: people were originally spherical
and now each half seeks to be reunited with its essential partner—
"So you see how ancient is the mutual love implanted in mankind,
bringing together the parts of the original body, and trying to
make one out of two, and to heal the natural structure of man"
(Plato, *Great Dialogues*, p. 87).   So Donne and his lady "possess
one world, each hath one, and is one. . . . Where can we find
two better hemispheres?"   The image draws also upon protestant
thought on matrimony, for Aristophanes asserts that the original
spherical people were hermaphroditic combinations of male and
female, and this was taken as an image of marital union (in the
original ending of *Fairy Queen* III, Scudamore and Britomart unite
and are compared to "that fair *Hermaphrodite")*.   The same implication is active in "The Canonization": "So to the one neutral thing
both sexes fit"; and at the end of "An Epithalamion on the Lady
Elizabeth and Count Palatine" the "act" of the two phoenixes
restores "but one phoenix still, as was before." In "The Good
Morrow" Donne plunders Platonic and protestant connotations
to establish a worldly, sexual relationship as the answer to a fundamental need for an ideal wholeness.
      The concluding figure, "What ever dies, was not mixed equally,"
runs exactly counter to the goal of ascent in the *Symposium*.
Socrates relates that we may contemplate "beauty undefiled,
pure, unmixed, not adulterated with human flesh and colours and
much other mortal rubbish" *(Great Dialogues*, p. 106).   The beauty
and love which Donne proclaims is mixed—but equally.   He insists
that the absolute is a function not of asexual transcendence but
of a reciprocal and physical relationship.   Yet his awareness
of the ambitiousness of the project is conveyed in the provisional
tone of the last two lines: "If our two loves be one, or thou and
I / Love so alike that none do slacken, none can die."   The condition is significant.   Donne knows that such harmony is a new
and hardly-tested ideal—rare, precious and precarious.
      Donne's conceits in "The Good Morrow" combine with the
exuberance of sexual union the idealistic implications of more
ascetic traditions of thought on love.   "Love's Growth" incorporates
sexual expression (with a tinge of Ovidian exploitation), a geo-
metrical figure of completeness and the romantic associations
of spring.
      The sexual meaning runs right through the poem.   When
Donne says, "Methinks I lied all winter, when I swore / My love
was infinite, if spring make it more," he evokes not so much the
passing of months as the (no doubt) briefer cycle of quiescence
and arousal.   "Love sometimes would contemplate, sometimes
do."   In the third stanza the circles which are "all concentric
unto thee" centre upon the lady's vagina ("we love the centric
part"—Elegy XVIII), and they are stirred by the poet's penis.

This is also the prince who gains more wealth with each "time of action": so the new power of the present experience will remain through the next period of quiescence.

The prince levying taxes introduces Ovidian language of domination and exploitation; Donne retains basically patriarchal assumptions. But we are not dealing with casual sexual conquest: the prince is established and accepted in office ("She' is all states, and all princes, I"—"The Sun Rising"). Donne is prepared to risk the implication, for he wants to bring sexual desire into a positive relationship with conventionally "elevated" feelings. He still has one line in which to balance out the tone with a more pleasant image: "No winter shall abate the spring's increase."

The circle usually figures absolute and unbreakable experience of a lofty character. That is how Donne uses it at the end of "A Valediction: forbidding Mourning"; in "Preached at a Marriage" he observes that although there is no eternity in this world, "yet we may consider a kind of eternity, a kind of circle without beginning, without end, even in this secular marriage" (*Sermons*, III, 247). This is his meaning in "Love's Growth," but he develops the circle to a series of widening ripples and plants in it a sexual pun. Thus he makes it comprise the intermittent climactic fulfilment of sexual union. This love is satisfied yet unabated, indeed it grows. It has the absolute quality of the circle, but each experience augments it. The sexual dimension enlarges the apparently infinite.

All this analysis of sexuality occurs within the context of spring growth. This ensures that we perceive the poem as primarily about the exalted feeling of being in love. It deploys the traditional association of spring and romantic love—as in the medieval lyric ("Now springs the spray"), in Surrey's "The soote season, that bud and bloom forth brings," the *Amoretti* ("The merry cuckoo, messenger of spring"—19) and Donne's own "Twicknam Garden." But whereas all those poems are about unrequited love, Donne here derives idealistic emotional intensity from sexual satisfaction, and their inter-involvement is proclaimed by the punning imagery.

> Gentle love deeds, as blossoms on the bough,
> From love's awakened root do bud out now.

The figure is extraordinarily delicate, and its careful construction implies the inter-involvement it celebrates. The first words are explicitly physical, though very tender—"Gentle love deeds"—but Donne at once regains the comparison with spring growth, and at its most evocative. Three meanings draw into one in "love's awakened root". They reawaken to their love for each other (compare "The Good Morrow" and "The Dream"), Donne experiences new sexual arousal, the root gives forth fresh leaf. All three involve swelling and growing as new life is stirred. Emotion and sexual excitement are fused together by the mediating image of spring growth.

My main theme is the cultural dislocation which accompanied Reformation Christianity, and we have seen its operation in the earnest repudiations of traditional modes of love by Sidney, Spenser and Milton.   But it was not an unproductive force, for it introduced a new and positive conception of fulfilled sexual love.   Writers struggled with the complications which accompanied this conception in the protestant doctrine of marriage; Donne alone achieved a significant and untrammelled assertion of human love.   But even he used it eventually as a mere illustration of insecurity in his relationship with God: "As humorous is my contrition / As my profane love, and as soon forgot" ("Holy Sonnet" 19). We don't know if Donne really forgot the love of "The Good Morrow," but if he did we may guess the reason from the conclusion to this sonnet: "Those are my best days, when I shake with fear."

5 Heroic assertion

Marlowe, Shakespeare, Seneca, Machiavelli, Ford,
Chapman, Webster

There are two principal ways of thinking about the tragic hero;
they are found both in Renaissance-Reformation thought and in
modern criticism.   According to one view the hero is typically
selfish and presumptuous.   He fails to control his passion as
he should, he refuses to accommodate himself to ordinary human
standards, he is prepared to harm others to fulfil his own needs.
Consequently he suffers in his life and meets an untimely death;
a more satisfactory social order is established by the survivors.
     In the main alternative approach much the same qualities
are observed in the hero, but they are given a positive interpretation.   He demonstrates the capacity of certain human beings
to achieve a pitch of greatness, to assert themselves within or
beyond a universal order—or disorder.   The refusal of the hero
to observe the norms of morality is a sign of his greatness and
of the inability of ordinary mortals to cope with the remarkable
case.   On this latter reading tragedy excites us by revealing
the extent of human potential; on the former, it calms and reassures us by showing how disruptive aspects of human experience
are eventually contained.
     The first reading is compatible with Christianity, especially
the stern Reformation variety.   Protestants were quite ready
to condemn the presumptuous hero.   Greville declared that contemporary tragedy emphasizes "God's revenging aspect upon every
particular sin, to the despair, or confusion of mortality" (*Life
of Sidney*, p. 163).   This was Milton's theme in *Samson Agonistes.*
The second interpretation of the tragic hero challenges protestantism at several points where it was particularly provocative
and problematic.   Writers of this period were fascinated by the
idea of the heroic assertion, I think because it offers expression
to attitudes and objectives which were given little scope in Reformation doctrine.   Very many tragedies do not clearly endorse or
condemn the hero; they encourage our admiration but allow also
the saving opinion that his aspiration is foolish and dangerous.
The Reformation sharpened the paradoxes of Christian dogma
and tragedians reacted, perhaps in a confused way, against its
rigours and limitations.   The ultimate excitement of their plays

is the delicacy with which they tread the line between a protestant and a humanist view of humankind. We are looking, finally, at the same kind of cultural dislocation that we observed in chapter III, but in tragedy it takes distinctive forms, deriving from the distinctive traditions, conventions and institutional opportunities of that medium.

The difficulty of assessing the hero is apparent in Marlowe's *Tamburlaine* (1587), which has always attracted rival interpretations. In part one the hero exhibits tyrannical cruelty and the utmost pretension—he justifies his thrust to power with a divine comparison, "What better precedent than mighty Jove?" (1; II.vii.17). He is surely among those who, in Calvin's opinion, must suffer God's judgment:

> Before his face shall fall and be crushed all kings and judges
> of the earth, who have not kissed his anointed, who have
> enacted unjust laws to oppress the poor in judgment, and
> do violence to the cause of the humble, to make widows
> a prey, and plunder the fatherless. (*Institutes*, IV.xx.29)

Yet within the play Tamburlaine has the support of Marlowe's exotic rhetoric and impresses even his enemies.

Marlowe's original audience must have expected *Tamburlaine* to follow the sequence of medieval *de casibus* tragedy, where the hero is God's cleansing agent on earth, engrossing all evil until he too eventually suffers for his crimes. This is the structure Shakespeare took from the chronicles and *The Mirror for Magistrates* for *Richard III* (1592-3). In that highly patterned play each of Richard's adult victims goes to his death lamenting his own crimes and cursing Richard; each death extends the list of murders mourned by the chorus of royal women. The pattern is summarised on the night before Bosworth when all the slain return, in order, to encourage Richmond and terrify Richard. "I shall despair," he cries (V.iii.200), exemplifying the fate which the seventeenth of the Thirty-nine Articles promises to the damned: "the Devil doth thrust them either into desperation, or into wretchlessness of most unclean living, no less perilous than desperation." Though, as I shall argue, even such a villain establishes a kind of heroic assertion, the whole pattern works to condemn Richard; his fall completes simultaneously the ethical and plot structures of the play.

Part one of *Tamburlaine* sets up to be that kind of sequence. Tamburlaine is cursed repeatedly: "Theridamus and Tamberlaine, I die: / And fearful vengeance light upon you both!" (II.vii.51), says Cosroe; Bajazeth makes an elaborate appeal that Tamburlaine should live in terror with tormented thoughts (V.i.293-99). But nothing like that happens. Even Zenocrate fears that Tamburlaine has gone too far:

> Behold the Turk and his great emperess!
> Ah mighty Jove and holy Mahomet,
> Pardon my love, O pardon his contempt
> Of earthly fortune and respect of pity.
>
> (V.i.360)

But she is reassured: "Your love hath Fortune so at his command, / That she shall stay and turn her wheel no more" (V.i.371), and in part one, which was perhaps intended to stand by itself, this seems to be true. Tamburlaine fails to fall.

The second part of *Tamburlaine* is even more provocatively constructed, for it teases the audience with hints that Tamburlaine's heroic power is insufficient and plays with the possibility of retribution. Zenocrate dies, his son proves effete, Theridamus fails to woo Olympia as Tamburlaine did Zenocrate. None of these episodes quite declares Tamburlaine's inadequacy and none of them is clearly the judgment of an outraged divinity; yet each tantalises us with the prospect of a critique of the hero. Finally Tamburlaine challenges religious authority in the person of Mahomet: "Now Mahomet, if thou have any power, / Come down thyself and work a miracle" (V.i.185). Nothing happens—for thirty lines—but then Tamburlaine is "distemper'd suddenly" (V.i.216). Is this coincidence or divine retribution? And if the latter, is it not even more strange that it is the heathen diety that responds? We are teased again.

Tamburlaine's initial reaction to his impending death invites ironic interpretation:

> Come, let us march against the powers of heaven,
> And set black streamers in the firmament,
> To signify the slaughter of the gods.
> Ah, friends, what shall I do? I cannot stand.
> Come, carry me to war against the gods,
> That envy thus the health of Tamburlaine.
>
> (V.iii.48)

He vaunts against the gods but cannot stand. Yet Tamburlaine's death is not necessarily a punishment. Every secularist must accept that we have to die; birth and death are the human limits which can be identified without recourse to supernatural speculation. Tamburlaine is shaken by the reminder of his mortality, but arguably recovers his self-possession through a sober recognition that his life has reached its natural end. He reaffirms the values by which he has lived and accepts the inevitable limits upon human aspiration:

> Let not thy love exceed thine honour, son,
> Nor bar thy mind that magnanimity
> That nobly must admit necessity.
>
> (V.iii.199)

Whether we should call this a defeat seems to me altogether
doubtful.   But in the context of Elizabethan doctrine the uncertainty itself promotes a radical questioning.

The basic challenge of Tamburlaine and other tragic heroes is
their determination to identify and pursue their own goals without
deference to God or humanity.   The heroic individual ascribes
his power to himself and is given to climactic statements of the
kind, "I am Antony yet" *(Antony and Cleopatra*, III.xiii.93); "at
myself I will begin and end" (Webster, *The White Devil*, V.vi.258);
"I'll be mine own example" *(The Duchess of Malfi*, V.vi.81); "I'll
trust myself, myself shall be my friend" (Kyd, *The Spanish Tragedy*,
III.ii.125);

> Would you have me
> False to my nature ?   Rather say I play
> The man I am.   *(Coriolanus*, III.ii.14)

The final confrontation with death finds him alone against the
rest but undeterred: "Welcome, come more of you whate'er you
be, / I dare your worst" (Ford, *'Tis Pity She's a Whore*, V.vi.81);

> Though Birnam wood be come to Dunsinane,
> And thou oppos'd, being of no woman born,
> Yet I will try the last.   *(Macbeth*, V.viii.30)

The hero will not sink his personality and objectives among those
which are generally accepted; he aims to be measured by the
quality of his defiance.
        Protestants reacted strongly against the notion that men
can be self-determining:

> We are not our own; therefore, neither is our own reason
> or will to rule our acts and counsels.   We are not our own;
> therefore, let us not make it our end to seek what may
> be agreeable to our carnal nature.   We are not our own;
> therefore, as far as possible, let us forget ourselves and
> the things that are ours.   On the other hand, we are God's;
> let us, therefore, live and die to him.   (Calvin, *Institutes*,
> III.vii.1)

Some critics have argued that the dominance of Christianity
in Elizabethan society was such that people must have disapproved
of the tragic hero.   But ideology is never totally overwhelming,
or how could change occur?—the Civil War, for instance?   Reformation doctrine actually stimulated questioning and anxiety.   There
were countervailing cultural forces in the period and although
their effect was muted it was not altogether suppressed.   The

theatre, of which so many protestants complained, is just where
we should expect subversive thought to emerge.

Dramatists found the heroic assertion powerfully rationalised
in two of the main influences upon tragedy: Seneca and Machiavelli
Seneca offered two models. His Hercules plays present the
image of a man who, like Tamburlaine, imposes himself upon
the world through his amoral but overwhelming prowess (see further
Eugene M. Waith, *The Herculean Hero* [Chatto and Windus, 1962]).
His stature seems to place him beyond conventional codes of
behaviour. Hercules has an unprincipled sexual appetite and
is given to random violence, but he overcomes all opposition
and is from the first a demi-god and destined for heaven. In
Hercules Furens Juno makes him mad so that he kills his wife
and children but no criticism of him is ventured; he is "of mind
unsound to see, / But yet full great" (*Tenne Tragedies*, I, 40).
Finally Hercules commits suicide, declaring:

> Forbear, forbear to moan for me, for virtue opened hath
> To me the passage to the stars, and set me in the path
> That guides to everlasting life.
>
> (*Tenne Tragedies*, II, 255)

Christians must regard this as absurd presumption, but Hercules'
apotheosis is meant straightforwardly by Seneca. Tamburlaine
and Shakespeare's Antony (who links himself with Hercules) may
be viewed similarly, as godlike heroes who arouse awe and wonderment by the sheer amoral scale of their heroic assertion. Seneca's
Elizabethan editor, Thomas Newton, denied that the plays tend
"sometime to the praise of ambition, sometime to the maintenance
of cruelty, now and then to the approbation of incontinency,
and here and there to the ratification of tyranny" (1581); *Tenne
Tragedies*, I, 4-5). But really there is no answer to these charges,
the Senecan hero cannot be drawn within the rules of protestant
society.

In his prose works especially Seneca developed an alternative
mode of human assertion, the Stoic goal of self-sufficiency.
He did not believe that people can control fortune, but he held
that they can render it irrelevant by cultivating a mental tranquill-
ity which events cannot touch:

> you see in what wretched and baneful bondage he must
> linger whom pleasures and pains, those most capricious and
> tyrannical of masters, shall in turn enslave. Therefore
> we must make our escape to freedom. But the only means
> of procuring this is through indifference to Fortune. Then
> will be born the one inestimable blessing, the peace and
> exaltation of a mind now safely anchored. ("The Happy
> Life," *Moral Essays*, II,111)

This Stoic answer to vicissitude appears again and again in tragedy:

> Though in our miseries Fortune have a part,
> Yet in our noble suff'rings she hath none—
> Contempt of pain, that we may call our own.
> <div align="right">(<i>Duchess of Malfi</i>, V.iii.56)</div>

Seneca never reconciled his two models of the hero; it seems that the plays represent his lack of confidence in the practicability of rational self-sufficiency. Many Christians and some protestants have thought the Stoic approach compatible with their faith, but Calvin believed that even this quiescent attempt to gain a hold on life arrogates too much power to humankind. He termed "absurd" the Stoic hero ,"who, divested of humanity, was affected in the same way by adversity and prosperity, grief and joy; or, rather, like a stone, was not affected by anything" (<i>Institutes</i>, III.viii.9). Philosophers like Seneca, he said, were wrong to imagine that "human reason is sufficient for right government" (II.ii.3).

Machiavelli was not simply the apostle of villainy; he was taken seriously as a historian and political thinker by many people, including Philip Sidney and Milton. He disputed the kind of position held by protestants, that events are beyond human control : "fortune is the arbiter of half the things we do, leaving the other half or so to be controlled by ourselves" (<i>The Prince</i>, 1513, p. 130; notice that "fortune" suggests an arbitrary force, not a caring providence). The right person, in the right circumstances, may dominate his or her fate.

Machiavelli is associated with the scheming villain but he admired above all the heroic figure who is raised above ordinary ethical considerations by a fulness of self. He gives an instance of the priority of greatness over morality which illustrates precisely the more admiring approach to the tragic hero. In 1505 Giovampagolo Baglioni of Perugia had the opportunity to seize his enemy, Pope Julius II, together with all his cardinals. But he shrank from that bold deed. The reason, "prudent men" concluded, is that we do not know "how to be either magnificently bad or perfectly good; and that, since evil deeds have a certain grandeur and are open-handed in their way, Giovampagolo was incapable of performing them." The sheer audacity and scope of the action excites Machiavelli and, he says, other people. Giovampagolo "would have done a thing the greatness of which would have obliterated any in infamy and any danger that might arise from it" (<i>Discourses</i>, 1531; p. 178). This suggests one way of thinking about Tamburlaine.

The cunning villain, the stage Machiavel, may also manifest a form of heroic assertion. Flamineo in <i>The White Devil</i> (1612) credits him with stature superior to the straightforward hero:

> Those are found weighty strokes which come from th'hand,
> But those are killing strokes which come from th'head.
> O the rare tricks of a Machivillian!
> He doth not come like a gross plodding slave
> And buffet you to death: no, my quaint knave,

He tickles you to death; makes you die laughing.
(V.iii.191)

The point is ratified in the dramatic context, for Flamineo is speaking, unwittingly, to the man who has just poisoned his patron.

The Machiavel, like the grand hero, is being himself. Marlowe's Barabas maintains a weird integrity, for instance in the vicious asides when he is talking with Lodowick about his daughter: "Pointed it is, good sir, (*Aside*) but not for you"; "And I will giv't your honour (*Aside*) with a vengeance" (*The Jew Of Malta*, 1589-90; II.iii.60, 67). He cannot allow Lodowick's presumption of his favour to pass without at least a secret reservation. There is a bitter absoluteness behind his ghoulish zest. He tells Ithamore, "First be thou void of these affections: / Compassion, love, vain hope, and heartless fear" (II.iii.167), and with fearful consistency he applies the doctrine to his daughter. Moreover, his downfall, as with many heroes, is caused by his commitment to his own chosen approach to life (Machiavelli argues that for total success one must meet flexibly the needs of each situation—*The Prince*, p. 131). When Barabas has gained control of Malta he rejects the straightforward exercise of power expected of the governor:

No, Barabas, this must be look'd into:
And, since by wrong thou got'st authority,
Maintain it bravely by firm policy.
(V.ii.34)

His self-assertion has been constructed entirely around villainy and circumspection and he is unable to relinquish it. As with the straightforwardly heroic Coriolanus, his determination to sustain his own identity is the source of his power but also of his ultimate weakness.

I am not saying that Barabas is admirable, but that there is a quality in his commitment which challenges the conformity and submission required by protestant doctrine. Machiavelli set out explicitly the disjunction between the heroic assertion and Christianity. He believed that an ethic of humility, as opposed to the glory which pagans bestowed upon heroic achievement, impoverishes human experience and weakens society. Christianity "has assigned as man's highest good humility, abnegation, and contempt for mundane things, whereas the other identified it with magnanimity, bodily strength, and everything else that conduces to make men very bold" (*Discourses*, p. 278). Elizabethans found this a shocking sentiment, but it had at least a surreptitious appeal for the major tragedians.

* * * * * *

In Seneca and Machiavelli Elizabethans found forceful proponents
of heroic assertion.   As well as the admonitions from pulpits
they assimilated the restrained but idealistic Stoic programme,
the awesome model of Hercules, and the extraordinarily intelligent
and practical analysis of Machiavelli.   But the relationship between
tragedy and protestantism operates at a more fundamental level
than a conflict of moral principles.   Protestants regarded human
presumption as a direct challenge to God.   Henry Smith declared
in "A Dissuasion from Pride" (1592) that the proud man "maketh
himself equal with God, because he doth all without God, and
craves no help of him; he exalteth himself above God, because
he will have his own will, though it be contrary to God's will"
(*Works*, I. 205).

      God's prerogative is so complete that *any* human assertion
infringes it.   Tragedians realized this: in the plays divine qualities
are often claimed for the protagonist.   Tamburlaine explains
his aspiration beyond his shepherd origins by a comparison with
his deity:

> Jove sometimes masked in a shepherd's weed,
> And by those steps that he hath scal'd the heavens
> May we become immortal like the gods.
> (1; I.ii.199)

Dr. Faustus thinks "A sound magician is a demi-god" and tires
his brains to get a deity (I.i.60); Coriolanus' admirers believe
"He wants nothing of a god but eternity, and a heaven to throne
in" (V.iv.24); the Steward says Timon's generosity is divine
(*Timon of Athens*, IV.ii.41); Orgilus in Ford's *The Broken Heart*
links his plotting with "The riddles which are purposed by the
gods" (I.iii.181).

      Such claims are of a piece with the humanistic estimate
of mankind which we discussed in chapter three.   Ficino declared:
"In certain ages there are great and powerful men, gods in the
guise of humans, or humans who are gods, but they are rarer
than the Phoenix" (*Letters*, II, 77-78).   More particularly, Seneca's
Hercules is a demi-god, and he says often that the tranquil, self-
sufficient person is godlike: "the wise man is next-door neighbour
to the gods and like a god in all save his mortality" ("On Firmness,"
Moral Essays, I, 73).   But for protestants the idea of the godlike
person merely recalls the original sin of Adam and Eve, who
fell because they aspired to divinity (Genesis, 3: 22).   Du Plessis-
Mornay explained the existence of human suffering and error
as God's way of discouraging the heroic assertion: otherwise

> we would think at the length, that it was of our own
> steadiness, and not of God's upholding of us, not only
> that we tripped not, but also that we tumbled not down.
> For what made us fall but pride: and what manner of pride,

but that we thought we would be gods without God, yea
even of ourselves? (*Trueness of the Christian Religion*, pp.
209-10)

Some critics believe that this is the moral of many tragedies;
others that it is outweighed by the human vitality of the protagonist. My argument is that the major tragedians were deeply engaged with the gap between the two positions.

In several plays the self-assertive character justifies himself
with an exposition of atheistic principles. Edmund in *King Lear*
(1605-06) proclaims, "Thou, Nature, art my godess; to thy law
/ My services are bound" (I.ii.1). Thus he denies God's providential control of the universe and attributes everything merely
to natural process. As Calvin puts it, "Substituting nature as
the architect of the universe, he suppresses the name of God"
(*Institutes*, I.v.4). The hero is reluctant to grant room in the
universe for a superior sentient being; he will be his own god
and everything else is ascribed to an impersonal nature. The
same implication informs Machiavelli's work—Elizabethans were
right to call him atheistic. He treats politics as a study in cause
and effect, rather than as a branch of ethics which is a branch
of religion. He is the first social scientist; he examines human
affairs in and for themselves, as process.

D'Amville in Tourneur's play *The Atheist's Tragedy* (1611)
is eventually obliged by events to recognize that "there is some
power above [Nature] that controls her force" (V.i.103). The
Christian doctrine is pressed upon us. But Ford gives a more
equivocal view of the atheist in *'Tis Pity She's a Whore* (1633).
The Friar's opening words indicate the religious character of
Giovanni's challenge:

Dispute no more in this, for know, young man,
These are no school-points; nice philosophy
May tolerate unlikely arguments,
But Heaven admits no jest: wits that presumed
On wit too much, by striving how to prove
There was no God, with foolish grounds of art,
Discovered first the nearest way to hell,
And filled the world with devilish atheism.
(I.i.1)

This warning hovers over the whole play. Giovanni's incest
is not just a moral lapse. It follows upon his distrust of God,
for it was believed that there can be no ethical principles without
an ultimate divine sanction. Edmund and D'Amville attribute
moral restrictions to arbitrary custom (*King Lear*, I.ii.3; *Atheist's
Tragedy*, IV.iii.126). So Giovanni asks:

> Shall a peevish sound,
> A customary form, from man to man,
> Of brother and of sister, be a bar
> 'Twixt my perpetual happiness and me?
>
> (I.i.24)

The ironic threat in "perpetual happiness" recurs throughout the play, but two factors incline us towards Giovanni.   One is the unpleasantness of almost all the other characters.   Even the pious and solicitous Friar is compromised by his urging of Annabella's marriage, which is surely unfair to Soranzo, the husband.   The other factor is Giovanni's courage and integrity. He is not an atheist from greed and pride like D'Amville—he tries to follow the Friar's counsel:

> Lost.   I am lost.   My fates have doomed my death.
> The more I strive, I love; the more I love,
> The less I hope: I see my ruin, certain.
>
> (I.ii.139)

Giovanni tries to subdue his desires to the divine will, but fails; he experiences the ultimate protestant dilemma, an inability to make the initial leap of faith.   His struggle must arouse some respect; but, for a Christian audience, so must Annabella's repentance.

The clash of values is most potent at Giovanni's murder of his sister.

> Pray, Annabella, pray; since we must part,
> Go thou, white in thy soul, to fill a throne
> Of innocence and sanctity in Heaven.
>
> (V.v.63)

Giovanni at last acknowledges the power of God, and in respectful terms, but his wish for his sister to achieve a blessedness that he cannot share presents us at the same moment with an insane but strangely unselfish love.   Annabella's last words affirm God and indicate the perversity of Giovanni's act, but they also throw us back upon the intensity of their relationship:

> Forgive him, Heaven—and me my sins; farewell.
> Brother unkind, unkind !—Mercy, great Heaven —O !—O !
>
> (V.v.92)

Giovanni's atheistic assertion is selfish but on a scale which confuses conventional moral judgment.   He has, at great cost, made what he wanted of his life:

> Fate or all the powers

> That guide the motions of immortal souls
> Could not prevent me.
>
>   (V.vi.11)

To condemn him is to ally ourselves with the corrupt Cardinal.

Thus far I have tried to identify the basic division in ways of regarding the tragic hero, and to establish its relationship with protestant doctrine. I want now to examine the issue in Chapman's *Bussy D'Ambois* (1604), a play which is perhaps too intellectual for the stage but which examines thoroughly the theoretical foundation of the heroic assertion; then to discuss *Hamlet* and *Macbeth*. All three plays present controversial heroes.

Bussy, from the beginning, sees the social system as arbitrary: "Fortune, not reason, rules the state of things; / Reward goes backwards, honour on his head." The "great men" of the kingdom are not heroic: they

> differ not from those colossic statues
> Which, with heroic forms without o'erspread,
> Within are nought but mortar, flint, and lead.
>
>   (I.i.15)

The image will recur at Bussy's death. There is, in his view, nothing given (i.e. God-given) in human existence: "Man is a torch borne in the wind" (I.i.18). He resolves to act. His acknowledgement of ethical imperatives sounds cynical: "We must to Virtue for her guide resort" (I.i.32); also, "Virtue" means "prowess"; this is Machiavelli's programme for a significant life. Bussy is given all the characteristics of the self-assertive amoral hero. He impresses the court by the sheer force of his anarchic personality, enters into a murderous quarrel upon little provocation, insults the mightiest nobles and claims as his right the (married) lady of his choice. Like Giovanni, he regards morality as convention:

> Sin, is a coward, madam, and insults
> But on our weakness, in his truest valour;
> And so our ignorance tames us that we let
> His shadows fright us.
>
>   (III.i.20)

At his death Bussy is said to be taken into the heavens like Hercules:

> Farewell, brave relics of a complete man,
> Look up and see thy spirit made a star;
> Join flames with Hercules. . . .
>
> (V.iv.146)

How should we assess such a hero? At first glance we assume
that "brave relics" refers merely to the fact that Bussy is dead,
but relics are what remain at death, not what we say "farewell"
to. Has Bussy ever been more than a bizarre remnant of a completeness which is no longer possible or even desirable?

Almost all the overt commentary in the play tends to support
the idea of Bussy's inherent nobility, but in bold and unusual
ways. The King, who is made to stand above the jealousies
of the lords, explains Bussy's significance in terms which flout
the protestant view of humanity. He is

> A man so proud that only would uphold
> Man in his native noblesse, from whose fall
> All our dissensions rise; that in himself
> (Without the outward patches of our frailty:
> Riches and honour) knows he comprehends
> Worth with the greatest.
>
> (III.ii.90)

Bussy's consciousness of his own worth implies the pagan sense
of the injunction, "Know thyself"; for Calvin, on the other hand,
true self-knowledge reveals "how great the excellence of our
nature would have been had its integrity remained" and "our
miserable condition since Adam's fall" (*Institutes*, II.i.1). That
the King ignores Calvin's interpretation of the human condition
is understandable, for he offers the remarkable suggestion that
Bussy has actually escaped the consequences of the fall—D'Ambois
alone represents "Man in his native noblesse." And the sign
of Bussy's prelapsarian quality is not the kind of virtue associated
with Christianity, but his anarchic pride.

The King has blended the Christian myth with Machiavelli's
account of the origin of tyranny—at first men made the strongest
their leader but eventually hereditary succession led to degeneration
(*Discourses*, pp. 106-07). The King declares:

> Kings had never borne
> Such boundless empire over other men
> Had all maintain'd the spirit and state of D'Ambois.
>
> (III.ii.95)

Heroic man would not tolerate arbitrary authority. Compare
the social theory of the English Church, for instance in the Homily
"Against Wilful Disobedience": God

> not only ordained that in families and households the wife
> should be obedient unto her husband, the children unto their
> parents, the servants unto their masters, but also, when
> mankind increased and spread itself more largely over the
> world, he by his holy word did constitute and ordain in
> cities and countries several and special governors and
> rulers, unto whom the residue of his people should be
> obedient. (589)

Everyone has someone to tell him or her what to do; there is
no scope for heroic initiatives.

Bussy's naive heroism leads inexorably to his death. The
political point is that he is an anachronism, almost an irrelevance.
The scheming lords admire him but they use him and dispose
of him when he becomes inconvenient. The traditional hero
cannot influence—can hardly comprehend—the diffuse, painstaking
and corrupt conduct of affairs in the modern state. Chapman's
observation is shrewd; compare the fall of Essex in 1601.

But Chapman is concerned equally with the religious implications of Bussy's career, and he does not allow us the simple
protestant moral, that anarchic aspirations will be defeated.
Monsieur and Guise discuss the fall of a person of Bussy's startling
powers as evidence for or against a constructive force working
in nature—that is, for or against the existence of God. Monsieur
is atheistic, he argues that there is no proportion or purpose
in nature:

> Now shall we see that Nature hath no end
> In her great works responsive to their worths,
> That she that makes so many eyes and souls
> To see and foresee is stark blind herself.
> (V.ii.1)

Guise cannot answer effectively. Monsieur reaffirms that the
fall of Bussy will be pointless and, moreover, that it is precisely
his heroic qualities which cause it.

How far are we expected to endorse such adventurous opinions?
It seems true that the death of Bussy makes little sense, and
the play contains no protestant reply to Monsieur's analysis (the
religious figures are corrupt to the point of necromancy). The
problem to which we feel directed is how far to accept the admiring view of Bussy which is taken eventually by all the characters.
Monsieur compares him to the solid tree which is blown down
whilst the hollow tree stands:

> So this whole man
> That will not wind with every crooked way
> Trod by the servile world shall reel and fall

> Before the frantic puffs of blind-born chance
> That pipes through empty men and makes them dance.
> (V.ii.41)

Here is the complete theory of the heroic assertion.   Bussy's
determination to be himself excites admiration but renders him
intolerable to the worldly and small-minded.   Such waste is
due merely to the perversity of natural process; there is no higher
appeal.

However, it is not difficult to construct a case from common
sense (let alone Christian theology) for Bussy's inadequacy: his
quarrelling is silly, his dismissal of sin as policy when wooing
Tamyra is itself politic, his inability to perceive the strength
of the plots against him is foolish.   We may recall Machiavelli's
argument that the complete person adapts to each situation.
Bussy's stature is bound up with an almost psychopathic impervious-
ness to the needs of others; this not only causes his fall, it also
restricts his humanity.

The suspicion that Bussy's heroism involves an unacceptable
inflexibility lurks behind the noble language of his death-speech:

> Prop me, true sword, as thou hast ever done!
> The equal thought I bear of life and death
> Shall make me faint on no side; I am up
> Here like a Roman statue! I will stand
> Till death hath made me marble. O, my fame,
> Live in despite of murder; take thy wings
> And haste thee where the gray-ey'd morn perfumes
> Her rosy chariot with Sabaean spices;
> Fly where the evening from th'Iberian vales
> Takes on her swarthy shoulders Hecate,
> Crown'd with a grove of oaks . . .
> (V.iv.93)

He claims to stand till he turns to marble but of course he can't;
and, anyway, the rigidity and posturing of statuary suggest that
he is posing, acting out his last great scene.   The imagery is
from the act IV chorus of Seneca's *Hercules Oetaeus*, but as
it develops we may find it incongruous in the contemporary setting
(compare *Tamburlaine*).   Has Bussy ever been more than a poser,
a superb player who has been more effective than the others
at disguising the emptiness of life beneath a grand though selfish
purpose?

These questions may seem to allow the protestant view to
take over the play.   So it may be held that Bussy is simply presumptuous, that his society is corrupt and that they will all go
to hell.   Perhaps some contemporaries saw the play like that,
but it must be emphasized that such a reading contradicts every-

thing said explicitly by the characters and that Chapman risks the pace of his action to develop alternative explanations. The unitary protestant interpretation depends on an assumption that the audience brought with them to the theatre a total commitment to official doctrine. My belief is that Chapman wanted his audience at least to consider subversive opinions about the hero; that he was attentive to contradictions in his culture.

Hamlet (1600-01) is fundamentally concerned with the nature of humankind:

> What a piece of work is a man! How noble in reason!
> how infinite in faculties! in form and moving, how
> express and admirable! in action, how like an angel!
> in apprehension, how like a god! the beauty of the
> world! the paragon of animals! And yet, to me, what
> is this quintessence of dust?
>
> (II.ii.301)

Protestant thinkers knew where they stood on the issue. Joseph Hall seems almost to take up Hamlet's speech:

> There is nothing more wretched than a mere man. We may
> brag what we will; how noble a creature man is above all
> the rest; how he is the lord of the world, a world within
> himself, the mirror of majesty, the visible model of his
> Maker; but let me tell you, if we be but men,it had been
> a thousand times better for us to have been the worst of
> beasts. (*Works,* V, 292)

Hamlet is reluctant to accept the protestant view of humanity. He wants urgently to believe in our noble reason as an instrument by which we may assert ourselves in the world:

> Sure he that made us with such large discourse,
> Looking before and after, gave us not
> That capability and godlike reason
> To fust in us unus'd.
>
> (IV.iv.36)

He admires Horatio because he is the perfect Stoic—"A man that Fortune's buffets and rewards / Hast ta'en with equal thanks . . . not passion's slave" (III.ii.65). The play brings into

question the ideal of the self-sufficient individual.
  Seneca explains how one should undertake revenge:

> The good man will perform his duties undisturbed and
> unafraid; and he will in such a way do all that is worthy
> of a good man as to do nothing that is unworthy of a man.
> My father is being murdered—I will defend him; he is slain
> — I will avenge him, not because I grieve, but because
> it is my duty. ("On Anger," *Moral Essays*, I, 137)

The person who could achieve such calm would be independent
of fate and even of God.   But Hamlet is quite unable to command
his emotions.   He can hardly focus coolly upon any matter; he
swings between icy detachment and nervous excitement; his most
sustained venture is the mouse-trap play but it is all brilliant
improvisation and he cannot follow it through.   Godlike indifference is unattainable for Hamlet.   We must reflect that if a
person of his intelligence and sensitivity cannot assert himself
or herself in this life then we are perhaps not "the beauty of
the world" but a mere "quintessence of dust."   It is usual to
contrast with him the other young men in the play, but they
are no more successful.   Laertes kills Hamlet but wishes he
had not, and though Fortinbras is presumably elected king of
Denmark it is by chance not design—the throne he and his father
fought and schemed for is gained not through their heroic qualities
but by default.
  The plausibility of the Stoic ideal is questioned similarly
by Marston in the Antonio plays (1599).   In *Antonio and Mellida*
Andrugio affects indifference to the loss of his kingdom but falls
at once into a rage when it is mentioned: "Name not the Genoese;
that very word / Unkings me quite, makes me vile passion's slave"
(IV.i.68).   In *Antonio's Revenge* Pandulpho is for a long time
tranquil about the murder of his son but finally declares, "Man
will break out, despite philosophy. . . . I spake more than a god,
/ Yet am less than a man" (IV.ii.69).
  Such derogation of mankind's godlike power for heroic assertion seems to throw us back upon the protestant view.   In Calvin's
words, "The human mind receives a humbling blow when all the
thoughts which proceed from it are derided as foolish, frivolous,
perverse, and insane" (*Institutes*, II.iii.1).   And, indeed, Hamlet
discovers that it is pointless to try to determine one's life:

> there is a special providence in the fall of a sparrow.
> If it be now, 'tis not to come; if it be not to come, it
> will be now; if it be not now, yet it will come—the
> readiness is all. Since no man owes of aught he leaves,
> what is't to leave betimes? Let be.
>
> (V.ii.212)

This is the conclusion Hamlet draws from the extraordinary events of the play—the appearance of the Ghost when Claudius seemed secure, the arrival of the players prompting the test of the King, the discovery of the plot against Hamlet's life, the amazing delivery through the pirates. Hamlet decides, "There's a divinity that shapes our ends, / Rough-hew them how we will" (V.ii.10). He seems to accept the protestant view.

But many critics have felt that Hamlet's tone, despite his reference to "special providence" and "a divinity," is fatalistic. This impression is strengthened when we observe that he makes no attempt either to avert the threatening danger or to cooperate with God's will. Although protestants argued that human efforts are irrelevant, they also insisted that the good Christian will seek enthusiastically to further the divine plan (Calvin, *Institutes*, I.xvii.3, 4). Hamlet believes that providence wants Claudius removed and that he should do it (V.ii.63-74), but he plays with Osric, competes with Laertes and makes no move against the King. He accords to the divinity respect but little love. He must accept human impotence before divine power, but he cannot be made to cooperate. His inactivity at the end of the play maintains a critical space between the determining power and himself, a space which he occupies with his own identity.

This is perhaps a minimal human assertion, but it is won out of a full awareness of the strength of the opposition—Hamlet is not, like Tamburlaine, a grandiose fantasy upon human potential. He abandons the notoriously optimistic Stoic programme, but goes on living and questioning. By this cool acceptance of the limits upon human power Hamlet gains a new independence and integrity of spirit in the face of external pressures—from society and the shaping divinity alike. At the end of the play he manifests an indifference to events which makes no claims but offers no oblation.

Macbeth is another kind of hero, but a comparable ambivalence about his self-assertion remains at the end of the day. He is a regicide who maintains his rule with further murders—not an uncommon type among British monarchs. Shakespeare makes of him an ultimate Satanic challenge to divine authority. Calvin explained that "as believers are recognized to be the sons of God by bearing his image, so the wicked are properly regarded as the children of Satan, from having degenerated into his image" (*Institutes*, I.xiv.18). We are told repeatedly that this is what has happened to Macbeth:

> Not in the legions
> Of horrid Hell can come a devil more damn'd

> In evils, to top Macbeth.
> (IV.iii.55)

This is not a metaphor; Macbeth has called upon "Night's black agents" (III.ii.53) and a Jacobean audience might properly see him as devilish.

Such polarisation of good and evil is characteristic of protestantism. Catholics and humanists posited a sequence of careful gradations between the extremes of good and evil, with mediatory agents and the continuous opportunity to repent. Protestants replaced this complicated structure with a dichotomy, all or nothing: a person either has grace or has not. Luther declared, "there are two kingdoms in the world, which are bitterly opposed to each other. In one of them Satan reigns. . . . In the other kingdom, Christ reigns, and his kingdom ceaselessly resists and makes war on the kingdom of Satan" (*Luther and Erasmus*, pp. 327-28). In the play the devilish Macbeth is set against the saintly Duncan and Edward and it seems that there is no significant ground between them.

Yet a paradoxical consequence of identifying the Satanic implications of the tragic hero is that he gains stature; his confrontation with God is made explicit. In Marston's play *Antonio's Revenge* the bloody tyrant Piero is analysed in these terms:

> Still striving to be more than man, he proves
> More than a devil; devilish suspect,
> Devilish cruelty, all hell-strain'd juice
> Is poured into his veins, making him drunk
> With fuming surquedries, contempt of heaven,
> Untam'd arrogance, lust, state, pride, murder.
> (III.i.119)

This is a condemnation phrased as powerfully as Antonio can manage; but Piero inevitably gains stature as a monstrous variation upon human nature, exciting awe and wonderment by crimes whose grossness exceeds the generally expected range and depth of human capacity. When Macbeth makes his final stand it is in the face of known odds entirely beyond those which confront, say, Coriolanus:

> Though Birnam wood be come to Dunsinane,
> And thou oppos'd, being of no woman born,
> Yet I will try the last.
> (V.viii.30)

Macbeth maintains his determination though he recognizes that supernatural forces oppose him. Joseph Hall declared, "It is one of the mad principles of wickedness, that it is a weakness to relent, and rather to die than yield" (*Works*, I, 373). Hall's

language reluctantly acknowledges the stature of evil and evokes
the heroic stance he means to condemn; there is something we
may admire in Macbeth's stand against the whole universe.
We may call him subhuman rather than superhuman, but he nevertheless exceeds the merely mortal.

But whilst he uses the implications of Macbeth's Satanic
challenge, Shakespeare's more remarkable project is to undermine
the protestant polarisation by making Macbeth (unlike Piero or
his own Richard III) human as well as devilish. Macbeth's assertion
of self is monstrous, and in a sense great, because he is aware
of the human feeling he is violating. At every step he faces
the wickedness of his life with a depth of response which exceeds
that even of his victims. He yields

> to that suggestion
> Whose horrid image doth unfix my hair,
> And make my seated heart knock at my ribs,
> Against the use of nature.
>
> (I.iii.134)

Compare Lady Macbeth: she imagines that "A little water clears
us of this deed" (II.ii.66). If immediate revulsion at the thought
of evil is a test of moral sensitivity then Macbeth is the most
moral person in the play. Even at the killing of Lady Macduff
and her children it takes an act of will to close off the scope
for scruples: "This deed I'll do, before this purpose cool" (IV.i.154).
Macbeth knows that he is stifling one part of himself in order
to express the other. He says when he hears a cry within of
women,

> I have supp'd full with horrors:
> Direness, familiar to my slaughterous thoughts,
> Cannot once start me.
>
> (V.v.13)

But the man who perceives himself as devoid of feeling cannot
be without sensitivity, and we see it finally when he is confronted
by Macduff: "But get thee back, my soul is too much charg'd
/ With blood of thine already" (V.viii.5).

Macbeth never succeeds in quelling altogether his humanity.
He stands at one limit of human experience, he is porter of hell-
gate, his actions are those of a devil; but he experiences them
as a human being.

The question, "What is a man?" rings through the play.
Lady Macbeth challenges Macbeth on his manhood both before
the murder of Duncan and at the appearance of Banquo's ghost
(I.vii.46-51; III.iv.57, 72). To her it is a matter simply of bravery—
the kind of daring expected of the traditional heroic leader.
But Macbeth recognizes the spiritual implications: to him the

murders of Duncan and Banquo have more than mortal significance
and require more than heroic courage.

> I dare do all that may become a man:
> Who dares do more, is none.
>
> (I.vii.46)

> What man dare, I dare:
> Approach thou like the rugged Russian bear,
> The arm'd rhinoceros, or th'Hyrcan tiger;
> Take any shape but that, and my firm nerves
> Shall never tremble.
>
> . (III.iv.98)

Macbeth is terrified by his own conscience; it is his own human
feeling that he is confronting. To Macduff this is as it should
be:

> *Malcolm.* Dispute it like a man.
> *Macduff.*   I shall do so;
>   But I must also feel it as a man.
>
> (IV.iii.220)

   Macbeth in his suppression of feeling pushes beyond the bound-
aries of human experience. He takes from the Witches the idea
that he can actually cross them and escape mortality:

> Be bloody, bold and resolute: laugh to scorn
> The power of man, for none of woman born
> Shall harm Macbeth.
>
> (IV.i.79)

But it cannot be; Macbeth can presume upon divine power but
he is finally shown to be mortal.
   The protestant polarisation of Christ and Satan is called
into question by Macbeth's courage and his residual, inextinguish-
able humanity. The play's enquiry into the nature of mankind
prompts three statements. Macbeth is less than human in his
brutality, more than human in his daring to assert his will in
the face of the most potent opposition. But finally, we are obliged
to recognize, he is human. We cannot, like Malcolm and Macduff,
simply excise him from the race by calling him devilish. We must
accept, for better and for worse, that he is within the possible
range of human behaviour.

Bussy D'Ambois, Hamlet and *Macbeth* discriminate with delicacy,

from within an awareness of protestant theology, the possibilities
of heroic assertion. .They attempt no clear decision upon either
the scope or the validity of the protagonist's pretensions.   Rather,
they encourage an ambivalent response, setting statement against
statement and statement against action.   The challenge is ultimately to divine authority, and for a Christian audience it arouses
both wonderment and alarm.   The hero is defeated but not bowed;
God is victorious but it is hard to suppress our identification
with the human.   We will look lastly at the gloomier vision of
human potential offered in the main plays of John Webster.

It is obvious that the characters of *The White Devil* are,
with the exception of Isabella, of an especial viciousness.   They
might be designed to illustrate St Bernard's account of the miser-
ies of the unredeemed soul—"burdened with sin, obscured with
darkness, ensnared by allurements, teeming with lusts, ruled by
passion, filled with delusions, ever prone to evil, inclined to every
vice; lastly, full of ignominy and confusion" (Calvin, *Institutes*,
III.ii.25).   For the protestant the disaster is relieved, since God
raises us up again: "Let us breathe again, brethren.   Although
we are nothing in our hearts, perhaps something of us may lurk
in the heart of God" (III.ii.25).   But in *The White Devil* there
is very little sign of such redemption.   Webster evokes all the
protestant sense of human futility without the compensation of
God's saving grace.   Like other melancholic Jacobean intellectuals,
he goes half-way with Calvin: he is convinced that we are fallen
and in a fallen world but has only a nominal confidence in God's
redemptive goodness.

At the same time, Webster denies the heroic assertion.
He does not, like Marlowe, cast doubt upon mankind's relationship
with God in order to imply an intrinsic validity to human achievement.   He trusts neither in God nor humanity.

The derogation of human potential works in *The White Devil*
partly through the confusing plot, which permits no character
to establish his or her purposes and carry them through.   Even
Francisco's eventual murder of Bracciano, Vittoria and Flamineo
is blurred by his personal absence and by the attempt of Vittoria
and Flamineo to destroy each other.   We are never allowed to
feel a man or woman gaining a firm grip even upon their immediate
future.   It is often said that it is difficult for the audience
to build up a consistent notion of character in the play.   This
is because Webster puts his people so much at the mercy of circumstances that they can hardly apprehend their own personalities.

Repeatedly characters change direction in response to events
beyond their control.   Lodovico drops his melancholic stance
instantly when he hears that his banishment is repealed (III.iii.102);
Cornelia runs to stab Flamineo because he has killed Marcellus,
but realizes that he is her only remaining son and instead asks
God to forgive him (V.ii.53).   Vittoria is particularly elusive,
almost a different person at each appearance, and the reason
is .changing circumstances.   Act I scene ii is intimate and she
responds to Bracciano's initiative, act III scene ii is public and

she is the defendant, act IV scene ii is again intimate but now
she is at the mercy of great lords, in act V scene vi she faces
death.   At each stage her possibilities are limited by pressure
from powerful men.   Different roles are required of her and
she does her best to play them with vigour, but she is quite unable
to impose herself upon events.   The idea that identity is an
illusion and that we are no more than a sequence of responses
to successive ocurrences is modern.   Webster's point, I think,
is not one of psychological principle, but an implied assessment
of the capacity of people to control their lives.   Flamineo declares,
"Man may his fate foresee, but not prevent" (V.vi.180).

The sense of human powerless is enhanced in *The White
Devil* by a pattern of diverted benefits: repeatedly a character
conceives a course of action which has consequences directly
opposite to those desired.   Camillo refuses to sleep with Vittoria
because he thinks it will keep her chaste, but it facilitates her
adultery. Isabella pretends to be the cause of her separation
from Bracciano in the hope of bringing peace, but she leaves
him free to sleep with Vittoria and so to develop the quarrel
with her brothers.   Again, Bracciano's murder of Camillo only
anticipates Francisco's intention of getting rid of him by sending
him to fight pirates; and the escape from the Convertites, which
Bracciano and Vittoria regard as a triumph, is just what Francisco
wanted. So Bracciano plays into Francisco's hands, but Francisco
himself, conversely, can gain his revenge only by allowing Bracciano
the license he desires.   Their goals in fact coincide: neither
of them can succeed without granting a considerable measure
of success to the other.   The perversity of the play's action
may be summarised in one of Vittoria's most vivid images: "As
if a man should spit against the wind, / The filth returns in's
face" (III.ii.150).

The ultimate figure for human insecurity in *The White Devil*
is Bracciano's refusal to grant a pardon to Flamineo—

> Only a lease of your life.   And that shall last
> But for one day.   Thou shalt be forc'd each evening
> To renew it, or be hang'd.   (V.ii.74)

All these characters live under threat of violent death and none
can see surely more than a day ahead—indeed, not so much,
for Bracciano himself dies that night.   The brave deaths of
Flamineo and Vittoria represent only a minimal human assertion.
In fact, they exemplify again the pattern of perverted benefits
by suggesting that a noble life is possible only at the point of
death: in Flamineo's words, "We cease to grieve, cease to be
Fortune's slaves, / Nay cease to die by dying" (V.vi.252).

In *The Duchess of Malfi* (1614) Webster again shows human
purpose hindered and blighted.   Antonio is weak, Ferdinand is
mad, the Cardinal's "greatness was only outward" (V.v.42), Bosola
becomes his own man only when it is too late.   But in this play
Webster raises a substantially new mode of heroic assertion through

the figure of the Duchess.   At the close of act I Cariola states
precisely the ambivalent status of the tragic protagonist's challenge
to the ordinary:

> Whether the spirit of greatness or of woman
> Reign most in her, I know not, but it shows
> A fearful madness; I owe her much of pity.

Is the Duchess heroic, or weakly and foolishly passionate (that
is what "woman" meant)?   The question is rendered peculiarly
difficult by the special quality of the Duchess and her goal.
Like other tragic figures she asserts her own will, but she seeks
merely domestic happiness; this lowly objective is raised to the
gigantic by the amazing perversity of Ferdinand.   Her special
quality is a naivety which fails entirely to anticipate or comprehend
the hostility she provokes.   When Ferdinand comes to her bed-
chamber she is talking of persuading him to be godfather to
her children; "I pray sir, hear me: I am married," she tells him,
imagining he will be mollified; she even ventures the thought
that he is there with Antonio's connivance (III.ii.68, 82, 88).
The Duchess does not intend a heroic challenge; greatness is
thrust upon her.

In the scene where the Duchess is tormented and murdered
Webster, perhaps uniquely in the drama, represents a passive
greatness—a heroic assertion composed of a proud acceptance.
Bosola describes her:

> She's sad, as one long us'd to't; and she seems
> Rather to welcome the end of misery
> Than shun it:—a behaviour so noble
> As gives a majesty to adversity.   (IV.i.3)

Ferdinand adds, I think with perplexity: "Her melancholy seems
to be fortify'd / With a strange disdain" (IV.i.11).   By the completeness of her submission she shows herself superior to her captors.
The supposed death of Antonio causes her to curse the stars,
but her determination to endure returns: "Necessity makes me
suffer constantly, / And custom makes it easy" (IV.ii.29).   By
welcoming her death she deprives her tormentors of the satisfaction
of afflicting her; through self-abasement she asserts herself.

The heroism of humility is hardly attempted elsewhere in
the drama of the period.   At that time it could be posited perhaps
only of a woman, but Desdemona dies complaining, Cordelia
has no last speech, Cleopatra retains all her pride, and Mistress
Frankford at the end of Thomas Heywood's *A Woman Killed
with Kindness* is sickly and undignified.   The imprisoned princesses
in Sidney's *New Arcadia* are almost certainly the model.

It is difficult to decide how far we should identify the Duchess'
humility with the self-denial enjoined upon Christians.   Calvin
explains that God

visits us with disgrace, or poverty, or bereavement, or
disease, or other afflictions.   Feeling altogether unable
to support them, we forthwith, in so far as regards ourselves,
give way, and thus humbled learn to invoke his strength,
which alone can enable us to bear up under a weight of
affliction.   (*Institutes*, III.viii.2)

If we could feel confident that the Duchess dies in a manner
pleasing to God, Webster would have reconciled human assertion
and the protestant sense of human worthlessness.   He would
have dissolved the dichotomy which, I have argued, characterizes
other tragedies of the period.   But the Duchess does not invoke
God's strength.   Bosola tells her, "Thou art a box of worm-seed,
at best" (IV.ii.124); compare Henry Smith's "Dissuasion from Pride":
"We were earth, we are flesh, and we shall be worms' meat"
(*Works*, I, 208).   But she insists, "I am Duchess of Malfi still"
(IV.ii.142).   She does not repent her past life.   On the contrary,
when she revives for a moment she calls for Antonio, and Bosola
with a brilliantly sympathetic intuition assures her that he is
well.   Her exclamation, "Mercy!" locates her final consolation
in the marriage which has provoked her suffering (IV.ii.353).
        The most ambiguous moment is when the Duchess kneels
to her death:

> Yet stay; heaven-gates are not so highly arch'd
> As princes' palaces, they that enter there
> Must go upon their knees.--[*Kneels.*]   Come violent death,
> Serve for mandragora to make me sleep!
> Go tell my brothers when I am laid out,
> They then may feed in quiet.   *They strangle her.*
>   (IV.ii.232)

Compare Henry Smith again: "As the way to heaven is narrow
(Matthew, 7: 13), so the gate is low, and he had need to stoop
which entereth in at it" (*Works*, I, 213).   But then, notice the
Duchess' tone of command: she *demands* to kneel, it is her own,
regal gesture, Stoic as much as Christian.   Her goal, moreover, is
not blessedness but "sleep."   And surely disdainful irony outweighs
forgiveness in the reference to her brothers: "They then may feed
in quiet."   Their quiet will be unlike her sleep, for they will be
alive—and that, the Duchess implies, means indulging their appetites.
        The Duchess' death hovers between Christian submission and
an ultimate, irrepressible, human assertion.   Nevertheless, Webster
systematically dissipates her attainment in the confusion of the
play's last act.   The concluding impression is of the futility
and despair of Ferdinand, the Cardinal and Bosola.
        I have discussed the heroic assertion in this chapter in terms
of the scope claimed by and permitted to the tragic protagonist.
We have seen that dramatists rarely commit themselves without

qualification for or against the protestant view of humanity. Often they seem to draw us towards the assertive individual whilst allowing us also to condemn him or her.   But into the balance with—or, most often, against—the human we must throw the nature and power of the superhuman.   The theme of the opening page of Calvin's *Institutes* is "The knowledge of God and of ourselves mutually connected."   The next chapter is about the tragedians' reaction to the protestant God.

6 Providence and tragedy

Shakespeare, Marlowe, Tourneur, Kyd, Webster

Others apart sat on a hill retired,
In thoughts more elevate, and reasoned high
Of providence, foreknowledge, will, and fate,
Fixed fate, free will, foreknowledge absolute,
And found no end, in wand'ring mazes lost.

(Paradise Lost, II, 557)

In the previous chapter I argued that critical dispute about the attitude of tragedians to humanity reflects an ambivalence in the plays themselves. The same kind of contradiction occurs over the nature of the ultimate forces governing the universe.

Some scholars believe that most tragedies demonstrate the overriding power and concern of divine providence; many readers feel that the plays depict a world which, even though evil is eventually defeated, can hardly represent the best creative effort of a benign deity. This chapter comes down on the side of the latter opinion, but argues that the protestant conception of God is nevertheless crucial to the tragedies, which afforded expression to an anxiety (perhaps only vaguely apprehended) about contemporary Christian doctrine.

First, we must recognize that the violent action of Elizabethan and Jacobean tragedies does not necessarily preclude a Christian reading. Protestants insisted as keenly as any playwright upon the vileness of man and the world; they traced it to the fall:

Various diseases ever and anon attack us: at one time pestilence rages; at another we are involved in all the calamities of war. Frost and hail, destroying the promise of the year, cause sterility, which reduces us to penury; wife, parents, children, relatives, are carried off by death; our house is destroyed by fire. These are the events which make men curse their life, detest the day of their birth, execrate the light of heaven, even censure God, and (as they are eloquent in blasphemy) charge him with cruelty and injustice. (Calvin, *Institutes*, III.vii.10)

Protestants did not expect the world to be pleasant. Calvin actually grants that pagan tragedians, lacking the Christian revelation, were wise to despair of life: "I confess, indeed, that a most accurate opinion was formed by those who thought, that the best thing was not to be born, the next best to die early" (*Institutes*, III.ix.4). But Christians know better, and in the face of this potentially tragic appreciation of human misery Calvin asserts: "the rule of piety is, that the hand of God is the ruler and arbiter of the fortunes of all, and, instead of rushing on with thoughtless violence, dispenses good and evil with perfect regularity" (*Institutes*, III.vii.10). From God's perspective, though we are unable to share it, all is well.

Every theology which posits a good and omnipotent deity has a problem with evil: if God is good and in control, why does he let such dreadful things happen? Most Christians, like Calvin, claim that we fail to comprehend God's plan, but many also seek to establish God's goodness by diminishing his power—allowing much to hang upon human choice. The reformers took the opposite line and insisted, to the point of predestination, that God is the cause of everything. I discern three reasons for this: they recognized that, logically, everything must be ultimately the responsibility of the creator anyway; they believed people to be so wretched as to be incapable of good choices; and they feared the incoherence of a universe not controlled immediately by God.

George Herbert is usually presented as a gentle and saintly man and so he was, compared with many of his contemporaries. But he subscribed to the protestant conviction that providence determines everything, and was happy to attribute specific human disasters to God's direct wish—when people starve it is God's way of getting attention:

> it is observable that God delights to have men feel, and acknowledge, and reverence his power, and therefore he often overturns things when they are thought past danger: that is his time of interposing. . . . So that if a farmer should depend upon God all the year, and being ready to put hand to sickle, shall then secure himself, and think all cock sure; then God sends such weather as lays the corn and destroys it. (*Works*, p. 317)

The modern reader, even the modern Christian, may well be disconcerted by the degree of manipulative intrusion in human affairs which is attributed to God, and by the harsh means by which he is supposed to discipline mankind. But for protestants these were fundamental and necessary properties of the deity.

Human wickedness is equally part of the divine scheme. God does not merely permit bad people, they are "instruments of Divine Providence, being employed by the Lord himself to execute the judgments which he has resolved to inflict" (Calvin, *Institutes*, I.xvii.5).   Viewed in this light, Cornwall putting out Gloucester's eyes, for instance, or the murder of the Duchess of Malfi, appears not as evil running amock but as God carrying out his mysterious judgments.

Protestants felt able to resolve the paradox of human suffering and divine goodness because they readily accepted the rightness of a God whom we might call harsh and punitive.   Presumably their idea of God reflected their own hierarchical social relations: they expected those set in authority over them to behave in a selfish, violent, retributive and inexplicable fashion. It seems that they were reassured by the thought of divine vengeance.   Joseph Hall describes how God dealt with the Philistines when they captured in battle the Ark of the Lord:

> Every man was either dead, or sick: those that were left
> living, through their extremity of pain envied the dead;
> and the cry of their whole cities went up to heaven.
> It is happy that God hath such store of plagues and thunder-
> bolts for the wicked: if he had not a fire of judgment,
> wherewith the iron hearts of men might be made flexible,
> he would want obedience, and the world peace. (*Works*
> I, 274)

Mark the present tense in the last sentence: the Old Testament God of wrath has not been superseded for these Christians. On the contrary, his plagues and thunderbolts guarantee our "peace."

This stern outlook was held not only by Calvinists.   Lancelot Andrewes in his "Sermon Preached at Chiswick in the Time of Pestilence" (1603) asked (rhetorically) the cause of plague.   It can't be random chance (that seemed intolerable); it must be from God; and why? because of our sins.   Andrewes concludes: "So our inventions beget sin, sin provokes the wrath of God, the wrath of God sends the plague among us" (*Works*, V, 234). We may recall Bertrand Russell's comment that the justification of suffering as a purification from sin would not, in any decent person, survive a visit to a children's hospital.   Andrewes' explanation of the horrors of war was given on Ash Wednesday, 1599, as Essex set off for his Irish expedition: "God stirreth up the spirit of Princes abroad to take peace from the earth, thereby to chasten men by paring the growth of their wealth with his 'hired razor' (Isaiah 7: 20); by wasting their strong men, the hand of the enemies eating them up; by making widows and fatherless children, by other like consequents of war" (*Works*, I, 331).

The scope given to wickedness and suffering in tragedies need not, therefore, indicate the absence of God.   Rather, it may suggest that the Reformation deity is active.   Perhaps Elizabethans, like us, perceived tragic plays as replete with human

disaster, but what strikes us as an indictment of a malign or
purposeless universe they interpreted cheerfully as the working
out of God's providential plan.   We are surprised simply because
ideas of goodness and justice have altered.

Indeed some people, especially puritan humanists, did hold
that tragedy advances the protestant world view.   Fulke Greville
believed that it seeks "to point God's revenging aspect upon
every particular sin, to the despair, or confusion of mortality"
(*Life of Sidney*, p. 163).   This is Milton's idea of tragedy in
Samson Agonistes.   Samson has been passive and uncertain,
able only to repel attempts to use him, until he feels "Some
rousing motions in me" (line 1382).   We are to take his wholesale
destruction of the Philistines as a response to God's call; the
Chorus says at the end,

> All is best, though we oft doubt
> What th' unsearchable dispose
> Of Highest Wisdom brings about,
> And ever best found in the close.
> (line 1745)

However, in many plays written for the Elizabethan and
Jacobean stage the role of providence is more problematic.
The thesis towards which I am working is that playwrights express
alarm and uncertainty about the official explanation of the
universe as directed by a deity who is at once good and omnipotent.   Tragedy of the period was in part at least a reaction against
a provocative theology.

Some tragedies do seem to manifest the protestant world view
so as to invite audience approval for it.   *The Atheist's Tragedy*
has two blatantly virtuous characters, though the atheist,
D'Amville, murders and oppresses in the usual tragic manner.
At the end of the play, when he chooses to behead the good
characters in person, he swings up the axe and knocks out his
own brains.   We are invited to recognize the hand of God:

> | D'Amville. | What murderer was he |
> |---|---|
> | | That lifted up my hand against my head? |
> | First Judge. | None but yourself, my lord. |
> | D'Amville. | I thought he was |
> | | A murderer that did it. |
> | First Judge | God forbid. |
> | D'Amville. | Forbid?   You lie, judge; he commanded it |
> | | To tell thee that man's wisdom is a fool. |
> | | (V.ii.243) |

If God had forbidden it, it could not occur.   Such is "The
power of that eternal providence"   (V.ii.271).
    The pattern of bloody rise to power and appropriate fall
which (in the previous chapter) we observed in *Richard III* suggests
that the play is designed to exemplify the operation of retributive
providence—that is how the chronicle sources interpreted this
period of history.   Shakespeare works to render the doctrine
acceptable by making Richard so wicked that he attracts very
little humanitarian consideration, giving his victims little individuality and having each (except the princes) acknowledge his own
misdeeds, keeping the murder of the princes off the stage, and
presenting the response of the bereaved in a highly formal manner.
The stylization which gives the action such a strong sense of
divine process at the same time depersonalizes the suffering of
the characters.   Thus the audience may believe that a sequence
of unmitigated wickedness and misery reflects a benign deity.
Observe the way Richmond credits God with the ultimate violence
which is to sweep away the corrupt regime:

> O thou, whose captain I account myself,
> Look on my forces with a gracious eye;
> Put in their hands thy bruising irons of wrath,
> That they may crush down with a heavy fall
> The usurping helmets of our adversaries!
> Make us thy ministers of chastisement,
> That we may praise thee in the victory!
> (V.iii.108)

The "bruising irons of wrath" seem far removed from real weapons;
the "usurping helmets" hardly contain human heads.   We do not
think of the abstract "adversaries" as leaving widows and orphans
and (in Andrewes' words) "other like consequents of war."   We
feel that God is doing well by his creation.
    However, most tragedies do not permit such endorsement
of protestant dogma.   Richmond calls himself God's minister
of chastisement and Tamburlaine says he is the scourge of God,
but the divine connection comes more provocatively from
Tamburlaine, who has just murdered his son:

> Villains, these terrors and these tyrannies
> (If tyrannies war's justice ye repute)
> I execute, enjoin'd me from above,
> To scourge the pride of such as Heaven abhors;
> Nor am I made arch-monarch of the world,
> Crown'd and invested by the hand of Jove,
> For deeds of bounty or nobility;
> But, since I exercise a greater name,
> The scourge of God and terror of the world,
> I must apply myself to fit those terms,
> In war, in blood, in death, in cruelty,
> And plague such peasants as resist in me

> The power of heaven's eternal majesty.   (2: IV.i.144)

From what has been said thus far it will be appreciated that
it is not easy, from a Reformation point of view, to fault
Tamburlaine's assertion that he is God's instrument.   But there
are hints that the claimed divine endorsement of violent power
is problematic.   Tamburlaine grants the term "tyranny" before
he repudiates it; he admits to "cruelty," which seems to go beyond
punishment; he implies that his divine role requires him to be
more vicious than he might: "I must apply myself to fit those
terms"; and we notice that God's power not, say, his justice,
is invoked.   Add to these hints the killing of Tamburlaine's son,
and even the sternest protestant may be moved to wonder what
kind of God is responsible here.

Where *Richard III* suppresses problems about the nature of
providence, *Tamburlaine* provokes them.   For whilst Tamburlaine's
deity and the protestant version are distinguishable in emphasis,
they have enough in common to raise questions about the exercise
of power which was usually attributed to God.   The theologians
I have quoted do sound like Tamburlaine, or almost.   Briefly,
he includes all Calvin's sense of divine power, but omits to claim
that God is good as well.   By heightening one half of the power/
goodness paradox Marlowe obliges us to ponder how the missing
term can reasonably be reincorporated.   The consequence is
a subversion of protestant doctrine parallel to that we observed
in the previous chapter.   Marlowe takes the protestant claims
for God apart and challenges us to put them together again.
Difficulties which the Christian might justify as paradoxes are
exposed as contradictions.

Several major tragedies follow this pattern: the deity is invoked,
but in a manner which fails to reassure.   As *Antonio's Revenge*
approaches its bloody climax the ghost of Andrugio attributes
it to God:

> Now down looks providence
> T'attend the last act of my son's revenge.
> . . . Heaven's just; for I shall see
> The scourge of murder and impiety.   (V.i.10, 24)

But Antonio's revenge has already led him to murder before our
eyes the affectionate small son of his opponent and the closing
murder is bizarre and gruesome.   Marston seems determined
to attribute events to providence but insists nevertheless upon
their disproportionate violence.   The split is equally apparent
in Antonio's view of his action.   He says at one moment, "pity,
piety, remorse, / Be aliens to our thoughts"; and then, "Thus the
hand of heaven chokes / The throat of murder" (V.iii.89, 108).
It is God's work, we are told, but it is also lacking in "pity, piety,
remorse."

The Revenger's Tragedy is the subject of typical critical
debate about whether Tourneur is offering a protestant version

of evil corrected by providence or a cynical world without moral
or spiritual dimensions.   Both approaches can be argued from
the text; the point, surely, is their contradictory interaction.
God is appealed to repeatedly and the subtle working out of the
plot, replete with coincidence and ironic reversals, suggests the
manipulative control of the retributive protestant deity.   But
God's power again seems much more apparent than his goodness
and the characters who invoke him seem tainted with a prurient
and disproportionate involvement in the evil they condemn.
The theological reply to this last observation is that God works
through corrupt agents, but in the theatre it is difficult to keep
the distinction in mind.   We may feel that Vindice's temptation
of his sister is perverse, but it concludes with the triumphant
exclamation: "O angels, clap your wings upon the skies, / And
give this virgin crystal plaudities!" (II.i.239).   Heaven is invited
to endorse a disconcerting sequence for which (given its power)
it is responsible anyway, and if we are uneasy about Vindice then
we are liable to reflect also upon the motivation of his divine
master.   Such appeals to God make us refer the disturbing action
of the play to him, but the only resolution offered is general,
violent and unrepentant death.   A new duke is established but
he at once adopts the perspective of the previous tyrant: "You,
that would murder him, would murder me!" (V.iii.103).   We cannot
feel that providential intervention has lived up to expectation.

The disconcerting qualities of the protestant deity perhaps explain
Hamlet's fatalistic attitude after his return to Denmark (discussed
in the previous chapter).   He accepts that there is "a special
providence in the fall of a sparrow" (V.ii.212) but declines to
cooperate.   His terms are extremely close to Calvin's:

> The Christian . . . will have no doubt that a special providence
> is awake for his preservation. . . . Hence, our Saviour, after
> declaring that even a sparrow falls not to the ground without
> the will of his Father, immediately makes the application,
> that being more valuable than many sparrows, we ought to
> consider that God provides more carefully for us.   (*Institutes*,
> I.xvii.6)

Hamlet has the phrase "special providence" and the sparrow (Jesus'
remark about the sparrow in Matthew 10 is awkward for Christians
who assert free will; Erasmus is obliged to take it as "hyperbole"—
Luther and Erasmus, pp. 83-84).   Indeed, in the first quarto Hamlet
says "there's a predestinate providence in the fall of a sparrow";
this is probably only an actor's memorial reconstruction, but it
shows that one well-placed contemporary saw the Calvinist implications of the speech.
    Hamlet penetrates to the essential protestant conviction

about divine determination of human affairs but, I have argued, he expresses little enthusiasm either in word or action.   It is late in the day to be attributing motives to Hamlet, but the audience must reflect upon events and his attitudes to them.   At first it seems reassuring to commit oneself entirely to a controlling deity, but the divine system revealed in the action does not comfort and delight as Calvin thinks it should.   It makes Hamlet wonder and admire; temporarily, when he is sending Rosencrantz and Guildenstern to their deaths, it exhilarates him; but ultimately it depresses him.

The audience too, especially if it experiences some degree of identification with the charismatic Prince, must consider the divine dispensation as it is exposed in the play.   God seems to exercise all the immediate power which protestants attributed to him—Hamlet was even able to seal the altered instructions to England: "Why, even in that was heaven ordinant" (i.e. "directing, controlling"; V.ii.48).   But there is little to rejoice the heart in the world of *Hamlet* and we may feel as indifferent as the Prince towards the presiding deity.   The Christian terminology, linked to a violent action which runs counter to all the more precious and legitimate human concerns, again invites us to question the claim that God is good as well as powerful.   Does it really appear, as Calvin declares, that "being more valuable than many sparrows . . . God provides more carefully for us"?

I have demonstrated the attention to Stoic ideas of self-sufficiency in *Hamlet*; we may relate the Prince's fatalism to the Senecan concept of fate.   This is a highly provocative connection, for Calvin was worried that a predestinating God might sound merely like Stoic fate—an impersonal force operating only a crude, retributive justice, powerful but not particularly good: "Those who cast obloquy on this doctrine [special providence], calumniate it as the dogma of the Stoics concerning fate" (*Institutes*, I.xvi.8).   Hence Calvin's point about the sparrow: he is insisting upon God's intimate and personal concern for every human being, and on the precise responsiveness of divine justice.   These are essential aspects if God is to be good as well as powerful: Calvin must head off the thought that his rigorous deity is, like Stoic fate, indifferent to mankind.   He needs to claim that Stoics accept fate merely because "so it must be," whereas Christians joyfully embrace God's will "with calm and grateful minds" (*Institutes*, III.viii.11).

Hamlet accords to "special providence" the resigned acknowledgment which Stoics gave to fate: "Let be."   Thus he invites us to meditate upon the slender margin between pagan fate and a determining deity.   We should notice also that Tamburlaine, whilst he sometimes speaks of God, refers also to fate and fortune.   We are told at his death that "fate commands and proud necessity" (2: V.iii.205).   The controlling power in this play also hovers between the two concepts so as to blur the distinction which protestants thought so important.

Tragedy is as concerned as religion with the nature of the

forces which govern the universe, but it is less committed to
a coherent explanation. It is not necessary to suppose that Marlowe
and Shakespeare manipulated purposefully Stoic and Calvinist
conceptions. It is equally possible that when the dramatist reached
the point when it was appropriate to have some comment on the
kind of world in which such things happen, he expressed out of
his own mingled anxiety and wish to conform a contradictory
and subversive combination of protestant and pagan thought.
It is precisely through such inconsistencies that ideologies are
adapted in the complex conditions of real life, and it is by remarking
them that we can observe the lines of fault in a culture.

But I suspect that Marlowe, at least, intended to disturb.
Consider the concluding couplet of *The Jew of Malta:*

> So march away; and let due praise be given,
> Neither to Fate nor Fortune, but to Heaven.

This sounds like a triumphant clarification of the spiritual basis
of the play—it would suit Richmond at the end of *Richard III.*
But the action of *The Jew of Malta* reflects little credit upon
heaven, and the hypocritical Ferneze is an unreliable witness.
By preferring heaven to fate and fortune in such a context Marlowe
undermines its status.

I am uncertain how much conscious intention to attribute
to Kyd, but in *The Spanish Tragedy* (c.1589) protestant notions
are juxtaposed quite grotesquely with Senecan. The fate/predesti-
nation issue is clearly there, for the whole action is overseen
by the Ghost of Don Andrea and the Senecan figure, Revenge,
who anticipates the events of the play:

> thou shalt see the author of thy death,
> Don Balthazar the prince of Portingale,
> Depriv'd of life by Bel-imperia.   (I.i.87)

When the Ghost complains that matters are tending otherwise
Revenge reassures him:

> Nor dies Revenge although he sleep awhile,
> For in unquiet, quietness is feign'd,
> And slumb'ring is a common worldly wile.   (III.xv.23)

That the revenge plot is predetermined is analogically implied
by the tragedy which Hieronimo devises to contain his culminating
vengeance. Villains and aggrieved act out together preordained
parts, mirroring the subjection of the characters in the larger
play to an external scheme.

But although Revenge is a pagan figure based upon Seneca's
Thyestes, the play is set in contemporary Spain and Portugal
and its language often asserts a Christian world view. Hieronimo
challenges the heavens:

> If this incomparable murder thus
> Of mine, but now no more my son,
> Shall unreveal'd and unrevenged pass,
> How should we term your dealings to be just,
> If you unjustly deal with those that in your justice trust?
> (III.ii.7)

He pleads for help and, lo and behold, a letter is dropped from above informing him of the villain.   He does not at once believe the letter—it may be a trap—but eventually his faith is restored:

> Why then, I see that heaven applies our drift,
> And all the saints do sit soliciting
> For vengeance on those cursed murtherers.   (IV.i.32)

Pagan and Christian concepts and images jostle each other, and we may ponder just what the difference is between the manipulations and crude justice of Revenge on the one hand and providence on the other.   The slow but inexorable control exercised by Revenge is just like that which Calvin attributes to God: "though he often permits the guilty to exult for a time with impunity, and the innocent to be driven to and fro in adversity, nay, even to be wickedly and iniquitously oppressed, this ought not to produce any uncertainty as to the uniform justice of all his procedure" (*Institutes*, I.v.7).   Is the protestant God a more caring and merciful force than Seneca's Revenge?

The reader may suppose that Kyd was a happy, unreflecting Renaissance man of the theatre who liked an exciting plot and didn't really notice whether the platitudes he gave to his characters were Christian or Senecan.   If this were so it would not detract from my argument that this play, like so many, is sited at an ideological disjunction; for such a disjunction is indeed more likely to speak through divergent literary or dramatic conventions than through individual awareness.   But Kyd seems purposely to fore-ground the issue.   Hieronimo enters with a book:

> *Vindicta mihi !*
> Ay, heaven will be reveng'd of every ill,
> Nor will they suffer murder unrepaid:
> Then stay, Hieronimo, attend their will,
> For mortal men may not appoint their time.
> *Per scelus semper tutum est sceleribus iter.*
> Strike, and strike home, where wrong is offer'd thee.
> (III.xiii.1)

The first quotation is the biblical claim that vengeance is God's alone; the second is the Senecan dictum that the answer to crime is crime.   Calvin offers attitudes to revenge as a test case of Christian versus pagan morality (*Institutes*, II.ii.24).   We are obliged to consider the disjunction.

Hieronimo's decision is for personal vengeance.   This would

seem to set him at odds with Christianity, inviting us to view
him as a man driven by passion wickedly to ignore God's injunction.
Yet, bewilderingly, the divine power we are shown in the play
is not God but Revenge, and it appears to endorse Hieronimo.
Various explanations are possible. Those who believe in free will
within the Christian dispensation may see Revenge as a mood
which infects wicked people. Those who believe in Christian
predestination may see Revenge as a spirit delegated by God
to execute his just judgments. But the most immediate interpretation for the spectator who is not a theologian is that the characters
live vicious lives in submission to the will of vindictive powers
which hover disconcertingly (for the Elizabethan protestant) between
pagan fate and the Calvinist God. The play ends with a distribution
of the characters which parodies the Christian. Hieronimo's
friends will consort together happily in Proserpina's underworld
and his enemies, Revenge promises, will be further punished in
"deepest hell, / Where none but furies, bugs and tortures dwell"
(IV.v.27). It sounds very like the protestant dispensation, despite
the admixture of pagan imagery. Is the Reformation God to
all intents identifiable with Revenge? The question occurred
to Erasmus; it may well have occurred to Kyd.

Reformation doctrine has a crucial impact upon our understanding
of *Dr Faustus*. Traditionally readers have felt that Marlowe's
hero is unfairly treated by God, but discussion usually hinges
round whether he was unduly influenced in his choice, or whether
choosing God requires the exclusion of too much else. But perhaps
Faustus had no choice: perhaps the play shows the life of one
of the reprobate whom God has, from everlasting, condemned
to hell. It is a reading which the historical context obliges us
to entertain and I propose initially to explore its implications.
    Mephostophilis says, though admittedly only in the "B" text,
that Faustus had no choice:

> 'Twas I that, when thou were't i' the way to heaven,
> Damm'd up thy passage; when thou took'st the book
> To view the scriptures, then I turn'd the leaves
> And led thine eye.   (V.ii.86)

If this is true (and Mephostophilis could be making it up), then
to the Calvinist it must signify a divine decision to damn Faustus,
for God controls the devils as he does everything else: "God,
therefore, does not allow Satan to have dominion over the souls
of believers, but only gives over to his sway the impious and un-
believing, whom he deigns not to number among his flock"
(*Institutes*, I.xiv.18). In this view Faustus is not damned because
he makes a pact with the Devil, he makes a pact with the Devil
because he is damned.

The issue is focussed in Faustus' first speech when he juxtaposes two texts: "The reward of sin is death. . . . If we say that we have no sin we deceive ourselves, and there is no truth in us" (I.i.40).   He concludes:

> Why then, belike we must sin, and so consequently die.
> Ay, we must die an everlasting death.
> What doctrine call you this?   *Che sera, sera.*
> What will be, shall be.   (I.i.42)

Christians who wish have little difficulty in evading this discouraging implication, but most protestants did not wish.   Faustus' conclusion is bold in form, but it catches correctly the consequence of Reformation theology.   Just these passages of Scripture were offered as evidence of election and reprobation.   Calvin used the text "The wages of sin is death; but the gift of God is eternal life" to emphasize that salvation is utterly within God's gift (*Institutes*, III.xiv.21).   William Tyndale in his *Exposition of the First Epistle of John* (1531) uses the other text, about everyone sinning, to demonstrate that we have no choice in the matter of mortal sin: "our nature cannot but sin, if occasions be given, except that God of his especial grace keep us back: which pronity to sin is damnable sin in the law of God" (*English Reformers*, p. 111).   Tyndale is quite clear that people are damned for sin to which they have, of their nature, a "pronity."   God chooses to save the elect despite their depravity; the others go to hell. Faustus' summary, "What will be, shall be," is doctrinally satisfactory.

What, then, of Faustus' efforts to repent?   Protestants generally agreed that apostasy is irrevocable.   The Homily "Of Repentance" declares, "they that do utterly forsake the known truth do hate Christ and his word, they do crucify and mock him (but to their utter destruction), and therefore fall into desperation, and cannot repent" (*Homilies*, p. 568).   So too Calvin and Hooker (*Institutes*, III,iii.22; *Of Ecclesiastical Polity*, I, 295).   Tyndale says that we should not even pray for such people, except for their destruction, "as Paul prayed for Alexander the coppersmith (the ii Timothy, the last), 'that God would reward him according to his works'" (*English Reformers*, p. 142).

Anyway, repentance is not something the Christian does for and of herself or himself--that would impute merit to her or him.   It is a gift from God, and if Faustus does not have it there is nothing he can do.   Phillip Stubbes declared, "it is not in our powers to repent when we will.   It is the Lord that giveth the gift, when, where, and to whom it pleaseth him" (*The Anatomy of Abuses*, 1583; I, 190).   Faustus' inability to repent must, like everything else, be God's will.   Donne gave the matter classic formulation:

> Yet grace, if thou repent, thou canst not lack;
> But who shall give thee that grace to begin?   (Holy Sonnet IV)

Faustus has not the grace to begin.
Yet the Good Angel calls repeatedly upon Faustus to repent:

> *Faustus.* Be I a devil, yet God may pity me;
> Yea, God will pity me if I repent.
> *Bad Angel.* Ay, but Faustus never shall repent. *Exeunt Angels.*
> *Faustus.* My heart's so harden'd I cannot repent. (II.ii.15)

The polarity of the Angels appears to represent, like the personifi-
cations in medieval morality plays, a choice which is open to
Faustus. But how real is it? God might indeed pity the devils,
but it is well-known that they remain in hell. God would pity
Faustus if he repented, but can he? Who has hardened his heart?
The line alludes to the sequence in Exodus (chapters 7-14) where
it is stated repeatedly that God hardened Pharoah's heart against
the Hebrews. St Paul used it to demonstrate that God has "mercy
on whom he will have mercy, and whom he will he hardeneth"
(Romans, 9:18). Luther stressed the text and Erasmus admitted
that it seems to leave nothing to choice *(Luther and Erasmus,*
p. 64). For Calvin it afforded key evidence that election and
reprobation are sheerly God's decision: "When God is said to visit
in mercy or harden whom he will, men are reminded that they
are not to seek for any cause beyond his will" *(Institutes,* III.xxii.11).
According to this theology it is God who hardens Faustus' heart
and that is why he cannot repent. When the Angels next appear
Faustus actually calls upon Jesus: "Ah, Christ my saviour, my
saviour, / Help to save distressed Faustus' soul." But the response
is the entrance of Lucifer, Belzebub and Mephostophilis (II.ii.83).
Why, then, the appeals of the Good Angel? The question
is of a piece with the whole problem of why the Bible is full
of exhortations to goodness which, according to protestants, are
beyond the powers of everyone, and especially of the reprobate.

> What purpose, then, is served by exhortations? It is this:
> As the wicked, with obstinate heart, despise them, they will
> be a testimony against them when they stand at the judgment-
> seat of God; nay, they even now strike and lash their con-
> sciences. *(Institutes,* II.v.5)

On this analysis, the role of the Good Angel is to tell Faustus
what he ought to do but cannot, so that he will be unable to claim
ignorance when God taxes him with his wickedness. This may
seem perverse to the modern reader, but it is entirely characteristic
of the strategies by which the protestant deity was said to
manoeuvre himself into the right and mankind into the wrong.
Dr Faustus is susceptible, I think at every point, to a rigorous
Reformation reading: the Thirty-nine Articles declare that salvation
comes only through grace and that grace is withheld from some;
Faustus is one of the latter. This faith was preached from pulpits
and an Elizabethan might well interpret the play through it.
However, my case is not that Marlowe wanted to present

a simple dramatization of Calvinism.   Two further things are
happening.   First, the play is entirely open also to the more
usual modern reading, which some Elizabethans, especially the
less intellectual, might also hold: namely that God gives Faustus
a choice and he chooses evil rather than good.   The fact that
both readings are possible brings into implicit confrontation
Calvinistic and Arminian Christianity, and this makes manifest
the contradiction in the hypothesis that God is good and omnipotent.
The Arminian reading maintains God's goodness by diminishing
his responsibility.   It grants large scope to Faustus and
Mephostophilis and God becomes just one factor in the equation—he
may be good but he is weak.   The Calvinist reading locates power
firmly with God, but it has trouble establishing his goodness.
Historically each version has fed upon the inadequacy of the other.
When both are present they contradict each other.
        The second way in which *Dr Faustus* disrupts any complacent
view of Reformation doctrine is through its very nature as a dramatic fiction.   It is perhaps very well to argue in principle that
the reprobate are destined for everlasting torment, but when
we see Faustus panic-stricken in his last hour we may think again
about the God who has ordained it.   Drawing out the protestant
scheme through a dramatic sequence with the immediate presence
of an actor tends to make apparent its inhumanity.   No-one can
prove or disprove that Elizabethans experienced such feelings.
Given the play and the dominant theology, it seems a good hypothesis.
        But we can remark that Marlowe, particularly in the Good
Angel's exhortations, leads us straight to the most embarrassing
aspects of Reformation protestantism.   He surely wants the audience to ask questions.   Calvin knows that he has a problem—watch
him wriggle:

> To some it seems harsh, and at variance with the divine
> mercy, utterly to deny forgiveness to any who betake them-
> selves to it.   This is easily disposed of.   It is not said that
> pardon will be refused if they turn to the Lord, but it is
> altogether denied that they can turn to repentance, inasmuch
> as for their ingratitude they are struck by the just judgment
> of God with eternal blindness.   *(Institutes,* III.iii.24)

God evades the moral dilemma of turning away penitent sinners
by refusing to allow it to arise.   He blinds and hardens them
so that they cannot repent.   But can they fairly be punished?

> But what, you will ask, can a miserable mortal do, when
> softness of heart, which is necessary to obedience, is denied
> him?   I ask, in reply, Why have recourse to evasion, since
> hardness of heart cannot be imputed to any but the sinner
> himself?   *(Institutes,* II.v.5)

Well, the hard heart does belong to the sinner in the way, say,

that rottenness belongs to a bough, so perhaps he or she should
be cut down.   But God has created sinners thus, he has created
them in order to condemn them.   All this is implicit in Faustus'
career; Marlowe directs us to the dilemma which Calvin tries
to obscure.

Responsibility for the fall of Faustus and all the reprobate
can lie only with God: he is the cause of the suffering.   That
is what Marlowe dramatizes.   There are two traps in the play.
One is set by God for Faustus; the other is set by Marlowe, for
God.

The plays considered thus far posit a harsh, intrusive and predestinating supernatural force, and I have argued that this draws attention to problematic aspects of Reformation Christianity.   Another
group of tragedies takes an opposite direction.   It undermines
protestantism by implying that, so far from being divinely ordered
and controlled, the world lacks any external principle of spiritual
or moral coherence.   I shall discuss particularly *The Duchess
of Malfi* and *King Lear*.

There are three fundamental theories in western thought
about the ultimate force which dominates humanity and the universe:
a mechanistic fate which operates only a crude, retributive moral
scheme; a God who cares for mankind; and arbitrary chance (the
latter appears most recently in "theatre of the absurd").
Elizabethans were acquainted with this distinction; in his sixteenth
Moral Epistle Seneca wonders whether "Fate binds us down by
an inexorable law, or whether God as arbiter of the universe has
arranged everything, or whether Chance drives and tosses human
affairs without method" (XVI,5).   The plays discussed so far work
partly by running together the first two theories, suggesting that
the protestant doctrine of providence is hardly distinct from or
preferable to an impersonal fate.

I have shown that Reformation theologians tried to resist
the connection of providence and fate; they were equally worried
by the idea of chance or fortune.   The Homily "For Rogation
Week" seeks to discourage it in church congregations:

> Which of these two should be most believed? fortune, whom
> they paint to be blind of both eyes, ever unstable and unconstant
> in her wheel, in whose hands they say these things be? or
> God, [whose] sight looketh thorough heaven and earth, and
> seeth all things presently with his eyes. *(Homilies,* p. 512)

Medieval thinkers sought to reconcile pagan and Christian by
making fortune a systematic power subordinate to God (that is
the assumption in the Monk's definition of tragedy in *Canterbury
Tales).*   But protestants wanted to cast out non-biblical accretions,
to insist on God's immediate providential concern, and to deny

any random element in human affairs:

> the providence of God, as taught in Scripture, is opposed
> to fortune and fortuitous causes.   By an erroneous opinion
> prevailing in all ages, an opinion almost universally prevailing
> in our own day—viz. that all things happen fortuitously—the
> true doctrine of providence has not only been obscured, but
> almost buried.   *(Institutes,* I.xvi.2)

Belief in the fortuitous determination of events, we are told,
is both widespread and antipathetic to protestantism.   It is also
the most reasonable inference to be drawn from several major
tragedies.
    Arbitrary fortune is implied when the action is contrived
so as to arouse expectations of human benefits, or merely of
retributive justice, and then those expectations are frustrated.
The process is the opposite of that we have discussed previously,
where it is the systematic rigour of the supernatural power that
raises questions.   By denying any coherence in the distribution
of human suffering the playwright forces us to contemplate the
notion that the universe is without purpose.
    This is the main theme of Webster's tragedies.   It might
seem that *The Duchess of Malfi* is the more optimistic because
the Duchess (as we have seen) manages to maintain even to death
her human assertion.   But, on the other hand, this achievement
is at once undercut by our awareness that her suffering was unnecessary.   The crazy Ferdinand immediately disavows the murder
and Bosola repents.   Had they considered longer it need not
have happened.   This is Bosola's lament:

> > That we cannot be suffer'd
> To do good when we have a mind to it!
> .   .   .   .   where were
> These penitent fountains while she was living?   (IV.ii.359)

There is no sense to it.   Bosola is inspired by the Duchess' death
to work for Antonio's safety and revenge, but kills him in mistake
for the Cardinal:

> > Antonio!
> The man I would have sav'd 'bove mine own life!
> We are merely the stars' tennis-balls, struck and banded
> Which way please them.   (V.iv.52)

This is a credible account of the world as the play has presented
it; we must entertain the depressing possibility that the Duchess
submitted herself to a divine power which cares nothing for human
pain and aspirations.
    The image of the stars' tennis-balls occurs in strikingly relevant
form in Calvin's *Institutes:*

occasionally as the causes of events are concealed, the thought
is apt to rise, that human affairs are whirled about by the
blind impulse of Fortune, or our carnal nature inclines us
to speak as if God were amusing himself by tossing men up
and down like balls. (I.xvii.1).

Thomas Norton's translation of 1561 has "toss them like tennis
balls." But this, Calvin says, is mistaken: "the issue would at
length make it manifest that the counsel of God was in accordance
with the highest reason" (I.xvii.1). Christians trust and partly
perceive the divine purpose in all things.

But in *The Duchess of Malfi* God's purpose is not apparent.
There is bizarre poetic justice in the entrapment of the Cardinal
in his own, characteristic command that cries for help should
be disregarded, but the outcome seems haphazard when the lunatic
Ferdinand "wounds the Cardinal, and in the scuffle gives Bosola
his death-wound" (V.v.53). The survivors find no satisfaction
in "this great ruin" (V.v.111). Bosola declares,

> Oh, this gloomy world!
> In what a shadow, or deep pit of darkness,
> Doth womanish and fearful mankind live!   (V.v.100)

The revealing context for both Bosola's complaints is Sidney's
Arcadia. The princes agree to conceal their names because the
man who is to try them is Euarchus, father of one and uncle of
the other:

> the chief man they considered was Euarchus, whom the strange
> and secret working of justice had brought to be the judge
> over them. In such a shadow or rather pit of darkness the
> wormish mankind lives, that neither they know how to forsee
> nor what to fear, and are but like tennis balls, tossed by
> the racket of the higher powers. *(New Arcadia*, p. 817)

Sidney's point is made quite different by the reference to "the
strange and secret working of justice," which proclaims an ultimately
fair deity in Calvin's manner; the pit of darkness and tennis-balls
express human worthlessness within the divine dispensation.
The marvellous and intricate conclusion of the story confirms
this interpretation and Basilius declares that "all had fallen out
by the highest providence" (p. 846). Webster perceives chaos
where the puritan humanist insists on divine order.

King Lear also implies an incoherent universe, and *Arcadia*
bears a similarly contrastive relation to it. The main point of
connection is the episode of the Paphlagonian King (II.10) which
furnished the Gloucester subplot, but in Sidney's work the blind
man and his good son are saved by the virtuous princes. When
the rescue is briefly in doubt a friendly monarch appears, summoned
by a dream to what was otherwise "a fit place enough to make
the stage of any tragedy" *(New Arcadia*, p. 280). There is no

such providential aversion of disaster in *King Lear*.

Many opinions of the gods are offered in the play—so many that their nature becomes an open question. Only the wicked Edmund can tolerate the idea that there are none. Lear assumes that they will sanction his punitive banishment of Cordelia; he expects them to keep a stern, retributive justice:

> Let the great Gods,
> That keep this dreadful pudder o'er our heads,
> Find out their enemies now. Tremble, thou wretch,
> That hast within thee undivulged crimes,
> Unwhipp'd of Justice; hide thee, thou bloody hand,
> Thou perjur'd, and thou simular of virtue
> That art incestuous . . .   (III.ii.49)

The prospect of such violent, retributive gods (reminiscent of Tamburlaine's) is alarming enough, but the action of the play does not confirm it. Lear loses his sense of a purpose in the divine powers—"Is there any cause in nature that make these hard hearts?" (III.vi.78). Human agents must improve the work of the gods:

> Take physic, Pomp;
> Expose thyself to feel what wretches feel,
> That thou mayst shake the superflux to them,
> And show the Heavens more just.   (III.iv.33)

Edgar's simple good nature wants to think well of the gods but the ground slides from under him. At the start of act IV scene i he declares that as an outcast he has at least reached the lowest depth, but then he sees his father "poorly led." He consoles himself for this further disaster by asserting that misfortunes have at least the virtue of making death tolerable, but then he realizes that his father is blind and is forced to exclaim, "O Gods! Who is't can say 'I am at the worst'? / I am worse than e'er I was" (IV.i.25). He is obliged to fabricate Dover cliff to cure Gloucester's despair because undoctored reality is too harsh.

Yet Edgar is determined to find purpose in the world, and he offers finally the punitive deity with which Lear began:

> The Gods are just, and of our pleasant vices
> Make instruments to plague us;
> The dark and vicious place where thee he got
> Cost him his eyes.   (V.iii.169)

There could be such gods and, as we have seen, they would not be altogether alien to protestantism. They might punish fornication with blinding, Cordelia's inability to humour her father with violent and premature death, Lear's pathetic love game with madness. But we may reflect that the immediate cause of Gloucester's blinding was his help for the mad and shelterless Lear.

If the action supported Edgar's vision of a retributive deity, we might class *King Lear* with *Tamburlaine* and *The Revenger's Tragedy* as exposing the problem of a god of power and goodness. But, even more than *The Duchess of Malfi*, *Lear* seems designed to disconcert by arousing and disappointing optimistic expectations. The return of Cordelia to rescue her crazed old father and their affecting reunion promises a fairy-tale outcome—it happens in the chronicle sources—but Shakespeare will not permit it. At the end of the play Albany sends to rescue Cordelia and Lear, exclaiming, "The Gods defend her!" (V.iii.255), but she is dead. Edmund's one attempt to do good is rendered futile—like Bosola's repentance, it comes too late. Lear is deranged again and has lost all he found on the heath and in the reunion with Cordelia; we are denied even his recognition of Kent's devotion. Yet Albany hopes to administer justice:

> All friends shall taste
> The wages of their virtue, and all foes
> The cup of their deservings.   (V.iii.302)

Lear's death speech follows at once: it is not in Albany's power to "show the Heavens more just."

We cannot safely dismiss Gloucester's image for the gods:

> As flies to wanton boys, are we to th' Gods;
> They kill us for their sport.   (IV.i.36)

In the *New Arcadia* Pamela insisted, against the atheistic Cecropia, that "not the estate of flies" must be "unknown" to the "mind of wisdom" which governs the world (pp. 491-92). *King Lear* obliges the audience to take seriously the possibility that the universe is governed not by providence, or even by a consistent though unsympathetic fate, but by inscrutable and arbitrary forces.

Fate and fortune are not as contrary to the protestant God as Marlowe's Ferneze assumed. Rather, they are subversive tendencies within any providential theory, and the classical discourses inherited by Reformation culture deposited them within it as an unassimilable residue. If God is omnipotent and good there are two ways to cope with evil. One is to assert free will, thus diminishing God's responsibility. The danger here is secularism: God loses relevance, we might forget him or attribute events to blind fortune. The other alternative is a high level of divine intervention, culminating in predestination. This approach maintains God's immediate control, but at the expense of making him appear rigorous and impersonal; here providence drifts towards fate. Tragedians picked at the seam of this ill-fashioned garment and for the thoughtful audience it splits apart.

But despite the exposure of contradictions in Christianity, Elizabethan and Jacobean plays never transcend the anxiety about a godless universe which has always been the mainstay of theistic religion.   They do not suggest that arbitrary forces can command no respect; that we need not worry about pleasing or displeasing them; that we might as well assume them not to exist and build our lives as best we can within the limitations of this world. We never find an unfettered secularist delight in the freedom available to people in an absurd universe.

This step was not historically impossible—Machiavelli made it, for one.   He nominates fortune as the external pressure upon human affairs, but he offers it no allegiance and makes no complaint.   It is simply the condition within which we operate: "fortune is the arbiter of half the things we do, leaving the other half or so to be controlled by ourselves" (The Prince, p. 130).   Fortune sweeps on like a violent river, but its effect may be altered by the building of embankments; either circumspection or an impetuous leap may, depending on the situation, gain a human triumph. In the plays there are moments of exhilaration for Barabas, Edmund and Flamineo but, as we saw in the previous chapter, they are accompanied by a sense that the heroic assertion is sinful.   The Machiavel is the villain.

I have argued that the rigorous form of Christianity preached in the period stimulated questioning; it must, also, have discouraged the bold thought of a Machiavelli.   Tragedians were unable to let go of the idea of a God who would confer from above a dignity and meaning upon life.   Instead they reproach providence for not living up to the claims made for it by contemporary religion.

The weakness in the theory presented in this chapter is my assumption that incidents like Tamburlaine killing his son and the blinding of Gloucester are, however those victims may have erred, repugnant to humanity.   Upon it rests my assertion that appeals to providence in such contexts provoke doubt rather than faith in the dogmas of contemporary religion.   However, the Elizabethans were, by modern standards, a harsh and punitive people.   Their treatment of the poor, children and criminals was violent and retributive, and we cannot be altogether confident that they would find anything questionable about the divinity that shapes the ends of these plays. But some tragedies offer from within themselves, though perhaps only tentatively, the ideal of a generous love between people; it is perhaps structurally related to the idea of mutual love (discussed in chapter IV).   This alternative ethic is highly subversive; it puts to shame the protestant God.

Othello's murder of his wife is related by him to a punitive concept of the deity: "this sorrow's heavenly, / It strikes when it does love" (V.ii.21).   At least he is consistent when he applies the same criterion to himself:

> when we shall meet at count,
> This look of thine will hurl my soul from heaven,
> And fiends will snatch at it: cold, cold, my girl,
> Even like thy chastity; O cursed slave!
> Whip me, ye devils,
> From the possession of this heavenly sight,
> Blow me about in winds, roast me in sulphur,
> Wash me in steep-down gulfs of liquid fire!   (V.ii.274)

Elizabethan theologians would have contemplated with equanimity the operation of providential justice through Othello's eternal damnation and, indeed, the play ends with good, responsible and typical bystanders promising to inflict abnormal torments upon Iago.

Yet notice that it is Desdemona's look which is supposed to hurl Othello from heaven.   If this happens, it will not be her wish, for her last human action was an attempt to save him:

> *Emilia.*   O, who has done this deed?
> *Desdemona.*   Nobody, I myself, farewell:
>   Commend me to my kind lord, O, farewell!   (V.ii.124)

This astounding act of unmerited love is a standing rebuke to the retributive God assumed by Othello and by the contemporary church.   It opens the play to the interpretation that Othello's vengeful stance permits the murder of Desdemona, and that the continuance of such an ethos into eternity is no answer.

The modern reader is liable to assume that Desdemona's attitude is Christian and Othello's horrible, but that is unhistorical. Certainly protestants attributed to God an amazing act of generosity in granting salvation to any sinful human being; but at the same time—precisely in order to demonstrate God's free gift—they asserted that he sends the majority to hell.   Unless these two factors are foregrounded in a particular context, we cannot be sure that they were experienced as a contradiction.   Thomas Heywood intended no irony when he showed a woman killed with kindness: most Elizabethans saw no reprehensible manipulation in "forgiving" one's wife in a manner which causes her to pine away and die.

In this context the entirely selfless love represented in some plays is subversive.   The juxtaposition of Desdemona's generosity and Othello's self-condemnation obliges us to unpack the paradox of love and damnation in protestantism, and to realize that for the best human being in the play forgiveness and mercy can be truly total.   Desdemona is a reproach to the divine being posited in the play and by most contemporary Christians.   Her attitude is properly described as more humane.

In *Dr Faustus*, amidst the theological abstractions and the dominating supernatural forces, the Old Man's human wish to

save Faustus persists beyond the Good Angel's.   Faustus himself
displays a generous concern for others.   As he anticipates his
last hour, when human support might seem essential, he refuses
the help of the Scholars: "Gentlemen, away, lest you perish with
me. . . . Talk not of me, but save yourselves and depart" (V.ii.67).
In the "B" text, between Faustus' horrifying death and the sharp
moral of the epilogue, the human response intrudes.   The sympathetic Scholars agree to hold a noble funeral; we may recall
the conclusions of Euripides' *Hippolytus* and *Bacchae,* where
the gods stand aside after their disastrous intrusions upon human
affairs and the people draw together with tenderness and compassion.

In *The Duchess of Malfi* also the human rebukes the divine.
The Duchess' care for her children at the point of her own death
sets off the arbitrary divine order:

> I pray thee, look thou giv'st my little boy
> Some syrup for his cold, and let the girl
> Say her prayers, ere she sleep.   (IV.ii.203)

The child has no chance to pray before she is strangled.

King Lear offers the fullest comparative analysis of human
and divine goodness.   Lear's demand for protestations of love
from his daughters invites us to contemplate more generous
ideas of relations between man and the deity than anyone in
the play actually puts into words.   Lear wants love but, consistently with his retributive gods, thinks it necessary to offer something
in exchange (see further my article, "Lear and Laing," *Essays
in Criticism,* XXVI [1976], 1-16).   Cordelia is caught in a double-
bind by his confusion of love and profit: to the question, "what
can you say to draw / A third more opulent than your sisters?"
the only legitimate reply is "Nothing" (I.i.85).   She implies a
love freely given and incompatible with self-seeking, but Lear
can think only in terms of debt and payment.   He insists, "Mend
your speech a little, / Lest you may mar your fortunes," but
the more he threatens the less possible it is to respond freely
with love.   He compels Cordelia to join his game of profit and
loss, and her only honest option is to play it without the flattery
of her sisters: "You have begot me, bred me, lov'd me: I / Return
those duties back as are right fit" (I.i.96—Lear will not notice
how she catches her breath at the line break between "I" and
the verb).   Then Lear tries to set up a second, reversed love
auction between Burgundy and France:

>   What, in the least,
> Will you require in present dower with her,
> Or cease your quest of love?   (I.i.191)

But France (the only person with power equivalent to Lear's)
busts through the whole structure:

> Love's not love
> When it is mingled with regards that stand
> Aloof from th'entire point.   Will you have her?
> She is herself a dowry.   (I.i.238)

The last sentence locates value firmly in the human being.

The gratuitous gift of love made by Cordelia, France, Kent and Edgar effects a critique of the harsh attitude shared by Lear in this scene and, it is severally asserted, his gods.   As with Desdemona's last words, it prompts an analogy with the mercy of the protestant God but not with his retribution.   From the security of its pagan setting *King Lear* focusses upon Reformation thought a three-pronged critique.   It requires us to consider the implications of a god of systematic retribution, rejects this for the idea that the world may be governed by blind fortune, and poses against these two versions of the divinity a subversive ethic of generosity.

The Reformation God must have sounded impressive, convincing, even inevitable in the highly developed sermon presentation of the time.   But when the implications are realized on the stage through characters of compelling humanity, they seem less satisfactory.   In *The Tempest* Prospero seems pleased at the discomfiture of his enemies, but Ariel invokes another standard:

> if you now beheld them, your affections
> Would become tender.
> *Prospero.*   Dost thou think so, spirit?
> *Ariel.*   Mine would, sir, were I human.   (V.i.18)

Calvin ends his treatment of predestination in the *Institutes* by observing, "Truly does Augustine maintain that it is perverse to measure divine by the standard of human justice" (III.xxiv.17). By placing human aspirations and suffering vividly before our eyes tragedians invite us to do just that.

7 The reformation and secular society
Bacon, Perkins, Hobbes, Chillingworth, Milton

> Princes' images on their tombs do not lie, as they were
> wont, seeming to pray up to heaven, but with their hands
> under their cheeks, as if they died of the tooth-ache;
> they are not carved with their eyes fixed upon the stars,
> but as if their minds were wholly bent upon the world, the
> selfsame way they seem to turn their faces.
> (Webster, *The Duchess of Malfi*, IV.ii.156)

The seventeenth century was critical in the development of modern
attitudes.   How we assess this change—even how we describe
it—will depend on our own values.   I should call it the beginnings
of secularism—a disbelief in or disregard for a spiritual or supernatural dimension.   Since 1600 ever-increasing areas of thought
have gained independence from the domination of religious attitudes.   The first stage is generally a relative distancing of God
from human affairs rather than a positive exclusion; often it
leaves a vague belief that there must be "something more"; but
certainly what remains is quite unlike the Reformation faith.
This demystification of experience has of course not been a smooth
process, but from the present perspective it looks all of a piece
and an awareness of its genesis may help us to appreciate what
we have gained.
    As I showed in chapter two, the Reformation was essentially
a movement to intensify spiritual experience by ascribing overwhelming power to an intrusive personalized God.   It was a
reaction against the Roman church, which seemed to weaken
God's role and our relationship with him by allowing works to
contribute to salvation and interpreting satisfaction in a mechanical
way; and against Renaissance tendencies to fashion from Christianity a humane programme of ethical self-development.   In its
origins, therefore, protestantism was an attempt to combat the
threat that people might free themselves from the supernatural.
Nevertheless, the secularist impulse reasserted itself.
    The argument of this chapter is that seventeenth-century
secularism was not just a counter-movement to protestantism,
but was actually a response to inherent contradictions.   Some
people found ways of drawing out secularist implications from

protestant thought, others came upon them unawares. The adjust-
ment and negotiation of divergent cultural tendencies which
we have traced in the period gave way, increasingly, to explicit
confrontation and the break up of the fragile protestant ideological
hegemony.

Ultimately, the Reformation stimulated the development
of the secularist outlook which many now enjoy. By releasing
human effort in natural science and ethics, by encouraging a
pragmatic attention to actual human behaviour, by destroying
final authority for belief, and by exposing contradictions in the
concept of an omnipotent and beneficent deity, protestant doctrine
weakened the credit of the God hypothesis. Even so, the punitive
and authoritarian approach which ratified Reformation theology
is still active, and it is salutary to observe its structure in seventeenth-century writing.

Protestantism created space for the study of the world on its
own, natural terms by its insistence upon separating divine and
terrestial concerns. As we have seen, it was through this distinction that Sidney, Spenser and Milton tried to justify their interest
in secular and pagan letters. It was designed to establish the
total impotence of natural understanding in spiritual matters,
but could be reversed so as to exalt human capacity in the arts
and sciences. Calvin granted readily "an universal reason and
intelligence naturally implanted" and that "this capacity extends
not merely to the learning of the art, but to the devising of
something new" (*Institutes*, II.ii.14). God means us to develop
these abilities; he even assists us "by the work and ministry of
the ungodly in physics, dialectics, mathematics, and other similar
sciences" (II.ii.16).

All this promised good success in the study of the world
and it was only a step to Bacon's preface to *The Great Instauration*,
where he proposed that

> trial should be made, whether that commerce between the
> mind of man and the nature of things, which is more precious
> than anything on earth, or at least anything that is of the
> earth, might by any means be restored to its perfect and
> original condition, or if that may not be, yet reduced to
> a better condition than that in which it now is.
> (*Philosophical Works*, p. 241)

Calvin's justification of human capacity in worldly matters tips
over into a grand but entirely secular enquiry into the nature
of mankind and the world which might even—though Bacon does
not quite commit himself—recover the effects of the fall.
The discussion of human knowledge in *De Augmentis Scientiarum*

concludes with a paeon to the achievements of the age, raising "this hope, that this third period will far surpass the Greek and Roman in learning" *(Philosophical Works,* p. 630); the comparison straddles the period of the incarnation without noticing it.
The protestant doctrine which was supposed to proclaim human degradation in essential—that is, spiritual—matters allowed the secular to slip free from religious domination and, under its own impetus, to promise advances in human understanding and control of the physical world.

The famous procedure whereby Bacon in *De Augmentis Scientiarum* divides knowledge into the divine and worldly and postpones the former while he plunges into a large account of the latter is, therefore, quite in accord with Calvinist principle and not necessarily cynical. Nevertheless, we see clearly its tendency in a person of Bacon's interests to relegate the spiritual.

He considers the topic most closely in *Filum Labyrinthi,* where he recognizes that science is incompatible with traditional ideas of reverence ("he" is Bacon himself):

> He thought also, how great opposition and prejudice natural philosophy had received by superstition, and the immoderate and blind zeal of religion; for he found that some of the Grecians which first gave the reason of thunder, had been condemned of impiety. *(Philosophical Works,* pp. 208-09)

Bacon has put his finger on a tricky topic: we observed in chapter five that exclusive reliance upon natural process was identified by Elizabethans as atheism. Thunder was a test case: Cecropia in Sidney's *New Arcadia* says of foolish and ignorant men, "when they heard it thunder, not knowing the natural cause, they thought there was some angry body above that spake so loud" (p. 488); Tourneur has D'Amville in *The Atheist's Tragedy* explain thunder as "a mere effect of Nature" (II.iv.142). Nevertheless, Bacon "calls the opposition to science "superstition" and "blind zeal." He notes the opinion of "men of devout simplicity" that "the desire in men to attain to so great and hidden knowledge, hath a resemblance with that temptation which caused the original fall," but he also insinuates Machiavelli's point that the religious establishment has an interest in maintaining superstition: "in men of devout policy, he noted an inclination to have the people depend upon God the more, when they are less acquainted with second causes" (p. 209).

Bacon's tone here may make us doubt his respect for supernatural revelation, but he offers a string of arguments to legitimate natural science in Christian terms. The most promising is that by studying the universe we gain a better appreciation of God's goodness:

> all knowledge and specially that of natural philosophy tendeth highly to the magnifying of the glory of God in his power, providence, and benefits; appearing and engraven

in his works, which without this knowledge are beheld but as through a veil. (p. 209)

Many seventeenth-century protestants must have believed that this argument reconciles religion and science. It does, but in a manner which subverts the essence of Reformation doctrine, for Bacon's approach depends upon the assumption that natural process is systematic and comprehensible in its own terms. This raises the spectre which, as we saw in the previous chapter, troubled Calvin: that emphasis upon God's controlling providence might imply a marvellous machine, like the Stoics' impersonal fate, from which the great designer has withdrawn. Calvin insisted instead upon the detailed and immediate interventions of a special providence. For example, he called "meagre and heathenish" the view that God sets up the elements and the seasons but the weather on a particular day is the product of "natural causes"—"as if the fertility of one year were not a special blessing, the penury and dearth of another a special punishment and curse from God" (*Institutes*, 1.xvi.5). Or note a typical instance in Joseph Hall's autobiographical *Observations of some Specialities of Divine Providence*. Hall's patron is being influenced against him by "a witty and bold atheist":

> I bent my prayers against him; beseeching God daily, that he would be pleased to remove, by some means or other, that apparent hindrance of my faithful labours: who gave me an answer accordingly; for this malicious man, going hastily up to London to exasperate my patron against me, was then and there swept away by the pestilence, and never returned to do any farther mischief. (*Works*, I, xxvi)

This attitude is ultimately irreconcilable with scientific analysis, which demands a reliable relationship between material cause and effect. Study of crop failure and disease is hampered by the belief that they are determined individually by God's decision to curse a community or to advance Hall's ministry. Bacon refers repeatedly in a general way to providence and grants that there are mysteries which seem not to be within the ordinary course of nature, but he believes that natural process will eventually afford an explanation: "we are not to give up the investigation, until the properties and qualities found in such things as may be taken for miracles of nature be reduced and comprehended under some Form or Fixed Law" (*Philosophical Works*, p. 335).

Bacon's argument on religion is therefore not adequate in terms of contemporary orthodoxy; it opposes an intense implication of the deity in the universe. Yet the position is more complex, for Calvin himself, despite his belief that the universe fell with Adam, on occasion directed attention to the way God manifests "his perfections in the whole structure of the universe." He offered it as a way of justifying the condemnation of those to whom God has denied Christian revelation: it serves as proof of his existence and is given so that "none, however dull and illiterate, can plead ignorance [of him] as their excuse" (*Institutes*, I.v.i).   He even asks us to consider "how great the Architect must be who framed and ordered the multitude of the starry host so admirably, that it is impossible to imagine a more glorious sight" (I.xiv.21).   Bacon pivots upon a contradiction in protestantism.

Calvin's followers tended to overlook the fact that the argument from design is difficult to reconcile with the intervention of special providence.   In ardent protestant writing the universe is liable to appear as an efficient machine, often in the deistic image of a clock, which is used by William Perkins, John Preston and Richard Sibbes. Perkins in his *Treatise of the Vocations or Callings of Men* (1603) says the world is composed of many wheels—

> and every one hath his several motion—some turn this way, some that way, some go softly, some apace, and they are all ordered by the motion of the watch.   Behold here a notable resemblance of God's special providence over mankind, which is the watch of the great world, allotting to every man his motion and calling and in that calling his particular office and function.   (*Work*, p. 447)

Perkins means to assert God's personal and detailed concern— that is the force of "special providence" and "particular office and function."   But a good watch does not work because of the continual tinkering of the watchmaker.   The argument from design tends to filter out the role of the designer, leaving a world of material cause and effect for Bacon's followers to study.   The contradiction in protestant thought legitimated the development of secularism.

The Calvinist distinction between spiritual and natural concerns had a similar effect on ethics.   Reformers were determined to deny the role of works in salvation, but this freed them to grant that people, even pagans, could achieve some virtue through merely human power.   "Nothing, indeed, is more common, than for man to be sufficiently instructed in a right course of conduct by natural law," Calvin declared; we should not despise "those ancient lawgivers who arranged civil order and discipline with so much equity" (*Institutes*, II.ii.22, 15).   Thus at the same time as they derogated human potential in relation to the spiritual domain, reformers allowed the possibility of moral attainment which owes nothing to Christian revelation.   This contradiction helped to liberate secularism.

In a period when the existence and relevance of God was
hardly questioned this seemed a safe procedure: the individual's
spiritual life was to be conducted on an absolute plane directly
with God and mundane affairs were, merely, mundane.   What
the reformers did not foresee was that this strategy might rebound:
that the habit of treating worldly matters on their own terms
would lead eventually, for many people, to a disregard for the
spiritual domain.   We observe the phenomenon directly in the
theatre, where the abolition of religious plays on the ground
that the divine should not be profaned allowed the development
of a secular drama which achieved stature in its own right through
its substantially human treatment of life.   Similarly, the freeing
of ethics from total involvement with religion permitted people
to construct, with the help of pagan thought, an autonomous
secular morality not dependent upon spiritual sanctions.   Protestantism unwittingly made possible the modern position, especially
in those countries where it was most influential, where many
people conduct a moral life with little or no reference to a spiritual dimension.

Moreover, it is a familiar paradox that protestant emphasis
upon election, which ought to have rendered works irrelevant,
actually increased the attention which many gave to the ethical
quality of their lives, for they took moral attainment as a sign
of divine favour.   The Homily "Of the True, Lively, and Christian
Faith" urged: "be sure of your faith; try it by your living; look
upon the fruits that cometh of it; mark the increase of love
and charity by it toward God and your neighbour; and so you
shall perceive it to be a true lively faith" (p. 45).   So at the
same time that they released ethics from an entire dependence
upon religion, protestants gave a distinct value to human interactions and encouraged people to justify themselves in earthly
terms.

The main instrument of protestant engagement with the
world was the doctrine of callings, whereby each Christian was
to labour dutifully in the station of life that God had placed
him or her in.   This slotted human effort neatly in with God's
determining providence; the democratically minded will observe
that it also made for strong social control.   But, given a hierarchical society, the doctrine offered the dignity of mutual responsibility in worldly affairs to people of all callings:

> Now all societies of men are bodies . . . and in these bodies
> there be several members which are men walking in several
> callings and offices, the execution whereof must tend to
> the happy and good estate of the rest, yea, of all men every-
> where, as much as possible is.   The common good of all
> men stands in this; not only that they live, but that they
> live well, in righteousness and holiness and consequently
> in true happiness.   (Perkins, *Of the Vocations or Callings
> of Men, Work*, p. 449)

So Perkins exhorted men to find fulfilment in this world.
But the world tends to demand compromise.   Protestantism
promoted a further element which was ultimately contradictory.
Perkins managed to derive from protestant principles a pragmatism
almost as radical as Machiavelli's.

No doubt the primary impulse was mainly ideal.   Philip Sidney
tried to follow his own advice to his brother: "your purpose is,
being a gentleman born, to furnish yourself with the knowledge
of such things as may be serviceable to your country, and fit
for your calling" (*Prose Works*, III, 125).   Milton's alarm in his
blindness was that his ability would be

> Lodged with me useless, though my soul more bent
> To serve therewith my Maker, and present
> My true account.
>
> ("On His Blindness")

But in important respects protestant ethics were not idealistic
but pragmatic and relativist.   On the one hand the possibility
of significant achievement was denied; on the other, the faithful
were to undertake continual soul-searching.   Both for the sake
of consistency and to give comfort and practical advice, ministers
were obliged to credit good intentions and approximations.
Hence in Perkins' *Whole Treatise of the Cases of Conscience*
(c. 1600) the faithful were told, "give place to the sway of the
times"; and "be not too strict or curious, in effecting that which
thou intendest, exactly, when thou canst not; but rest contented
in this, that thou hast done thine endeavour" (*William Perkins*,
pp. 169, 170).

Furthermore, the involvement with the practical problems
of everyday life proposed by the doctrine of callings seemed to
demand a blurring of the absolute morality of the gospel.   Thus
Perkins evades Jesus' approval of a life of poverty and allows
us not just those goods "without which nature and life cannot
be well preserved" but also "those goods, without which a man's
state, condition, and dignity wherein he is, cannot be preserved"
(*William Perkins*, p. 189).   He even appeals beyond biblical
authority to nature: "the law of nature sets down and prescribes
distinction of professions and propriety of lands and goods, and
the gospel doth not abolish the law of nature" (p. 195).   Here
and in a whole range of problems Perkins does not shrink from
the knotty detail and its inevitable compromises. Games
involving a lottery are absolutely forbidden, but what about cards,
does the element of hazard in dealing them make them unlawful?—
no, "this casual distribution is not a lot, but only a casual auction"
(p. 221).

When Perkins permits the use of "policy" (p. 172) we perceive
how purposefully he is converging upon the pragmatic and secular
ethic which we associate with Machiavelli and Bacon.   He quickly

abjures Machiavelli as an atheistic villain, but we are not far from Bacon's admiration in *De Augmentis Scientiarum:* "we are much beholden to Machiavelli and other writers of that class, who openly and unfeignedly declare or describe what men do, and not what they ought to do" (*Philosophical Works*, p. 570). Bacon adds at once that we must understand evil in order to combat it, but this kind of hesitancy is characteristic and cannot obscure the revolutionary implications of his programme to base ethics upon human capacity. He begins: "First therefore in this, as in all things which are practical, we ought to cast up our account what is in our power and what not" (p. 572). He offers as "the most noble and effectual" means to virtue the principle of "electing and propounding unto a man's self good and virtuous ends of his life and actions; such as may be in a reasonable sort within his compass to attain" (pp. 576-77). What sounds at first like a lofty exhortation turns into sheer pragmatism. On occasion it is undisguised. The main need in politics, Bacon asserts, is to know ourselves, but he does not mean our essential worthlessness before God (the protestant interpretation of the phrase) but our tactical strengths and weaknesses. He adapts the scriptural image of a mirror but gives a brutal twist to Calvin's distinction between spiritual and natural: "the divine glass in which we ought to behold ourselves is the Word of God, but the political glass is nothing else than the state of the world or times wherein we live" (p. 598). In this sentence the divine and terrestial are not just distinct, they are opposed.

Perkins claimed to draw his ethical principles from scripture; an awareness on his part of the obliqueness of the derivation may only be inferred from his comment that "it is not a matter easy and at hand, but full of labour and difficulty" (*William Perkins*, p. 88). Bacon's thought on the relationship is often equivocal, giving with one hand and taking with the other. In the introduction to his discussion of ethics he sways about. "If it be objected that the cure of men's minds belongs to sacred divinity, it is most true," but moral philosophy may be her "wise servant and faithful handmaid"; this sounds like a clear statement of priorities. But at once the position is blurred: "and yet no doubt many things are left to the care and discretion of the handmaid"—perhaps, then, divinity should not intrude on ethics. The conclusion settles nothing by its suggestion that philosophy is independent but must keep an eye over its shoulder: it must give "a constant attention to the doctrines of divinity, and be obedient to them, and yet so as it may yield of itself within its own limits many sound and profitable directions" (*Philosophical Works*, p. 572). When Bacon comes on to theology he seems to feel that some reference back to his section on ethics would be appropriate. It takes the form of using the "more perfect interpretation of the moral law" in the New Testament as evidence that scripture is inspired by a divine revelation beyond man's natural understanding. This is, of course, orthodox, but Bacon

implies that the absolute injunctions of the Sermon on the Mount
are so far beyond our capacity as to be irrelevant: "'Love your
enemies'; 'do good to them that hate you,' and so on; . . .
To which words this applause may well be applied, 'that they
do not sound human'" (p. 632).   The natural and divine are again
not just separate but opposed.
    Pragmatism and independence of Christian principles in ethics
were taken further by the more adventurous thinkers of the period.
Lord Herbert of Cherbury worked out his own principles:

> the Christians and the heathens are in a manner agreed
> concerning the definitions of virtues . . . , they being doctrines
> imprinted in the soul in its first original and containing the
> principal and first notices by which man may attain his
> happiness here or hereafter.   (*Life*, p. 24)

Christian revelation adds little or nothing; good works, according
to innate principles, are sufficient for this life and the next.
Herbert's advice on actual behaviour is entirely pragmatic: "Discretion is required, for every virtue is not promiscuously to be used
but such only as is proper for the present occasion" (p. 25).
Hobbes in *Leviathan* (1651) derives moral authority not from
intuition but from the social order: "The desires and other passions
of man are in themselves no sin.   No more are the actions that
proceed from those passions, till they know a law that forbids
them: which till laws be made they cannot know" (p. 187).
Without a power to control them, men are in a state of war
and there is no moral order.   The ruler imposes laws and the
keeping of them is the basis of morality.   Within a given society,
therefore, Hobbes envisages a clear and potent ethical structure,
but its ultimate validity is relative and particular.
    By its insistence on the absolute quality of spiritual experience
the Reformation overreached itself.   Seventeenth-century thinkers
edged towards a secularist society by building upon almost legitimate implications of protestant doctrine on nature and mankind.
Thus they set up the rationale from within which the secular
might take a larger and larger share of thought, and eventually
become a self-sufficient approach to life.

In natural science and ethics, I have tried to show, protestantism
contained the seeds of secularism.   Positions which were propounded to sustain the structure in its relations with one set of ideological pressures were developed in unforeseen ways and became
key factors in new formations.
    The Reformation dependence on the inner light of the individ-
ual conscience was similarly far-reaching.   Luther declared
at the Diet of Worms (1521):

> Unless I am convicted by the testimony of scripture or plain
> reason (for I believe neither in Pope nor councils alone,
> since it is agreed that they have often erred and contradicted
> themselves), I am bound by the scriptures I have quoted,
> and my conscience is captive to the Word of God.   I neither
> can nor will revoke anything, for it is neither safe nor honest
> to act against one's conscience.   Amen. (*Martin Luther*,
> p. 60)

Any belief may be justified through an appeal to conscience.

It may seem that Luther limits the possibilities by his insistence upon scripture, but the succeeding century was to demonstrate that almost anything can be proved from the Bible.
Moreover the thoughtful, including Richard Hooker, observed
a logical difficulty: scripture cannot be self-defining, it cannot
tell us "what books we are to esteem holy" (*Of Ecclesiastical
Polity*, I, 215).   Hooker's answer was that we must rely on the
church, but of course the ultimate authority for the church is
the Bible! The more strenuous protestant response may be seen
in *An Abridgement of Calvin's Institutes* (trans. 1587) where
William Lawne introduces an objector who puts points to be answered with protestant orthodoxy.   It is asked: "Who can make us
believe that these things came from God, and that they came
safe and sound to our time? That one book is to be received
reverently, and another to be put out of the number?" The reply
is that "the scripture doth of itself carry the sense of truth,
which the Spirit of God doth firmly imprint in our minds" (p.
13).   We are thrown back upon the individual's personal conviction.

Luther's justification by conscience leads us to identify two
central paradoxes of protestantism.   The first is that, despite
their insistence upon the fall, Luther and Calvin in fact made
humanity the measure of God.   They declared that we can know
nothing of spiritual truth without the unmerited gift of revelation
but they presumed continually, and even in the act of making
that statement, to interpret divine will.   Similarly, they asserted
that no one can be among the elect without an unmerited access
of grace, but also that only the individual can have any idea
of whether he or she is chosen.   Thus they located within the
individual the criteria both for the comprehension of God and
for the conviction of election.   People interpret God's wishes
and judge their own spiritual condition.

The second paradox is that protestant leaders did all they
could to hinder appreciation of the profundity of their innovation.
In both doctrine and institutions they strove to clamp the lid
back upon the forces of individual thought which they had released.
They sought finality in doctrine and used any argument to cut
off the possibility of ambiguity or freedom of interpretation.
Where they held temporal authority they were intolerant of disagreement to the point of taking life.

Nevertheless, people of the sixteenth and seventeenth centuries exploited the vacuum of spiritual authority created by the

Reformation and professed all kinds of belief.   Often, as we
have seen, they moved in the direction of secularism.
    Some questioned the very basis of Christianity.   In "An
Apology of *Raymond Sebond"* Montaigne warned that "the new
fangles of *Luther*" would lead to atheism: once people learn "that
some articles of their religion be made doubtful and questionable,
they will soon and easily admit an equal uncertainty in all other
parts of their belief" (*Essays*, II, 126-27).   Montaigne himself
developed the case that we should take nothing on trust but make
"a perpetual confession of ignorance" (II, 207).   He recognized
that most people adopt the religion of the country where they
were born and that any heresy can be supported from scripture
(II, 133, 304).   His own profession of faith amounts to little more
than a combination of insecurity and inertia:

> And since I am not capable to choose, I take the choice from
> others; and keep myself in the seat that God hath placed
> me in.   Else could I hardly keep myself from continual rolling.
> Thus have I by the grace of God preserved myself whole
> (without agitation or trouble of conscience) in the ancient
> belief of our religion, in the midst of so many sects and
> divisions which our age hath brought forth.   (II, 285)

Montaigne saved his religion by his reliance upon faith and the
church, but it was his penetrating relativism which impressed
English tragedians.   He is behind Lear's statement that "A dog's
obey'd in office" (IV.vi.161) and Flamineo's remark that "they
that have the yellow jaundice, think all objects they look on to
be yellow" (*The White Devil*, I.ii.109).
    Others tried to return to first principles and devise a religion
that made sense to them.   Lord Herbert of Cherbury found that
the details of doctrine "were more contraverted than that the
age of any man could untie and dissolve the knots and intricacies
in them" and therefore decided "to begin upon the most certain
and unfallible principles I could find and from thence to proceed
unto the next" (*Life*, pp. 31, 29).   He found just five: that there is
one God, he is to be worshipped, he requires of us virtue, piety, faith
and love of himself, we must repent our sins and seek the right
way, there is reward and punishment in an afterlife.   In fact
these are the very notions which protestants allowed to pagans,
"that all to a man, being aware that there is a God, and that
he is their Maker, may be condemned by their own conscience
when they neither worship him nor consecrate their lives to his
service" (Calvin, *Institutes*, I.iii.1).   Lord Herbert found his way
back to a pre-Christian rational theism.
    The most corrosive independent thought was that which examin-
ed the social and psychological bases of religious belief.   This
was part of the threat posed by Machiavelli.   We noted in chapter
five his argument that Christian virtues damage society; he also
conducts a bland analysis of the political usefulness of religion
to the founders and rulers of Rome which slips repeatedly into

off-hand remarks about religion in general: "Nor in fact was there ever a legislator who, in introducing extraordinary laws to a people, did not have recourse to God"; "to whatever [miracles] owed their origin, sensible men made much of them, and their authority caused everybody to believe in them"; "the times were so impregnated with a religious spirit and the men with whom he had to deal so stupid . . . " (*Discourses*, pp. 141, 143).   The tracing of beliefs about God to human sources is the essence of secularism.

Hobbes saw no irreverence in considering religion as an agency of social control, for he took that as the main human need. He declares that both those who have invented religions and those who have worked "by God's commandment and direction . . . have done it, with a purpose to make those men that relied on them the more apt to obedience, laws, peace, charity and civil society" (*Leviathan*, p. 173).   Hobbes' approach is revolutionary in its secularism because he reasons not from God to humanity, but from humanity to God.   This is true even of his account of God, which he bases upon his theory of the worldly ruler and upon human psychology.   He argues that people are inclined to believe in God because "it is peculiar to the nature of man, to be inquisitive into the causes of the events they see"; and that in the absence of apparent causes "there is nothing to be seen, there is nothing to accuse, either of their good or evil fortune, but some *power*, or agent *invisible*" (pp. 168, 170).   He identifies four factors as "the natural seed of religion": "opinion of ghosts, ignorance of second causes, devotion towards what men fear, and taking of things casual for prognostics" (p. 172).

Hobbes is strongly aware of the implications of Luther's liberation of conscience.   To say that we believe in God, he explains, really means that we trust the person who has told us about God.   The Bible offers no security, for it is subject to the same limitation: "they that believe that which a prophet relates unto them in the name of God, take the word of the prophet . . . ; whether they be sent from God or not, is faith in men only" (pp. 133-34).   Hobbes is alarmed about this because he thinks it will produce anarchy, but his solution further undermines the status of spiritual experience by subjecting it to human considerations: we must accept the religion of the state,

> for if men were at liberty to take for God's commandments their own dreams and fancies, or the dreams and fancies of private men; scarce two men would agree upon what is God's commandment; and yet in respect of them, every man would despise the commandments of the commonwealth.
> (p. 333)

Community of belief is required to hold society together—the argument is still to be heard.   Hobbes invariably distinguishes reformed Christianity and other beliefs, but he conveys no sense of the reality of a spiritual dimension in life.   His views exposed him to continual condemnation and danger; Parliament even thought of blaming his atheism for the Plague and Great Fire of London.

As well as elevating – reluctantly – private judgment, protestantism stimulated secularist thought by making very plain the difficulties in the concept of a good and omnipotent deity.   I argued in the previous chapter that claims for the beneficence of a stern and intrusive providence threw up problems which tragedians exploited. These problems are implicit in all traditional Christian thought; protestantism was a turning point in the development of secularism partly because it presents them in a specially provocative form. Hobbes observed: "That which taketh away the reputation of wisdom in him that formeth a religion, or addeth to it when it is already formed, is the enjoining of a belief of contradictories" (Leviathan, p. 179).

Hobbes exposed the assumptions of protestantism by taking them to a logical conclusion.   He abandoned the claim that God is good, just and concerned about mankind, and identified as the source of divine sovereignty nothing more than power: "The right of nature, whereby God reigneth over men and punisheth those that break his laws, is to be derived, not from his creating them, as if he required obedience as of gratitude for his benefits; but from his *irresistible power*" (Leviathan, p. 397).   Calvinists declared that God does as he will with his creation, but they held neverthe-less that human afflictions are deserved and hence part of the divine beneficence.   Hobbes, more logically, retained only half the doctrine.   He denied that sufferings and deserts are related, pointing out that Job was innocent and that God used "arguments drawn from his power, such as this, *Where wast thou when I laid the foundations of the earth?*" (p. 398).   If afflictions are not punishments but simple manifestations of divine will, the whole apparatus of supernatural concern about human behaviour collapses. Hobbes cut the knot of God's power and goodness by dropping the goodness.

Most contemporaries could not endure the abandonment of the idea of a benevolent deity.   Ralph Cudworth said he would as soon contemplate traditional pagan atheism and a world governed by "the motions of senseless atoms furiously agitated, or of a rapid whirlwind" (*The True Intellectual System of the Universe*, IV, 161).   But Hobbes was only developing protestantism, which had always fallen back on God's power as the ultimate argument. In Lawne's *Abridgement of Calvin's Institutes* the objector com-plains, "to adjudge to destruction whom he will, is more agreeable to the lust of a tyrant, than to the lawful sentence of a judge"; the reply is, "It is a point of bold wickedness even so much as to inquire the causes of God's will" (p. 222).   The objector calls it "a fearful decree" to condemn so many simply "because it pleased God"; the answer is, "I grant: and yet no man can deny but that God knew before what end man should have before he created him" (p. 223).

Such a dialogue manifests a society poised at a crisis of
moral awareness.   Concepts of good and justice are shifting.
The protestant responder, whose point of view is shared by the
author, believes he has justified a deity which horrifies the question-
er.   Some people found comfort in an idea of God which others
felt bound to repudiate.

For us it is more difficult to understand the supporters of
the tyrannical deity (though I would repeat that he is logically
implicit in all traditional Christianity).   In the Elizabethan world
relations between the strong and the weak—in the family, at
school, at work, in the local community and in the state—were
characterized by personal cruelty and the exercise of autocratic
power.   Lawrence Stone in *The Family, Sex and Marriage* (London,
1977) argues that these attitudes were more pronounced in the
period 1500-1660 than before or after.   He relates them to aspects
of child-rearing, particularly a lack of affection in infancy and
the belief that the child's will had to be broken.   Certainly whip-
ping was the usual response to infringements at all levels of society,
and this is reflected in the continual references by divines to
God's "chastening rod."   Parents were advised to beat the Catechism into their children.

For as long as this kind of interaction between people was
thought satisfactory they had an excellent way of explaining the
afflictions which befell them.   Protestant emphasis upon depravity
enabled them to interpret any degree of suffering as God's just
punishment.   So Archbishop Grindal in his service of thanksgiving
for the abatement of the plague (1563) accepts the "severe rod
of this terrible plague, wherewith thou hast hitherto most justly
scourged us for our wickedness" and attributes to the surviving
faithful "the deadly plagues of sin and wickedness; by the which
inward infections of our minds these outward diseases of our
bodies have, by the order of thy justice, O Lord, issued and followed" (Grindal, *Remains*, pp. 113-14).

Already in Luther's time some people rejected this way of
thinking about human existence.   In the late seventeenth century
the reaction became pronounced; it marks the development of
a more humane pattern of relations between people.   Protestantism
may partly have helped here (for instance in its doctrine on
marriage); often imaginative literature was in the forefront, as
we have seen in some love poetry and tragedy.   In this more
humane context the authoritarian God posed too many problems
to afford an adequate explanation of the world.   The case made
by Lawne's objector seemed more and more compelling and people
tried to find a better theory.

(The repudiation of the justice of tyrannical relationships
was not, of course, uniform, and neither is it yet complete.
The attitude survives in those with what I should call a punitive
personality—to them sheer accident or social process is intolerable,
always someone must be blamed and punished).

In various ways, from triumphant defiance to anxious soul-searching, people of the period rejected the inevitability of sin and punishment and with it the intrusive providence. Some plunged into antinomianism, effectually denying sin and an exteriorized God; some attempted to construct a humane Christianity; many, unimpressed by these reactions, just let God slip out of the main part of their lives.

William Chillingworth may represent the liberal thinkers who met at Lord Falkland's house at Great Tew. He became briefly a Catholic (he hoped to find an infallible doctrine) and then, returning to protestantism, hestitated to subscribe to the Thirty-nine Articles because they make God seem unreasonable and vindictive. Chillingworth sought a more humane Christianity in two respects: he wanted to maintain human responsibility, and to make God appear fair. In *The Religion of Protestants a Safe Way to Salvation* (1637) he attacks the whole punitive stance:

> Take away this persecuting, burning, cursing, damning of men for not subscribing to the words of men as the words of God; require of Christians only to believe Christ, and to call no man master but him only; let those leave claiming infallibility that have no title to it, and let them that in their words disclaim it disclaim it likewise in their actions. In a word, take away tyranny. (*Works*, II, 38)

Chillingworth approaches the question of faith from the opposite direction to the usual authoritarian theology of the period. Instead of stating what we must believe, he asks which beliefs it is reasonable to condemn. His criteria are the Bible and individual judgment.

Chillingworth has been celebrated for his liberal Christianity, but his analysis shows how a good God must be a weak God and ultimately, for many, an unnecessary God. First, he professes the full protestant dependence upon the Bible rather than a church (II, 410-11) but admits not only that the scriptural canon cannot be decided out of scripture (I, 177-78), but also that uncertainty often occurs "about the sense of some place of scripture which is ambiguous, and with probability capable of divers senses" (I, 123). He has to fall back on the view that "the scripture is not a judge, nor cannot be, but only a sufficient rule for those to judge by that believe it to be the word of God" (I, 230). Second, he allows the full implications of the Lutheran appeal to the individual. A person can believe only that which presents itself forcibly to his or her mind as credible:

> God's Spirit, if he please, may work more, a certainty of adherence beyond a certainty of evidence: but neither God doth, nor man may, require of us, as our duty, to give a greater assent to the conclusion than the premises deserve; to build an infallible faith upon motives that are only highly credible and not infallible. (I, 267)

Each must do his or her best to work out a sincere faith; the integrity with which any belief is held becomes its justification. Hence Catholics should judge "the religion of protestants damnable to them only who profess it, being convicted in conscience that it is erroneous" (I, 103). Even pagans must have the same scope: "If, through want of means of instruction, incapacity, invincible or probable ignorance, a man die in error, he may be saved" (I, 91). No opinion can reasonably be forced upon anyone; Chillingworth inveighs against "this deifying our own interpretations, and tyrannous enforcing them upon others" (II, 38).

All this may sound only reasonable and it presents God in an amiable light, but in its period it is amazingly libertarian and it has far-reaching implications. Logically it permits atheism, though Chillingworth would say that evidence for the existence of God is so strong that everyone is bound to believe it; he could cope with the convinced atheist only be declaring him or her insane. But even within Chillingworth's theistic assumptions, the role of God is hugely weakened in comparison with orthodox protestant doctrine. He no longer determines events in the world, he does not guarantee their justice or intervene to support the faithful; he leaves us to decide who shall go to heaven; he has not made a clear revelation of himself and is not consistent in the guidance he offers through his spirit; indeed, no knowledge of him is required for salvation.

In this version of Christianity God withdraws to heaven and people take control of their own lives. Chillingworth can make God good only by making him less responsible, less *present*. The field is opened for the growth of secularism.

Whilst people like Chillingworth puzzled with rational modifications of authoritarian Christianity, the more audacious leapt into an antinomian rejection of sin and deification of humanity. They drew from the doctrine of predestination the inference that the elect are already of the kingdom of God, indeed are divine, and hence unable to sin. Consequent doctrines usually included an insistence on the overriding authority of the individual's inner light, a denial of the fall and of hell, and a denunciation of private property and the pretensions of ecclesiastical and civil institutions. Chillingworth made God good by making him more remote, the sectarians, in effect, by incorporating him into humanity.

The protestant establishment persecuted such views at every opportunity. Luther did not grant to Anabaptists the liberty of scriptural interpretation he claimed for himself. In his tract "Against the Robbing and Murdering Hordes of Peasants" he urged rulers to "stab, smite, slay, whoever can. If you die in doing it, well for you! A more blessed death can never be yours, for you die in obeying the divine Word" (*Martin Luther*, p. 126). Yet heresy was not suppressed. In 1563 we find Grindal putting down the Dutch sponsor of the Family of Love, Justus Velsius, who held that Christ is "God in man" and that "all Christians are gods" (Grindal, *Remains*, pp. 439-40). But the Family continued underground into the 1640s, when the removal of censorship permitted the exuberant growth of many similar sects—Diggers, Ranters, Grindletonians, Seekers, Quakers. In 1650 Parliament condemned to imprisonment or banishment those who asserted that "the eternal Majesty dwells in the creature and nowhere else . . . or that there is no such thing really and truly as unrighteousness, unholiness or sin, but as a man or woman judgeth thereof; or that there is neither heaven nor hell, neither salvation nor damnation."

Sectarians used the language of religious enthusiasm but their attitude was quite incompatible with the intrusive punishing providence. It is mistaken to speak of these people as "extremists," if that means a more thoroughgoing version of protestant doctrine. They drew God so completely into mankind that he became one with mankind, not a supernatural being but a vision of how people might be.

Chillingworth and the liberal theologians tried anxiously to modify protestantism to accommodate humane values; the sectarians were prepared to abandon the fall, hell and any external spiritual control. Both were in reaction against the tyrannical deity, and both weakened critically the foundations of theistic religion.

It has been argued by Christopher Hill in his book *Milton and the English Revolution* (London, 1977) that Milton belongs among the sectarians. He does and he does not. Milton strides across the categories developed in this chapter, bewildering us with massive inconsistencies. What does seem impossible is the traditional claim that he represents some central and enduring Christian orthodoxy. We observed in chapter three his struggle to contain puritan and humanist impulses; his engagement with the protestantism of his day is independent, sensitive, determined and unsuccessful.

Milton was entirely committed to the freedom of interpretation which was implicit in Luther's stand. We think of him as the poet of biblical myth, but in his unpublished treatise *Of Christian Doctrine* he recognized the problems of reliance upon scripture and asserted the superiority of "the internal scripture of the Holy Spirit which he, according to God's promise, has engraved upon the hearts of believers":

> I do not know why God's providence should have committed the contents of the New Testament to such wayward and uncertain guardians, unless it was so that this very fact might convince us that the Spirit which is given to us is a more certain guide than scripture, and that we ought to follow it. (*Complete Prose*, VI, 587, 589)

In the opening paragraph of *Paradise Lost* Milton alludes to Moses and the book of Genesis, but he invokes an independent inspiration directly from the Spirit—an inspiration not mediated by the words of Moses, but parallel to them:

> And chiefly thou, O Spirit, that dost prefer
> Before all temples th' upright heart and pure,
> Instruct me, for thou know'st; thou from the first
> Wast present.   (I, 17)

He appeals from "temples"—the symbols of institutional religion, where holy books are kept and priests pronounce on doctrine—to "th' upright heart and pure" of the individual believer. The appeal for inner illumination at the climax of the invocation to light at the start of book III implies, in the religious context of the time, a derogation of other authority. Samson gains a purely personal intimation of divine grace and responds to the summons of the Philistines because of an inner call (*Samson Agonistes*, lines 1168-77, 1381-89).

Milton's belief in individual inspiration led him to reject all worldly coercion in matters of faith. Michael's gloomy vision of the future condemns churchmen who "Spiritual laws by carnal power shall force / On every conscience":

> What will they then
> But force the Spirit of Grace itself, and bind
> His consort Liberty?
> > (*Paradise Lost*, XII, 521)

From our reading of Chillingworth and the sectarians we might expect this revolutionary freeing of the human spirit to be accompanied by a rejection of the punitive God, but this is by no means the case. From this split between the liberal and the authoritarian derives the peculiar theological and emotional character of *Paradise Lost*.

The issue is sharpened by Milton's awareness of the danger of making God appear tyrannical. He cannot, with Calvin, merely assert divine justice; he knows of the contemporary debate and sees a real need to "justify the ways of God to men" (I, 26). Orthodox Reformation doctrine was predestinarian; it was restated in the Confession of Westminster (1647). Milton's departure from it is evidently designed to make God appear fair:

> Whose fault?
> Whose but his own? Ingrate, he had of me
> All he could have; I made him just and right,
> Sufficient to have stood, though free to fall.   (III, 96)

The logical difficulties here are notorious: God knows in advance the behaviour of Adam, his creation, and it seems therefore that he must be responsible for the precise balance of Adam's nature and hence, ultimately, for his choice. Milton makes these issues even more problematic by devoting the whole of book III to God's anticipation of the fall so that it takes on an air of inevitability;

and by dwelling upon the paradox of making—*compelling*—freedom:

> I formed them free, and free they must remain,
> Till they enthrall themselves: I else must change
> Their nature, and revoke the high decree
> Unchangeable, eternal, which ordained
> Their freedom.   (III, 124)

Milton ran himself into these difficulties, I believe, because at the same time as wishing to justify God by relatively liberal and humane standards of goodness and justice, he also wished to retain the image of the all-powerful, intervening deity of the Reformation.   He was trying to resist the disintegration of the protestant God which was going on around him as men like Hobbes, Chillingworth and the sectarians pondered the relationship between divine power and goodness.   Milton's tyrannical God is not, therefore, a mere blunder or quirk of his temperament (though both may be factors).   With or without free will—and in some ways the Pelagian's cat-and-mouse game with human achievement is more objectionable than predestination—it is the usual authoritarian Reformation deity.   Even the Son presents his resurrection primarily as the delightful punishment of the enemy:

>   Thou at the sight
> Pleased, out of heaven shalt look down and smile,
> While by thee raised I ruin all my foes.   (III, 256)

Joseph Hall was Milton's opponent in Calvinism and episcopacy, but his God is the same: "There is nothing more lamentable, than to see a man laugh when he should fear: God shall laugh, when such a one's fear cometh" (Hall, *Works*, I, 344).

Milton's extreme personification of supernatural powers is often regarded as one of the problems with *Paradise Lost*.   It is part of the same determination to maintain the intrusive presence of the spiritual in the world.   Milton makes Satan into a character who can attract the admiration of many and has God justify himself to the Son because such anthropomorphism suggests the kind of direct intervention in human affairs which protestants intended in the doctrine of special providence.   There is no disagreement among critics that God is emphatically *there* in *Paradise Lost*. Milton resisted the intuition of liberal theologians that God had to be distant to appear good, that as soon as he is drawn into the afflictions of human life his power becomes an embarrassment. The undesirable effects of anthropomorphism had already been identified by William Davenant in his *Preface to Gondibert*, which he wrote in 1650 and dedicated to Hobbes.   As part of a thorough humanistic critique of contemporary religion, Davenant attacked the use of supernatural beings in epic because of its involvement with a crude and unsatisfactory punitive theology.   It is what we might expect of pagans,

> Yet a Christian poet (whose religion little needs the aids
> of invention) hath less occasion to imitate such fables as
> meanly illustrate a probable Heaven by the fashion and dignity
> of courts and make a resemblance of Hell out of the dreams
> of frighted women; by which they continue and increase the
> melancholy mistakes of the people. (*Gondibert*, p. 6).

The reader who admires Milton's intellect and verbal gift
will be on the lookout for hints of a softening of the implications
of the tyrannical deity.   The notion that Milton's sympathies
are with Satan is no help, for Satan is entirely like God.   They
both conceive an implacable enmity towards those who infringe
what they take to be their rights; they both make proud, rigorous,
legalistic and equivocal speeches of self-justification.   The difference is that God is right and Satan is wrong; or, in Hobbesian
terms, God is the more powerful.   Milton may empathize with
Satan, but it does not help him to see beyond a punitive ethic.
Nor is there much cheer in God's legalistic presentation of the
doctrine of redemption:

> He with his whole posterity must die;
> Die he or justice must; unless for him
> Some other able, and as willing, pay
> The rigid satisfaction, death for death.   (III, 209)

Anyway, mercy is tied to the authoritarian deity, for only
someone who can condemn you can be merciful.   As Milton well
knew, many sectarians repudiated original sin and with it the
need for atonement.   Gerrard Winstanley in *The New Law of
Righteousness* and *Fire in the Bush* (1649) denied Milton's whole
assumption "that a man called *Adam*, that disobeyed 6000 years
ago, was the man that filled every man with sin and filth, by
eating an apple" (Winstanley, *Works*, p. 176).   Satan is a destructive
state of mind: "This imagination fears where no fear is: he rises
up to destroy others for fear lest others destroy him; he will
oppress others lest others oppress him; and fears he shall be in
want hereafter—therefore he takes by violence that which others
have laboured for" (pp. 456-57).   People can reject that condition
for a new and complete innocence and dignity: "then they begin
to appear and act like men; and rise up from the low earth of
a beastly and swinish nature, to acknowledge and honour their
Maker in the light of himself" (p. 157).   There will be no call
for a punitive deity, or for the worldly structures by which "everyone that gets an authority into his hands tyrannizes over others;
as many husbands, parents, masters, magistrates, that live after
the flesh, so carry themselves like oppressing lords over such
as are under them" (p. 158).   There is one glimpse of such a non-
punitive ethos in *Paradise Lost:* after the last judgment the just
will

> after all their tribulations long

> See golden days, fruitful of golden deeds,
> With joy and love triumphing, and fair truth.
> Then thou thy regal sceptre shalt lay by,
> For regal sceptre then no more shall need;
> God shall be all in all.   (III, 336)

Milton does recognize the ideal of a release from the pressure of divine disapproval, but it is not for this life.

Yet—I have said the topic is full of contradictions—Milton introduces, right at the end of the poem, a disconcertingly strong version of the traditional paradox of the fortunate fall:

> only add
> Deeds to thy knowledge answerable, add faith,
> Add virtue, patience, temperance, add love,
> By name to come called charity, the soul
> Of all the rest: then wilt thou not be loth
> To leave this Paradise, but shalt possess
> A paradise within thee, happier far.   (XII, 581)

There is little anticipation elsewhere in the poem of such a positive life on earth.   As Adam and Eve are about to be expelled from Eden—the very moment at which, as we saw in chapter four, he introduces his most generous notion of human relations—Milton reaches out towards Winstanley's goal of a second earthly paradise to be obtained through the liberating of the human mind:

> Christ the spirit of truth shall arise above the power of un-
> righteousness in me; that is, humility arises above pride,
> love above envy, a meek and quiet spirit above hasty, rash
> anger, chastity above unclean lusts, and light above darkness.
> Now the second *Adam*, Christ, hath taken the kingdom,
> my body, and rules in it. (Winstanley, *Works*, pp. 173-74)

Both men challenge the whole spirit of the Reformation by suggest-ing—more boldly than Bacon—that the fall may be retrieved in this world.   The difference is obvious: Winstanley envisages an intrepid leap from the oppression of guilt into a state of harmony and well-being, Milton cannot offer more than a long grind towards a virtue which may appease the angry God:

> Henceforth I learn that to obey is best,
> And love with fear the only God, to walk
> As in his presence, ever to observe
> His providence, and on him sole depend. (XII, 561)

Milton's intense realization of the essential contradiction in Reformation theology—the freeing of the human mind from worldly authority and the suppression of it by a punitive deïty—helps us to identify the characteristic emotional timbre of *Paradise Lost*.   The impression is of a vast energy almost smothered.

The poem's huge scope is narrowed down into its petty theology;
the surpassing image of Eden is almost stifled by Adam's restrained
speech; the expansive similes are nipped off by Christian interpretations; the massive, unravelling syntax is tortured by inversions.
The whole poem bespeaks a power and range continually clipped
back and controlled, as Milton's natural, human capacity is forcibly
subjected to the will of his God.

The gardening which Milton imposes upon Adam and Eve
epitomizes it all:

> To-morrow ere fresh morning streak the east
> With first approach of light, we must be ris'n,
> And at our pleasant labour, to reform
> Yon flow'ry arbours, yonder alleys green,
> Our walk at noon, with branches overgrown,
> That mock our scant manuring [sc. cultivating], and require
> More hands than ours to lop their wanton growth.
> Those blossoms also, and those dropping gums,
> That lie bestrown unsightly and unsmooth,
> Ask riddance, if we mean to tread with ease.   (IV, 623)

Blossoms lying about on the path, it can't be endured.   Paradise,
like the poem, can't be allowed to burgeon, it must be kept in
control.   Perhaps the initial idea is pruning to ensure fuller growth—
"reform" may mean that, though it more often means, more
negatively, "cut back" and "correct."   But "wanton," whose range
of meaning runs from "frolicsome" through "undisciplined" to "lascivious," displays Milton's anxiety at the exuberant and unrestrained,
and implies a connection between it and sexuality.

Hair, too, is wanton and must be cut back.   As St Paul com-
manded, Adam's is cut above his shoulders; Eve's is long and disordered and hence threatening—it shows that she must be kept
in hand:

> She as a veil down to the slender waist
> Her unadorned golden tresses wore
> Disheveled, but in wanton ringlets waved
> As the vine curls her tendrils, which implied
> Subjection.   (IV, 304)

Eve's dishevelment is of a piece with her sexual attraction and
it implies, of itself, that she must be subjected; the final word
chops off the waving, curling syntax.   Sexuality, disobedience
and liberty are organized into a pattern of inhibition, which Milton
identifies as evil.

Samson's hair was long and it was the source of his superhuman
power, but he couldn't manage it and now he is trapped "To grind
in brazen fetters under task / With this Heav'n-gifted strength"
(*Samson Agonistes*, line 35).   Milton's hero has divine capability
but his failure to keep a reverent hold over it has angered God
and he is reduced to impotence, "these redundant locks, / Robust-

ious to no purpose, clust'ring down" (line 568). The only way
Samson can see to break through is by a more extreme and self-
destructive identification with the punitive deity: he pleases God
by pulling the whole building down upon the enemy and himself.

Milton suffered a bondage which no longer troubled those of his
contemporaries who were prepared to live without a dominant
and intrusive deity. Davenant in his *Preface to Gondibert* brings
our study of the confrontation between Renaissance and Reformation to a pointed conclusion, for he purposefully denies the con-
cordat which puritan humanists like Sidney and Milton so carefully
constructed. Like them, Davenant says that poetry tempts us
into virtue. But instead of being embarrassed by the rival claim
of religion, he contrasts its lack of success, blaming the punitive
stance of contemporary protestantism: "the persuasions of pulpits,
where is presented to the obstinate Hell after death" seem not
to work, and we would do much better with "the persuasions of
poesy instead of menaces"—"harmonious and delightful insinuations,
and never any constraint; unless the ravishment of reason may
be called force" (*Gondibert*, p. 38). Davenant denies the social
efficacy, the common sense and the humanity of punitive theology:
"morality is sweetened and made more amiable by poesy. And
the austerity of some divines may be the cause why religion hath
not more prevailed upon the manners of men" (p. 41). Poets
need no longer apologize for distracting people from God: they
are performing a service.

Like Bacon and Hobbes, Davenant appeals beyond religion
to nature: "And as poesy is the best expositor of nature (nature
being mysterious to such as use not to consider) so nature is the
best interpreter of God; and more cannot be said of religion"
(pp. 40-41). This precisely reverses the assertion of puritan humanists that poetry may penetrate beyond nature to the divine.
Davenant's case is provocatively and hence perhaps insecurely
stated, but it points to Restoration and modern modes of thought.
God becomes perhaps an ultimate referent, certainly not a very
immediate presence; people make what they can of the world;
"nature" becomes a principal agency of ideological mystification.
Unfortunately *Gondibert* is a boring poem.

This book has been occupied with the privileged, educated
sector of society, but it would be wrong to leave matters quite
there. Certain seventeenth-century intellectuals were reaching,
as I think, a more sensible view of the world, but it is likely that
many ordinary people never held anything else. Whilst divines
erected elaborate theological structures and writers wrestled
to accommodate them to a wider intellectual tradition and to
human life, most men and women probably made sense of existence
on a reasonable day to day basis, as they always had. William
Perkins prefaced *The Foundation of Christian Religion* (1590)

with a list of "common opinions" which "poor people" maintained despite the efforts of preachers.   Some of them are very reassuring:

> That it is the safest thing to do in religion as most do;
> That drinking and bezeling [guzzling] in the alehouse or tavern is good fellowship, and shows a good, kind nature and maintains neighbourhood;
> That every man must be for himself and God for us all;
> That if a man be no adulterer, no thief, no murderer and do no man harm, he is a right honest man;
> That a man need not have any knowledge of religion, because he is not book-learned;
> That ye are to be excused in all your doings, because the best men are sinners.   (Perkins, *Work*, pp. 142-44)

Vox populi, vox dei.

Editions Cited

Lancelot Andrewes, *Works*, 11 vols., Oxford, 1841

Ludovico Ariosto, *Orlando Furioso*, trans. Guido Waldman, Oxford, 1974

Roger Ascham, *Whole Works*, ed. the Rev. Dr Giles, 4 vols., London, 1864

Francis Bacon, *Philosophical Works*, ed. John M. Robertson, London, 1905

Du Bartas. See James VI; Sylvester

Thomas Becon, *The Catechism*, ed. John Ayre, Cambridge, 1844

The Bible, King James' Version, Cambridge, n.d.

Sir Thomas Browne, *Religio Medici*, ed. W.A. Greenhill, London, 1892

Sir Thomas Browne, *Selected Writings*, ed. Sir Geoffrey Keynes, London, 1968

Henry Bullinger, *The Christian State of Matrimony*, trans. Miles Coverdale, 1541

Robert Burton, *The Anatomy of Melancholy*, ed. Holbrook Jackson, 3 vols., London, 1932

John Calvin, *Calvin's Institutes*, [trans. Henry Beveridge], Florida, n.d.

Jean Calvin, *Commentaries on the Psalms*, trans. Arthur Golding, 1571

George Chapman, *Bussy D'Ambois*, ed. Robert J. Lordi, London, 1964

William Chillingworth, *Works*, 3 vols., Oxford, 1838

Common Prayer, Oxford, 1865

Ralph Cudworth, *The True Intellectual System of the Universe*, ed. Thomas Birch, 4 vols., London, 1820

E.D., *A Brief and Necessary Instruction*, ed. H.R.D. Anders, *Shakespeare Jahrbuch*, XL (1940), 228-29

Sir William Davenant, *Gondibert*, ed. David F. Gladish, Oxford, 1971

John Donne, *The Complete English Poems*, ed. A.J. Smith, Harmondsworth, 1971

John Donne, *Sermons*, ed. George R. Potter and Evelyn M. Simpson, 10 vols., Berkeley and Los Angeles, 1953-62

Desiderius Erasmus, *Luther and Erasmus: Free Will and Salvation*,
    ed. E.G. Rupp and P.S. Watson, London, 1969
Marsilio Ficino, *Commentary on Plato's Symposium*, trans. Sears
    Reynolds Jayne, Missouri, 1944
Marsilio Ficino, *Letters*, 2 vols., trans. Members of the Language
    Department of the School of Economic Science, London,
    1975
Marsilio Ficino, *Platonic Theology*, trans. Josephine L. Burroughs,
    Journal of the History of Ideas, V (1944), 227-39
John Ford, *The Broken Heart*, ed. Brian Morris, London, 1965
John Ford, *'Tis Pity She's a Whore*, ed. Brian Morris, London and
    Tonbridge, 1968
Sir Fulke Grevil, *The Life of the Renowned Sir Philip Sidney*,
    London, 1906
Edmund Grindal, *Remains*, Cambridge, 1843
John Hall, *The Court of Virtue*, ed. Russell A. Fraser, London,
    1961
Joseph Hall, *Collected Poems*, ed. A. Davenport, Liverpool, 1949
Joseph Hall, *Works*, 10 vols., ed. Josiah Pratt, London, 1808
George Herbert, *The English Poems*, ed. C.A. Patrides, London,
    1974
George Herbert, *Works in Prose and Verse*, London, n.d.
Lord Herbert of Cherbury, *Life*, ed. J.M. Shuttleworth, London,
    1976
Thomas Hobbes, *Leviathan*, ed. C.B. Macpherson, Harmondsworth,
    1968
Homilies: *Certain Sermons or Homilies*, London, 1899
Richard Hooker, *Of the Laws of Ecclesiastical Polity*, ed.
    Christopher Morris, 2 vols., London, 1965
Lawrence Humphrey, *The Nobles*, 1563
James VI, *The Essayes of a Prentise*, ed. Edward Arber, London,
    1869
Thomas Kyd, *The Spanish Tragedy*, ed. Philip Edwards, London,
    1959
Hugh Latimer, *Selected Sermons*, ed. A.R. Buckland, London,
    1904
William Lawne, *An Abridgement of the Institution of Christian
    Religion*, trans. Christopher Fetherstone, Edinburgh, 1587
Sidney Lee, ed., *Elizabethan Sonnets*, 2 vols., New York, 1964
Martin Luther, *Luther and Erasmus: Free Will and Salvation*, ed.
    E.G. Rupp and P.S. Watson, London, 1969
Martin Luther, ed. E.G. Rupp and Benjamin Drewery, London
    1970
Niccolo' Machiavelli, *The Discourses*, ed. Bernard Crick,
    Harmondsworth, 1970
Niccolo' Machiavelli, *The Prince*, trans. George Bull, Harmondsworth,
    1961
Christopher Marlowe, *Plays*, ed. Roma Gill, Oxford, 1971
John Marston, *Antonio and Mellida*, ed. G.K. Hunter, London, 1965
John Marston, *Antonio's Revenge*, ed. G.K. Hunter, London, 1966
John Milton, *Complete Prose Works*, 7 out of 8 vols., Yale, 1953-

John Milton, *Poetical Works*, ed. Douglas Bush, Oxford, 1966
Michel de Montaigne, *Essays*, trans. John Florio, 3 vols., London, 1965
Jorge de Montemayor, *Diana: A Critical Edition of Yong's Translation of Montemayor's Diana and Gil Polo's Enamoured Diana*, Oxford, 1968
Philippe du Plessis-Mornay, *The True Knowledge of a Man's Own Self*, trans. Anthony Munday, 1602
Philippe du Plessis-Mornay, *The Trueness of the Christian Religion*, trans. Arthur Golding, London, 1857
Thomas Nashe, *Works*, 5 vols., ed. Ronald B. McKerrow, revised F.P. Wilson, Oxford, 1958
Ovid, *The Art of Love and Other Poems*, trans. J.H. Mozley, London and Cambridge, Mass., 1962
Ovid's Metamorphoses, trans. Arthur Golding, ed. John Frederick Nims, New York, 1965
William Perkins, ed. Thomas F. Merrill, Nieuwkoop, 1966
William Perkins, *The Work*, ed. Ian Breward, Abingdon, 1970
Plato, *Great Dialogues*, trans. W.H.D. Rouse, New York, 1956
Plato, *Phaedrus and Letters*, trans. Walter Hamilton, Harmondsworth, 1973
Pierre de Ronsard, *Oeuvres Complètes*, ed. Paul Laumonier, 20 vols., Paris, 1921-75
Jacopo Sannazaro, *Arcadia and Piscatorial Eclogues*, trans. Ralph Nash, Detroit, 1966
Seneca, his Tenne Tragedies, ed. Thomas Newton, 2 vols., New York, 1967
Lucius Annaeus Seneca, *Moral Epistles*, trans. Richard M. Gunmere, 3 vols., London, 1961
Lucius Annaeus Seneca, *Moral Essays*, trans. John W. Basore, 3 vols., London and Cambridge, Mass., 1958
William Shakespeare's plays are quoted from the New Arden editions when available (all published in London):
    Antony and Cleopatra, ed. M.R. Ridley, 1954;
    As You Like It, ed. Agnes Latham, 1975;
    Coriolanus, ed. Philip Brockbank, 1976;
    King Lear, ed. Kenneth Muir, 1964;
    1 King Henry IV, ed. A.R. Humphreys, 1961;
    Macbeth, ed. Kenneth Muir, 1962;
    Measure for Measure, ed. J.W. Lever, 1965;
    Othello, ed. M.R. Ridley, 1962;
    The Tempest, ed. Frank Kermode, 1962;
    Timon of Athens, ed. H.J. Oliver, 1959;
    Twelfth Night, ed. J.M. Lothian and T.W. Craik, 1975;
    The Winter's Tale, ed. J.H.P. Pafford, 1963.
    Hamlet, Richard III and *The Taming of the Shrew* are quoted from *The Complete Works*, ed. Peter Alexander, London and Glasgow, 1951
Richard Sibbes, *The Soul's Conflict*, London, 1837
Sir Philip Sidney, *A Defence of Poetry*, ed. J.A. van Dorsten, Oxford, 1966

Sir Philip Sidney, *Old Arcadia: The Countess of Pembroke's Arcadia*, ed. Jean Robertson, Oxford, 1973

Sir Philip Sidney, *New Arcadia: Arcadia*, ed. Maurice Evans, Harmondsworth, 1977

Sir Philip Sidney, *Prose Works*, ed. Albert Feuillerat, 4 vols., Cambridge, 1963

Sir Philip Sidney, *Selected Poetry and Prose*, ed. David Kalstone, New York, 1970

G. Gregory Smith, *Elizabethan Critical Essays*, 2 vols., Oxford, 1904

Henry Smith, *Works*, 2 vols., ed. Thomas Fuller, Edinburgh, 1866

Robert Southwell, S.J., *Poems*, ed. James H. McDonald and Nancy Pollard Brown, Oxford, 1967

Edmund Spenser, *Poetical Works*, ed. J.C. Smith and E. de Selincourt, Oxford, 1912

Phillip Stubbes, *The Anatomie of Abuses*, ed. Frederick J. Furnivall, 2 vols., London, 1877-79

Joshua Sylvester, *The Complete Works*, ed. Alexander B. Grosart, 2 vols., Hildesheim, 1969

Torquato Tasso, *Discourses on the Heroic Poem*, trans. Mariella Cavalchini and Irene Samuel, Oxford, 1973

Torquato Tasso, *Jerusalem Delivered*, trans. Edward Fairfax, London, 1962

Cyril Tourneur, *The Atheist's Tragedy*, ed. Brian Morris and Roma Gill, London, 1976

Cyril Tourneur, *The Revenger's Tragedy*, ed. Lawrence J. Ross, London, 1967

William Tyndale, *An Answer to Sir Thomas More's Dialogue*, ed. Henry Walter, Cambridge, 1850

William Tyndale: *English Reformers*, ed. T.H.L. Parker, London, 1966

William Tyndale, *Writings of Tindal, Frith and Barnes*, London, n.d.

Isaac Walton, *The Lives of Dr John Donne, Sir Henry Wotton, Mr George Herbert and Dr Robert Sanderson*, ed. Charles Hill Dick, London and Felling-on-Tyne, 1899

John Webster, *The Duchess of Malfi*, ed. John Russell Brown, London, 1964

John Webster, *The White Devil*, ed. John Russell Brown, Manchester, 1977

John Whitgift, *Works*, ed. John Ayre, 3 vols., Cambridge, 1853

Willobie His Avisa, ed. G.B. Harrison, Edinburgh, 1966

Gerrard Winstanley, *Works*, ed. G.H. Sabine, Cornell, 1941

Sir Thomas Wyatt, *Collected Poems*, ed. Kenneth Muir, London, 1963

Index

Index

E.D. 49
education 3, 12, 20, 24-6,
   37-8, 58, 151
election *see* grace, predestination
Elizabeth I, Queen 12-13, 46-7
Elton, W.R. 6
empiricism 3, 130-7
epic *see* heroes
Erasmus, D. 2, 8-9, 17, 21, 24,
   112, 116, 118
ethics 10, 16, 20-8, 33-43, 49-60,
   81-2, 85-9, 91, 99, 125-8,
   133-7
Euripides 127

fall 8-11, 14-15, 22, 24, 26, 28,
   30-1, 33, 37-9, 42-7, 69-70,
   88, 92, 101, 106, 132-3, 138,
   144-9
fate 83, 90, 97, 102, 112-14,
   120, 124
Ficino, M. 21, 31, 49, 63, 77,
   88
Fish, S.E. 6
Fletcher, G. 55
Ford, J. 71, 84, 88-91
fortune 2, 83, 86, 91, 95, 120-4,
   128
Frye, R.M. 6

George, C. and K. 1
Gifford, G. 23
God *see* divine power and goodness;
   Jesus Christ
Golding, A. 51-2, 60, 63
Gouge, W. 64
grace 8-11, 13-15, 18-19, 29-31,
   44-7, 64, 98, 101, 117-20,
   138; *see also* predestination
Greville, Sir F. 26-7, 81, 109
Grindal, E. 12, 142, 144

Hagstrum, J. H. 69
Halewood, W.G. 6
Hall, John 50
Hall, Joseph 26, 54, 95, 98-9,
   108, 132, 147
Hall, S. 4, 6
Harington, Sir J. 24, 51
Heinemann, M. 6

Herbert, Lord E. of Cherbury
   137, 139
Herbert, G. 8, 15-17, 20, 25
   60, 107
Hercules 27-8, 85, 88, 91-2,
   94
heroes 24, 37-48, 81-105
Heywood, T. 103, 126
hierarchy *see* authority
Hill, C. 1, 145
Hobbes, T. 7, 11, 137, 140-1,
   147-8, 151
Hooker, R. 13-14, 31, 117,
   138
homilies 7-8, 12-13, 20, 52,
   56, 61, 66, 92-3, 117, 120,
   134
Homer 24, 28, 33, 37-9
Humphrey, L. 22
humanism 3, 5, 17, 19-48,
   50, 60, 62, 81-105, 109,
   122, 151
Hunter, R.G. 6

James VI and I, King 14, 25
Jefferson, T. 6
Jesus Christ 2, 21, 26, 28,
   39-41, 43, 57, 75, 98, 100,
   112, 118, 135, 137, 147
Joannes Secundus 24
Julius II, Pope 86

Kinsman, R.S. 6
Kyd, T. 84, 114-16

Laing, R.D. 127
Latimer, H. 9, 75
Lawne, W. 10-11, 16, 18, 138,
   141-2
Lee, S. 55
Leicester, R. Earl of 23
Lewalski, B.K. 6
Lewis, C.S. 70
literature 2-6, 12, 19-33, 142,
   151
love 3, 5, 16, 19, 27-8, 34-7,
   49-80, 89-90, 125-8, 149-50
Lucan 29
Lucian 22
Luther, M. 8-9, 13, 17, 21,
   37, 98, 112, 118, 137-40, 142-4

Index